HEARTMIND WISDOM
Collection #1

**An anthology of Inspiring Wisdom
from those who have been there.**

Kindness Is Key Training Inc.

BALBOA
PRESS
A DIVISION OF HAY HOUSE

Balboa Press books may be ordered through booksellers or by contacting:

Balboa Press
A Division of Hay House
1663 Liberty Drive
Bloomington, IN 47403
www.balboapress.com
1-(877) 407-4847

Because of the dynamic nature of the Internet, any web addresses or links contained in this book may have changed since publication and may no longer be valid. The views expressed in this work are solely those of the author and do not necessarily reflect the views of the publisher, and the publisher hereby disclaims any responsibility for them.

The author of this book does not dispense medical advice or prescribe the use of any technique as a form of treatment for physical, emotional, or medical problems without the advice of a physician, either directly or indirectly. The intent of the author is only to offer information of a general nature to help you in your quest for emotional and spiritual well-being. In the event you use any of the information in this book for yourself, which is your constitutional right, the author and the publisher assume no responsibility for your actions.

Any people depicted in stock imagery provided by Thinkstock are models, and such images are being used for illustrative purposes only.
Certain stock imagery © Thinkstock.

Printed in the United States of America

ISBN: 978-1-4525-6718-1 (sc)
ISBN: 978-1-4525-6719-8 (e)
ISBN: 978-1-4525-6720-4 (hc)

Library of Congress Control Number: 2013900994

Balboa Press rev. date: 2/26/2013

Contents

Five percent of retail sales from the
Heartmind Wisdom Collection
goes to

MERCY SHIPS CANADA

Mercy Ships, an international faith-based organization, uses hospital ships to deliver *free* health care services, capacity building, and sustainable development to those without access in the developing world. Founded in 1978, Mercy Ships has worked in more than 70 countries providing services valued at over $1 Billion, directly impacting some 2.35 million lives. Each year up to 1,200 volunteers from over 40 nations—including surgeons, nurses, health care trainers, seamen, cooks, and agriculturalists—pay their own board and room while donating their time and skills to the effort.

Mercy Ship seeks to become the face of love in action, bringing hope and healing to the world's poorest—transforming one life at a time. To learn more about our organization or to donate, please contact:

Mercy Ships Canada
5 – 3318 Oak Street
Victoria, B.C. V8X 1R1
1-866-900-7447
www.mercyships.ca

Dedicated to our mentor and friend

RAY HELM.

(1953 – 2012)

HEARTMIND WISDOM

AUTHORS

DECADES OF WISDOM

Heartmind Wisdom offers more than sweet platitudes and anecdotes. Each chapter in this collection of 21 true and inspiring stories details how a particular coauthor overcame his or her shadow(s) to live the life we are each meant to love. To assist you in finding the wisdom that will speak to your soul, we have created five restorative categories: Bouncing Back, Divine Connection, Healing from Loss, Hope, and Self-Actualization.

Bouncing Back

Divine Connection

Healing from Loss

Hope

Self-Actualization

Published through

Kindness is Key Training Inc.

www.kindnessiskey.com

www.kindnessiskey.com

HEARTMIND WISDOM PROMISE

No matter where you are on your personal healing journey, and regardless of what challenges currently stand between you and your light, Heartmind Wisdom Collection #1 promises to brighten your path toward wholeness, happiness, health—and the

Life You Are Meant to Love!

KINDNESS IS KEY
CONTESTS, COURSES & EVENTS

DISCLAIMER

The intention of Kindness Is Key (*KiK*) is to provide inspiration and 'food for thought' by sharing personal experiences and life-gained wisdoms. *KiK* believes that the chapters in this Heartmind Wisdom collection are an accurate, honest and personal account of each author's recollections, interpretations and conclusions regarding persons, events and circumstances. However, it is acknowledged that recounted events, circumstances and conclusions are subjective and may or may not be recollected, interpreted or concluded in the same way by all persons.

www.kindnessiskey.com

Kind Welcome from the Cofounders of Kindness is Key Training Inc.

Joyce M. Ross and E. Patricia Connor

Written by Joyce M. Ross

In 2010, when Patricia and I started Kindness is Key Training Inc., we originally planned to offer seminars based on the *13 Kindness Keys to Living the Life You Are Meant to Love*. As well, we wanted to offer courses to empower heart-centered visionaries to share their healing messages with the world. Our intended course lineup included: purpose, platform and profit; journaling and writing; speaking from the heart; and, traditional and social media promotion. (We love the Internet because it has literally placed the world at our fingertips. All you need is a 'magic box' (aka a computer) to instantly explore, connect, communicate, and promote yourself and your creations globe-wide.)

As part of our mission, I wrote, and Patricia helped inspire and edit, *The Kindness Ambassador and the Sugarholic Prosecutor*. Loosely based on our lives and challenges, this inspirational novel was written with the intention of helping to heal and inspire our global brothers and sisters. After a year of diligent preparation, we were finally ready to begin sharing what we each hold dear in our hearts. Then we froze.

"It feels like I have cement for shoes," I confessed to Patricia. "*The Kindness Ambassador* is finished and our courses are ready to teach. But I have a sense of being stuck and not ready to proceed."

Patricia smiled and nodded, before saying, "I'm feeling the same way."

"I guess we're supposed to wait," I suggested.

"When it's time to get started, we'll know," Patricia added.

We let the matter drop. Within about a week, sitting outside enjoying the late fall sunshine, I suddenly knew why we'd frozen pre-launch.

"Patricia, I know why we're feeling immobilized and what we're intended to do!" I excitedly began. "We're supposed to take others on our global healing journey."

"We are?" she responded, narrowing her gaze and readying for what I'd say next.

"Yes! I heard it in my mind's ear just a few seconds ago."

"Go on," she encouraged, accustomed to me receiving what I truly believe are divinely inspired messages from the universe.

"We're supposed to take a number of healing and inspirational stories to the world via an inspirational anthology."

"I like it!" she said, glee dancing in her hazel eyes. "We should call the book *Coffee Wisdom*."

Recalling the title of the book we'd considered writing a few years earlier, I nodded. *Coffee Wisdom* was to be a collection of our personal wisdoms, shared with the reader in the way one would impart personal experiences over a cup of coffee with a friend.

For the next few weeks, Patricia and I busied ourselves with preparing our universe-inspired mission. Then we slowly introduced the concept to a group of mature singles we were coaching on the Joy of Being Single. (At the time, I ran singles dances for the forty-plus crowd. Patricia has been happily married for over twenty years.) Within a few weeks of introducing the concept of an anthology of educational, healing and inspirational wisdom from those who have been there, we had twenty-one coauthors for twenty-one chapters. The book full, it was time to teach our new friends and fellow authors how to identify and write about their life-gained knowledge.

About three months into our Inspirational Authorship course, impressed by the incredible 'heart' and 'mind' wisdom of our coauthors, we changed the name of the anthology to *Heartmind Wisdom*. (We had also noticed that someone else on the Internet was promoting a project called Coffee Wisdom.)

The Heartmind Wisdom Inspirational Anthology Collection
Having each faced personal challenges, Patricia and I know that healing

is an ongoing process that requires much more than hearing or reading about sweet platitudes and heartwarming anecdotes. We also realize that:

- Our emotional nature combined with our physical nature creates a myriad of possible circumstances to confuse, hurt and frighten us.
- Challenge, illness and loss are natural consequences of the human condition—of life. As the Heartmind Wisdom coauthors share in this book, finding your way out of darkness requires hope, love and belief—hope that you will find your way to the light; love to sustain your mind, body and soul; and, belief in your divine deservedness and earthly purpose.
- Though no one can truly know what it is to walk in someone else's shoes, there is great comfort, perhaps even answers and solutions, in reading about the trials and healing pathways of others.

Knowing the above is why each of our Heartmind Wisdom anthologies offers a collection of 21 authentic stories, with each chapter detailing how a particular coauthor overcame his or her shadow(s) to live the life we are each meant to love. To assist you in finding the wisdom that will speak to your soul, we have created five restorative categories: Bouncing Back, Divine Connection, Healing from Loss, Hope, and Self-Actualization. Reading the inspiring accounts of our Heartmind Wisdom coauthors' triumphs over various challenges— body weight, personal missteps, depression, emptiness, self-devaluing, illness, and loss—will lift you emotionally; however, it will also equip you with practical knowledge.

Our combined Heartmind Wisdom wish is that by reading our personal journeys, you will find your way to the life you are meant to love.

indness is Key

The 13 Kindness Keys

Key # 1: HARMONY
"Live in harmony within: mind, heart and soul." —Joyce M. Ross: Author, Teacher and Speaker.

Key # 2: GRATITUDE
"Be grateful for your shadows, light and dark, as they are your compass to the life you are meant to love." —Joyce M. Ross: Author, Teacher and Speaker.

Key # 3: LOVE
"Even after all this time, the sun never says to the earth, 'You owe me.' Look what happens with a love like that...it lights the whole sky." —Hafiz: 14th Century Poet.

Key # 4: INTEGRITY
"My word is my contract; my handshake, my seal; and, my conscience, my witness." —E. Patricia Connor: Ordained Minister, Author, Teacher, and Speaker.

Key # 5: FORGIVENESS
"You are loved, not for anything you did or didn't do; but because at Source, there is only love." —Anonymous

Key # 6: ACCEPTANCE
"My truth is but mine alone; as yours is yours. For this reason, I hear and see you free of judgment, fear, anger, and resentment. This is my promise to you. This is my gift to me." —E. Patricia Connor: Ordained Minister, Author, Teacher, and Speaker.

Key # 7: EGO
"As a sense of self, ego is a great protector. As a sense of being separate from others, the universe and Creation, ego enhances the illusion that you are alone." —E. Patricia Connor: Ordained Minister, Author, Teacher, and Speaker.

Key # 8: LIVE

"Sing like no one's listening. Love like you've never been hurt. Dance like nobody's watching. And live like it's Heaven on earth." —Mark Twain: American Author and Humorist.

Key # 9: DREAM

"Dreams are the seeds still in the universal storehouse. To become a reality they must be chosen, planted, tended, and harvested." —Reverend Barbara Leonard: Author of *Don't Just Stand There Sucking Your Thumb*.

Key # 10: BELIEVE

"Belief in your dreams, yourself, others, and the guiding love of Source—chart the walkway to true meaning, the highway to greatness, and the flight path to the Life You Are Meant to Love." —Joyce M. Ross: Author, Teacher and Speaker.

Key # 11: ACTION

"Once I have mastered peace within, only then will I experience peace in my family, my community, my country, and finally, the world." —Ted Kuntz: Psychotherapist, Speaker & Author of *Peace Begins with Me*.

Key # 12: PROSPERITY

"There is no way to prosperity, prosperity is the way." —Dr. Wayne Dyer: Spiritual Teacher, Author and Speaker.

Key # 13: PURPOSE

"Everything in the universe has a purpose. Indeed, the invisible intelligence that flows through everything in a purposeful fashion is also flowing through you." —Dr. Wayne Dyer: Spiritual Teacher, Author and Speaker.

Bouncing Back

www.kindnessiskey.com

Bankrupt!
What I learned about Life

Katharine Fahlman

"Katharine," my husband said, a catch in his voice.

Whatever Dwayne was about to say, intuition told me that I wasn't going to like it. "I'm listening," I answered, leaving the floor his.

"I need you to come to the bank with me and sign some forms."

Mostly my husband was a strong and proud man. At that moment, he seemed more lost. "Okay," I agreed, not bothering to ask what kind of forms. Banks lent people money; we obviously needed a quick cash influx.

"What time?" I asked, sensing his deep sadness and not mentioning the lone tear edging his clouded brown eyes. Protective instincts kicking in, I momentarily considered closing the distance between us and hugging him. But I knew my husband well enough to know what he needed was space.

"Ten, tomorrow morning," he supplied, lowering his head as he turned and exited the room.

"Your debt-to-asset ratio has greatly affected your credit rating," the loans officer said, his expression sober as his shoulders squared off with Dwayne. "Quite frankly, we can't grant you a consolidation loan, because we aren't confident that you'd be able to fulfill your payment obligations."

We wouldn't be able to fulfill our payment obligations! Did I hear him correctly? Nervously reaching for the papers I studied our bleak financial picture. "There must be some mistake," I said aloud, inwardly realizing that there wasn't. My husband hadn't revealed *all* the facts and figures before our appointment; nevertheless, I knew our financial situation wasn't ideal.

Turning to face me, the loans officer said, "There's no mistake. I completed your financial profile myself. It's accurate."

Deafened by the hysterical trample of inner screams, I'm not certain if either the loans officer or my husband responded. Like a thousand horses stampeding, hoofbeat after hoofbeat, clatter pounded against my temples as the room teetered and my face flushed red hot.

"Excuse me," I muttered, standing and heading for the office door. *Things like this happened to other people, not to us.*

Somehow having found my way to the ladies room, I gaped in the mirror. The sweat-speckled crimson 'me' looking back seemed foreign and odd. My legs too weak to support the shock of my mangled new reality, I braced against the sink before splashing cold water on my face. I still couldn't ground, seemingly floating out of my physical body and into a weightless dimension. Taking deep breaths helped to somewhat reconnect my mind and body. Counting to ten slightly calmed my anger, as my overwhelmed mind frantically sought to assign blame elsewhere...anywhere.

Our financial safety was gone. Sad, hollowed and numb, I dragged my sandbagged feet down the hall and back into the reality room. A quick glance at my husband told me that while I was absent, his conversation with the loans officer had been strained. Locking eyes with Dwayne, my heart flipped upside down, but landed safely. *There had to be a way out of this mess.*

On the way home from the bank that day, I recalled how many weeks earlier, Dwayne and I had talked to a debt management consultant, only to be told that our situation was *not bad enough.* So we carried on for a few more months, bearing the brunt of abusive debt collectors and wage garnisheeing threats.

On weekends, we went camping to escape our worries. The scent of the pine trees was our aromatherapy. The sound of the birds singing calmed our anxiety. The antics of the squirrels made us laugh, which was the best medicine of all.

Camping with friends helped us forget what was waiting for us at home. We could de-stress and regain some sanity for a couple of days. I believe that this *hugely* contributed to saving our marriage, because it allowed us to connect without the constant bombardment of financial gloom.

"Let's call John," I said to my husband as we walked into our house, knowing our trusted friend, who was a certified general accountant, would be able to advise us of our options.

A nod of approval from my husband was all I needed to fuel my determination. I immediately called John, and he suggested we contact a bankruptcy trustee. Glancing through the telephone book, I intuitively chose one. Through our initial phone consultation we learned what we needed to do to prepare for going bankrupt, including bracing ourselves for life without credit cards. We were also advised to stop making payments on everything.

A few months later, we turned our financial predicament over to our trustee. Within a few days, the harassing phone calls and collection letters stopped. From there forward, anyone inquiring about our non-payment was referred to his office. Our sense of peace, relief and hope for the future was somewhat restored.

Feeling he needed more space and time to think, my husband left our house for a short time to live in a camper parked on the street. It took caring intervention and a pep-talk from his daughter to bring him back home.

As we didn't want all of our friends and family knowing our predicament, my husband took solace in venting and sharing with his closest sister and brother, who were both as supportive as possible. Our shame and sense of failure was not something we wanted to talk about with just anyone.

The feeling of having been financially irresponsible was always present. Prior to our bankruptcy, wanting to avoid an unpleasant discussion that might lead to an argument, I didn't discuss our finances with my husband. After filing, I berated myself for not having taken a more assertive role regarding money matters.

Though we were forced to sell our home, because only one of us went bankrupt, we were allowed to keep half of the net proceeds. The other half went toward our outstanding debts. It was a step taken among a gamut of emotions—we were excited because we'd be on better financial footing; sad, because we were losing our home; and, stressed, because we needed to find somewhere else to live.

I'll forever remember and be grateful for our real estate agent and the way she negotiated our first serious offer from a potential buyer. I'd attended a budgeting workshop, and thanks to their system of financial strategizing based on income percentages, I had a specific figure in mind that would allow us to carry out our recovery plan. The initial purchase offer was too low. Spitfire speed, the potential buyer's agent and ours negotiated back and forth on the phone, while I paced caged-animal style. With a bottom price firm in my mind, when the buyer neared that number, I started to fret. *Should I give in? What if they back out?* Aware of my secret bottom figure, my agent kept countering, until BINGO! I had my price. (I'd never want to be a stockbroker...spitfire negotiation is way too stressful.)

From there, we moved into a basement suite with such narrow hallways that traffic lights would have been helpful. Whenever we met midway, one of us had to back up so the other could pass by. The people above us were so noisy at night we couldn't sleep. One evening, my husband took out the trumpet that he used to play in high school.

"Just what are you planning on doing with that?" I asked, hands on hips, lips slightly upturned, head cocked sideways.

"I'm going to give them a taste of their own medicine," Dwayne stated, determination glistening in the brown eyes I so loved.

Imagining how our inconsiderate, raucously annoying neighbors would respond, I just laughed.

Sure enough, the loud commotion started upstairs, Dwayne puckered and blew, and I covered my ears. The noise that came from his trumpet wasn't music. It sounded more like a sick elephant. Eventually my husband put down his weapon, delighted that the noise upstairs had stopped.

Talking with neighbors the next morning, we learned that the people from upstairs had moved out in a midnight run. The joke was on us; they'd missed the latter half of Dwayne's serenade. How lucky for them—my husband's backup plan included a duet with his chainsaw.

One night, impacted by all we'd endured and unable to sleep, I wondered—"Is this what God wants for me...for us?" Normally an optimistic person, but feeling particularly overwhelmed that night, I slowly accepted that if our current state of existence was God's will, then so-be-it, and relinquished my earthly destiny to Him. Divinely relieved of the stress and burden of unending worry, I drifted into a peaceful sleep.

The next day, my husband came home very excited. He was back to his usual social self, and in conversation with a neighbor had learned of a vacant townhouse for sale. Currently in foreclosure, it would be on the market soon and likely listed at a very cheap price. We immediately contacted the real estate agent to make viewing arrangements, only to learn that other agents were hot on this listing too.

Walking into the townhouse, we were greeted by a dizzying mix of gaudy mustard, purple and green walls standing like colorful sentinels over a black and white checkered floor. Not exactly our dream home, but the place was livable. And then I saw it! Shining through the window was a big white moon, its positive energy beaming through the darkness to smile upon us. I immediately realized that it was a divine sign that we should buy this townhouse and make it our own.

After a short discussion, Dwayne and I decided to put in an offer, surprised when the agent advised us to sleep on it. *Did the real estate salesman have a hidden agenda?*

"Nope, let's write it up!" I insisted, growing more certain that this place was meant to be our new home.

Twenty-four hours passed without a word from the agent. Expecting and hoping for a counteroffer, the waiting was unbearable. Dwayne and I had a down-payment garnered from the forced sale of our home. However, unless our offer was accepted, it would likely be a long time before we found another somewhat suitable house—in foreclosure and below market value—for which we could qualify at the bank.

Finally, on Halloween night, we learned we'd been accepted. Between handing out trick-or-treats, I signed the purchase agreement. More excited than the goblins, witches and clowns, I thanked the universe for our good fortune. We were on our financial feet again.

The tragedy in declaring bankruptcy is *not* the financial loss, or the *imagined* stigma. The real casualty risks are the personal relationships that may be affected, including spouses, children, coworkers, family, and friends. Money can be replaced—people cannot.

While in bankruptcy, if you strive to keep your relationships intact through the process, you will come out richer beyond measure. The less value you place on material belongings, the better. Being able to release your attachment to 'things' will greatly determine how well you survive emotionally and health-wise.

Forget about laying blame. The *truth* is that no single factor caused your bankruptcy. Reviewing your financial history will hold some valuable lessons for future money management. Focus on the solutions and consult a professional bankruptcy trustee.

I wish Dwayne and I had sought personal and financial counseling before our debt burden threatened all we held dear. I now see how important it is for every couple to discuss their money situation on a regular basis. A financial consultant can strengthen communication by acting as a liaison and offering suggestions; thereby, reducing resistance and avoiding unnecessary arguments with someone you love.

Should you be faced with bankruptcy, the first step I recommend is taking an inventory of your assets and resources. Add up *what you do have, not what you owe or don't have.* You will be surprised at your tally.

We still had our jobs and were allowed to keep some assets. However, our debts were not completely wiped out. We were required to pay a predetermined 'outstanding debt balance' which we'd earlier negotiated with the help of our trustee. Thanks to an old boss, who helped rather than judged, Dwayne secured a second job. That money went toward reducing our residual debt balance.

FYI: Reestablishing your après bankruptcy credit rating is less complicated than you might think. My husband's longtime bank lending-officer advised and approved a Registered Retirement Savings Plan loan for Dwayne. Thanks to this earth angel, my husband's credit rating began an immediate upward swing. You should also know that, while waiting to again become a good financial risk, prepaid credit cards and cell phone plans are still attainable.

Dwayne and I learned about bankruptcy the hard way—we couldn't maintain our debt load. Don't let that become you. Within the world of finance there are many escape hatches and solutions for ordinary folk. Our government is acutely aware that thanks to the constant onslaught of media fueled consumerism, and credit card companies willing to fulfill our lifestyle dreams via unsecured debt, personal bankruptcies continue to rise. To this end, legislation is in place to ensure citizens caught within the buy-buy-buy frenzy, or who find themselves in an unforeseeable monetary bind, have a chance to recover financially and start over again.

But long before you get to where you need to be bailed out, take personal financial control. One safeguard we now use is dealing in cash, rather than bank and credit cards. Counting out what you pay for groceries, clothes and entertainment keeps you aware that your hard-earned dollars are slipping away.

When declaring bankruptcy, be mindful that your self-respect and confidence are at risk of plummeting out of control. Should anyone close to you measure your value as being the sum total of your assets and bank balance, take a deep-hearted look at whether to continue with that particular relationship. Those who empathize and support you, in spite of your financial troubles, are worthy of your continued friendship. Those who don't, obviously need to re-evaluate their priorities.

No one enters bankruptcy easily. It's an anxious, guilt-ridden ordeal, during which the financially stressed person continually berates him or herself. Should bankruptcy become the unfortunate fate of someone you know, regardless of anything you might think about his or her financial irresponsibility, trust me, your loved one is doing a much more thorough job of self-admonishment than you ever could. My advice regarding any time you find yourself considering saying something hurtful to someone: stop and think—it only takes a second to wound a heart that may take a lifetime to heal.

The most valuable asset Dwayne and I saved was our marriage. So take heart and feel the hope…*there is life after bankruptcy*. What your life will look like, will be up to you. Count your blessings and be thankful for your truly precious assets—health, love, family, and friends—all will be instrumental and invaluable in helping you get through.

The chain of positive events that has occurred since I turned my earthly destiny over to God continues to amaze and inspire me. Every morning, I wake up and read a sign that I posted on my wall: "*Good morning. Know that today you are in good hands. You can relax. Thank you for your trust and understanding.*"

Our spiritual guides are always with us. Ask your higher power for guidance; then watch carefully and listen openly. I think you will be pleasantly surprised by the people and answers that come to you.

Bouncing Back from Brock-Bottom

Brock Tully
Founder of the World Kindness Concert

"…when i thought the light was at the end of the tunnel, i got
'tunnel-vision';
when i see that the light is within, there are no longer any
tunnels visible."

In 1970, at age twenty-three, I was totally disconnected from myself, deeply depressed and daily struggling with nagging thoughts of taking my life. Remarkably, over time, I came to see that this seemingly bleak existence was truly a blessing.

Being at *Brock-bottom* forced me to make a choice—either get on with it and take my life; or, as it turned out, spend time alone on my bicycle in the quiet of the mountains and deserts of North America. Alone, I was finally able to hear the even quieter, yet powerful and profound, voice of my heart.

At first, it was a foreign voice, hedging thoughts of not being good enough and cries for love once numbed and muted with alcohol, drugs, loud music, and empty *busy*-ness. But as the miles cycled by, from a mere seven inches below the chatter came a beautiful truth—I'm not here to 'take my life' but 'to give with my life.'

Raised in a family that never hugged, shared feelings, or said 'I love you,' harbored within was always an extreme sense of unworthiness. No matter what was going my way, even being captain of the basketball team, I remained caught in the fears of my head. There were so many overlapping and conflicting voices from family and others telling me what I *should do or be*, that I actually went to a counselor to figure out which voice had the best advice!

During the bicycle trip, the peaceful, joyful yearnings of my heart overrode the doubts and confusion of my mind, connecting me to happiness, so I penned…

> "…i thought i'd be
> 'out-of-my-mind'
> to go after my dreams…
> now that i've gotten
> out of my mind
> by following my heart
> i'm living my dreams."

The more I followed my heart, the more excited I became about life, and the more I realized that my depression came from losing touch with *my*-self first, and then others. Disconnected from my heart, the very essence of life, there was no way to truly connect with others, for this vital organ is the 'source' of our interconnected oneness.

Previously, I viewed others not as people I wanted to love and to be loved by, but as a collective group to *be better than*, so I could feel safe within a false sense of being okay and worthy. My *best*-striving naturally cocooned me in separateness, making love seem elusive, or at best, a fleeting source of admiration. It was incredibly freeing to discover that disconnected from others was a slow death to nowhere; yet, heart-connected, life became exciting.

The Disappearing of One's Authentic Self

> "…i do enjoy things…
> but joy comes from
> loving the things I do."

Growing up, my well-meaning parents and others constantly told me that I needed certain things 'out there' to make me happy. They really did want the best for me, sincerely believing that the more money I made, the more 'things' I'd be able to have to make happiness possible.

Many of us are brought up with this belief, and as our conditioning is slow and constant, we willingly meander the established pathways so eagerly charted and championed by others—pathways that too often lead us away from our true nature and toward our *false*-self.

As we learn that pleasing others gleans love, and being different repels love, we entrench ourselves in a continual pursuit of *normalness*. Having tasted the sweet nectar of 'fitting in,' with the exception of peer-sanctioned wardrobe experimentation, most of us stay the course of striving for approval. From school grades to trophies, to career, purchase and mate choices—many people convert everything one does or doesn't *do, accomplish* and *own* into a measure of worth.

Though we may suspect that prescribed remedies for happiness may actually be tonics for despair, fearing change and loss of love, we become masters of denial, and simply close our eyes to our unique truths and selves. At the root, is that we feel that by changing or being 'different' we will lose family and friends. In truth, it is *listening to* and *following* one's heart that actually creates the opportunity for becoming closer to family and friends. You can't *lose* family and friends by being your authentic self, because until you live authentically, you are never the 'real' you, but rather an 'actor' you think is loveable—a mere illusion of you.

It is by taking time alone, or with others that completely support and understand journeying inward, that one can truly listen to the quiet and powerful voice of his or her soul.

It took my first 10,000 mile bicycle trek, where, for six months, I was generally alone and in silence in the 'middle-of-nowhere,' for me to listen inward, instead of outward. By hearing and feeling my heart's yearnings, and by thinking about *how* and *why* I lost touch, I realized that happiness, or true peace, is within. As a result, I became happier—*not because I went away, but because while away I went within.*

I may never have gone away on my bicycle journey, if I hadn't earlier started to question what I observed, was told and intuitively suspected. On my summer breaks from college, I was fortunate to have the opportunity to be a lifeguard at a beach in West Vancouver, British Columbia. There were many quiet days when the ocean was free of swimmers, affording me time to sit on the 'guard' chair in quiet reflection.

Every day of those summers, many children came to the beach for hours on end. Never once did I see a child under the age of ten who was bored. In fact, at the end of the day, it was a challenge for parents to get their young ones to leave. Totally at peace with the sand, the driftwood, the rocks, the seaweed, the shells, and the water, the children were 'one' with nature and continually created their own fun and treasures.

I also noticed that parents often bought toys for their children; unfortunately, as they approached their preteen years, the kids seemed to want for more and more. At around age fourteen, most appeared to lose their connection with nature, their joy sadly slipping away to worry as they became concerned with their appearance and what others thought of them. Nature became unimportant as they obsessed with getting a tan. Like watching meat on a spit, I had a strange sense that I should somehow continually turn them all over before they became too roasted.

I thought it was the older people who enjoyed the beach the least. The litter they would leave at the end of the day was disgusting. Dogs, like the small children, gained much joy in playing by the sea. Unfortunately, as it was against the rules, I had to ask the owners to take their pets off the beach. I always wondered why dogs weren't allowed to visit the beach they so loved. At least the little bit of litter they left was biodegradable.

Some dog owners appeared to have spent a great deal of time getting dressed to impress. However, it was generally their pets who received compliments such as, "Oh, what a beautiful dog you have." Even babies, with dribble and drool all over their faces, poop in their pants, food everywhere, and all chubby and wrinkled, were honored with favorable comments like, "Wow, what a beautiful baby you have!" Unless it was a 'line' to win someone over, I hardly ever heard people say anything flattering about one another.

The dogs and children, so full of excitement and joy, were terrific happiness mentors. Ironically, it is we who teach them how to live, often with explanations, expectations and examples that rob their *joie de vivre*.

While a lifeguard, I would regularly hear the Royal Hudson steam train blowing its whistle on the way by the beach. People, of all ages, would jump up and run across the grassy area to wave wildly at the passengers. And those crammed together on the train's deck would enthusiastically wave back. Witnessing this ritual, I often pondered what would happen if the train suddenly came to a stop. Would the passengers remain high above the ground, safe from true human contact? Would the beachgoers retreat to their colorful blankets and picnic baskets? Or would both groups gleefully run toward one another, eager to become acquainted? I doubted that the answer was the latter scenario; for though people intrinsically desire and need community, we shy away out of fear, ensuring our separateness and loneliness. The impromptu display of friendly affection was made possible by the expectation that the train was merely passing by—a sense of *safety by distance*, which would quickly dissipate should the train actually stop.

My many summers of witnessing and analyzing human behavior did little to heal what ached within Brock Tully. I remained desperately lonely and separate from others. Looking back, my observations were only made possible because they were a reflection of my own disconnectedness—a disconnectedness that I naively tried to soothe with alcohol and drugs. When that didn't work, my contemplations turned to suicide.

It wasn't until my bicycle journey, that I realized that my loneliness and separateness from others were the direct results of being disconnected from my own heart. Conditioned to conform and seek approval above all else, prior to my journey within, I lacked the *courage to be authentic* and to stand *alone* when necessary.

Paradoxically, once I physically separated and faced my aloneness via a bicycle built for one, I connected with my heart and authentic self. Freed from my chatty head and calmly centered in my heart, I found compassion for myself and all others. Today, I no longer seek love for the sake of approval or a dread of being alone. Instead, I seek ways to be in *service to my love* for all beings, so that fewer souls will feel the separateness that once beckoned me to take my life.

Labeling: Helpful, Hurtful or Benign?

When young, we are just referred to as children. As we 'grow up' we are often labeled, which serves to separate us from one another, and therefore from our collective *oneness*. There is an array of labels for one's beliefs, affiliations, marital status, body type, achievements, education level, addiction(s), emotional stability, sexual orientation, etc. Some labels and titles are viewed as being more desirable than others—e.g., athlete, musician, actor, boss, writer, artist, minister, doctor, lawyer, etc. However, even desired labels serve to categorize, separate and invite comparison. Unwittingly, also moving us from the pure joy of just *being a being, interconnected with all beings.*

Why do humans, who from birth forward naturally seek connectedness, choose to conjure and foster descriptive tags that invite separation through comparative labels? Though it may be helpful to know which person's skills, knowledge and/or experience would best be able to meet our needs—is it helpful, hurtful or benign to view each of us by a *label* first and as a person second?

To answer this question, let's consider how freeing it might be if, rather than labeling, we each chose to view ourselves and others as *beings* performing functions and making choices based on where each of our hearts leads us at a given point in our personal growth. Instead of labeling or accepting a label of addict, thief or failure, what if we saw such circumstances for what they are—current circumstances, not forgone conclusions of a person's sum worth or absolute earthly path. If we didn't place professionals, actors and millionaires on pedestals, but instead viewed them as *beings* currently choosing to perform various tasks with varying results, each of our lives would become less limiting and more liberating.

People are *beings* first and labels second. To define our individual uniqueness with labels is limiting not only to others, but also to one's self. Considering, too, that the esteemed can fall from grace, and the scorned can rise to sainthood, from where I sit, labels are merely translucent transient tags.

Minus labels and their accompanying societal stigmatization, we are left to observe that people differ in their affinity or proclivity toward a variety of activities, beliefs, desires, habits, and such. Viewed in their entirety, we see that like a diamond, each being has many facets—not one could be defined merely by his or her acts, beliefs, achievements, sexual orientation, appearance, intelligence, choices, etc.

Labeling others with our perceptions actually shifts our self-perception. Though we may intellectually view ourselves as superior to someone we've labeled negatively, when we 'think' or 'voice' a judgment, we feel a little 'icky' inside. Likely, this is somewhat because we know that *there but for the grace of God, go I.* However, it is also because thinking in negative terms, registers as negativity in our bodies. Inwardly, it feels different and more freeing to view another as someone who—amid his or her many other qualities—currently has a challenge with reality, alcohol, drugs, cash, truth, heath choices, etc.

When we assign what we view as desired labels, the same truths apply. If doctors, professors and firemen, for example, are seen merely as symbolic icons of their esteemed professions, it becomes natural to compare their contributions against seemingly less virtuous job functions and titles. Much the same as when we think of others in negative terms, comparing one human's worth to another's opens the door to 'icky' feelings of inferiority, jealousy, fear, and resentment.

The same applies for adjectives such as *good* as compared to *bad*, *pretty* as contrasted with *ugly*, and such. Labels divide in the same way that judgments divide and separate. No matter what someone's accomplishments, habits and characteristics may be, the sum total of that person is much more than any adjective, title or label could ever accurately capture.

We are all diamonds: multifaceted, unique, and shining our brilliance exactly as the universe intended. Together, through our interconnected *oneness*, we are the light.

An Unexpected Lesson in Gratitude

> "...i want to work
> hard on my faults...
> but be easy on myself
> when i falter."

In the early eighties, while travelling in California, a new friend mentioned that Louise Hay, the author of *You Can Heal Your Life*, was speaking in Los Angeles. The event, as it turned out, was a weekly Wednesday night gathering of five hundred to a thousand people, including many who had been diagnosed with AIDS. Having just recently been discovered, there was tremendous fear and many misconceptions regarding the Human Immunodeficiency Virus (HIV) that causes AIDS (Acquired Immune Deficiency Syndrome).

Though mainly thought to be a 'gay' disease, even in the heterosexual community, fear of catching the virus was rampant among non-monogamous youth. Sexually active, and at that time having a lot of fear around both the issue of sexuality choices and the spread of AIDS, I entered the packed auditorium with much trepidation.

Louise Hay actually said very little. Instead, she encouraged people to address the audience and share their personal experiences regarding the virus. One by one, many a brave soul poured out his heart, while others massaged and held loved ones who were lying or sitting because they were too sick or weak to stand.

What struck me most was the incredible love that filled the auditorium. Sharing in the sadness and laughter laced with joy, I could no longer fear, or separate from, those victimized by an insidious disease no one saw coming.

The healing that took place in that room, and within me, was overwhelming. Witnessing the transformation as parent after parent was finally able to release fears and prejudices regarding a son's sexual orientation and lovingly accept him for who he was, touched me deeply. As did a young man who shared, "I am so thankful I got AIDS because for the first time in my life I am experiencing LOVE."

I was shocked at first, but as his message sunk in, I totally understood it. As sad a statement as it was about our culture and communities, hearing his wisdom helped me to further embrace the healing power of being *authentic*, in contrast to the pain and suffering caused from holding one's issues inside. As he finished sharing, about seven hundred people jumped to their feet, zealously clapping and cheering.

As I walked away from the meeting, there was no longer him, them or me—all of us were *one*.

Years later, reflecting on what purpose disease could possibly serve on our beautiful and plentiful planet, I realized that 'disease' is often a symptom, a kind of red flag that we're collectively or individually off course; and as such, are out of sync with our hearts, bodies, minds, one another, and/or our planet. Yet, we spend billions treating disease symptoms, not our skewed course or the 'at heart' root cause. Though it would be fantastic to discover a pill for whatever ails us, would having a quick fix permanently distort our sense of wellness, wholeness and oneness?

How easy it would be to just ignore those numbing and self-hurting through the use of tobacco, illicit drugs, prescription medications, over-eating, or alcohol. Rather than reaching out in love, we could just say, "Oh, well. When whoever figures it out, he/she can pop a pill and get back to working toward feeling well, loveable and whole."

Equally sad, if there were a quick fix for the cancerous effects of pollution, we could each just pile up the garbage to our heart's content.

The clutter might become a stinking eyesore, but we'd be able to just shrug our shoulders and utter a collective, "Oh, well. Pigs will be pigs. Pass me a pill, some dark shades and a gas mask, please. And while you're at it, be a dear and dump a bag of that cure-all tonic into the ocean."

Maladies of the mind and body often signal where we are astray of healthful and heart-centered living. Therefore, embracing disease as a governess is a crucial first step toward absolute health. Collectively and caringly, we can eradicate disease, one kind act at a time.

Toward the very attainable outcome of a disease-free planet, rather than merely offering platitudes for those suffering emotionally or physically, we could instead each ask questions such as: From cancer to bullying, what steps can I take to ease and prevent disease-related suffering? What's possibly the cause behind each type of disease? How am I contributing to the fostering and festering of disease?

An assault on one person—disease or otherwise—is an assault on all of humanity. Turning a blind eye to another's suffering is a symptom of our separateness and misguided perceptions of helplessness. Imagine how differently our human experience might unfold, if instead of ignoring a beggar seeking a handout or digging through trash bins, we, at a minimum, realized that one of us has fallen away from our flock's love. Envision living in a community where, instead of judging people self-hurting via an unhealthy lifestyle, we all sought ways to let them know they are loveable. How delightful it would be to live in a neighborhood where everyone: habitually smiled kindly at strangers who seem unhappy or lost; cared enough to present a floundering friend with an unexpected bouquet of bright flowers; and, regularly volunteered at organizations that offer aide.

There are a myriad of gestures we can each make toward absolute mental and physical health. *So why do so many of us continue to ignore the obvious steps we can take to be part of the prevention team?* I would venture that it's because we don't fully appreciate the significance of our personal impact. As a result, we become apathetic and forfeit the care of our health and planet to the government, scientists and assorted professionals, trusting that the illusory 'they' have our best interest at heart and will somehow find a magical cure for pollution and disease. *How crazy is that?*

Individually, we compound into either the problem or the solution. When we forfeit personal power by throwing our hands up in a 'What can I do?' attitude, we inadvertently contribute to the problem, making it possible for disease to flourish. Each time we claim personal significance and accept our infinitely vital role as co-protectors of our planet, animals, others, and ourselves—we move toward a disease-free planet. From consumption to kindness, our individual daily choices—actions and non-actions—make a lasting difference. As Mahatma Gandhi said: "Be the change you wish to see in the world."

Staying Grounded and Surrounded in Love

> "...i'm not excited about the challenge
> of winning someone else's heart
> so i'll feel good for
> a little while...
> i am excited about the challenge
> of staying in touch with my own heart
> so i'll know how to feel good forever."

It was when I *wasn't* feeling needy about having a relationship, and excited about my journey of *inner growth and awareness*, that I met Wilma. I was hobbling down the street on crutches (due to a knee operation) on my way to the beach where I planned to do some writing, when I came across this beautiful, vibrant woman from Austria who was waiting for her two travel companions who'd gone to find a restroom. The three women spoke very little English, but were able to convey that they were traveling North America to experience the beautiful nature, culture, and the kindness of the people of Canada and the United States. As was I, Wilma was healing from past relationships, and wasn't looking to become involved in a romantic partnership.

We became close rather quickly, which surprised and delighted us both. I was about to embark on a six month speaking and book tour around the U.S., and after only a few days of knowing each other, I asked Wilma if she wanted to accompany me. Thankfully, her answer was, "Yes!" Twenty-two years later, we are still happily together.

Being with Wilma is a joyous and delightful journey—not because she *makes* me happy, but because *I'm happier with myself.* As a result, I'm *openly* loving and nurturing toward Wilma. Equally important, I'm *open* to her love for me.

From my perspective, the secret to a lasting meaningful romantic union lies in refraining from thinking of yourself as being 'in love'—

and instead, as being 'loving in the moment.' As a result, I'm not keen making promises that happen in the elusive future, preferring instead to commit to staying 'fully present in the moment,' so that I will still be 'fully present in the moment' in the future.

> "...if i don't live in the 'now,'
> because i'm worried about my future,
> then in the future,
> i'll probably be worried about
> my future's future...
> ...if i live in the 'now'
> now,
> i'll probably be living in the 'now,'
> in the future,
> and i'll see that there was nothing
> to worry about,
> before."

Others simply aren't capable of making us *feel loved,* or even *okay* with who we each are. That honor is truly up to the beholder of unfulfilled needs and desires. I'm aware that should I choose to move back into my head, and away from my heart-sense, I run the risk of succumbing to fear, jealousy and anger. I know that I must listen inward, so that the 'hole' in my being won't again run and ruin my happiness experience. My hedge against creeping away from my *authentic* self is remaining *fully present and loving in the moment,* so that I can stay *grounded in the love I feel and the love I receive.*

> "...i don't want
> you
> to fill a hole
> in me...
> ...i want
> you
> to feel 'whole'
> with me."

The Miracle of Kindness

"...one kind act
by one kind person
is the kind of action
that shows kindred spirits
how kindness
can rekindle
our oneness."

Viewing our travelling time together as an adventure, and wanting to see how things progressed between us, after Wilma decided to trust her intuition and accept my invitation to accompany me on my speaking tour, she flew back to Austria to get her things. The plan for her return trip to North America, conveyed in spite of the inherent challenge of speaking two different languages, was for her to fly into Seattle, where I would meet her for our trip south. While she was away, I went to Orcas Island (off the coast near Seattle) where I oversaw the building of a new camper being made according to our mutual specifications: lots of wood, a fireplace, plant boxes, and a skylight.

A few hours before Wilma was due to land, I drove to the ferry terminal, excited about seeing her and our trip. But that quickly changed when I noted the lengthy lineup of vehicles, and then learned that the ferry only took about a hundred cars. With absolutely no way to reach Wilma, I panicked. Neither of us had a cell phone, she spoke very little English, hardly knew me, and was about to be stranded in a strange city. Undoubtedly, she'd be hurt and feel stupid for trusting someone she barely knew.

I frantically counted the lined up vehicles. There were a hundred and five cars—five more than there was normally room for on the ferry, which was quickly approaching from the distance. Running from car to car, explaining that I'd finally, after many years, found 'the woman of my dreams,' I pleaded with drivers, in a fun way, to please park as close as possible to the car in front of theirs, so that my vehicle would be able fit on the small ship. Though I admit to feeling guilty for appealing to their sensibilities with my woes worthy of country song lyrics, I didn't falter in my pursuit *not* to hurt and disappoint Wilma.

Heart in throat, I drummed my fingers on the camper steering wheel as vehicle after vehicle slowly filed onto the ship. As the first passengers onboard crowded onto the outside decks to watch and see if I made it onto the ferry, my heart swelled. Everyone was rooting for me—a total stranger, and a woman they'd never meet.

When I was finally crammed into the last available spot on the vehicle deck, there was a near deafening roar of clapping and cheering. As the cliché goes…the rest is history. I remain eternally grateful to those who helped save me from becoming *history* with Wilma before our relationship had a chance to truly begin.

Ponderings

"…i'd rather be seen for who i am and be alone…
than be accepted for someone i'm not and be lonely."

I've now cycled around North America two more times—altogether close to 30,000 miles in three trips—to raise awareness for a KINDER world. For our earthly experience to move forward in collective authenticity and happiness, we must daily practice being kind to ourselves, others, the planet, and animals. I hope that the words and poems I've shared here, and in my *Reflections* books, inspire you to listen to and follow your heart.

It's important to me that you relate to my ponderings from your *authentic self.* In school, I was always asked what a poem or story meant to the writer or the teacher—I was never asked what it meant to me. I write to stimulate thought, and to inspire others to *think* and *feel* independently of what I pen or what society expects. By each of us finding and responding to our own inner-truths, I believe we will come to see the oneness in our humanness. When we are truly willing and open to listening to our own and one another's heart's desires—and not the fears that too often escape our heads to form hurtful words—the world becomes a kindly place to call home.

"…when i think i need
to belong,
i often follow others…
…when i follow my heart
i feel i belong
regardless of others."

Decision Day—To Live or Die

Larry Chase

My eyes shot open. I couldn't breathe. It felt as if someone were on top of me, his murderous hands squeezing my throat closed. Gasping, I threw off the covers and bolted for the window. *I need air. I need air. I need air.*

Awakened by my dying man's wheeze, my wife called out, "Larry, are you okay?"

I couldn't answer.

Thrusting my head into the cold night, I tried for a breath of oxygen. I barely managed a wee wisp. My lungs ached for more. I prayed my next breath would be a little deeper. Scorched dry by stomach acid, my throat wouldn't open. *God, are you ready for me? Or are you going to let me breathe again?* I coaxed in another tiny wisp, then another, repeating the process for what seemed an eternity, until little by little my throat expanded and oxygen reached my lungs.

The next morning, staring at the ceiling, I listened to the Nova Scotia January wind howling around our house. I didn't move for quite some time. *What was the sense in getting out of bed?* I was exhausted.

The bedtime oxygen thief was acid reflux that seeped up my esophagus and burned my throat raw, dry and shut. The terrifying nighttime ritual was always the same—my wife panicked and me fighting for my life with no time to comfort her. The only possible salvation was shocking my system with crisp, damp air, as I prayed for mercy.

You've heard the saying *die a thousand deaths*—I lived it many nights, hour after hour, for months and years on end. Falling asleep, I'd know that within a short while I'd be in a fight for my life. *What if tonight I couldn't get out of bed on my own?* I knew my wife wouldn't be able to help me to the window. I weighed four hundred and fifty pounds.

My weight was also a problem for the poor bed. It had center support legs, but they were no match for me. The frame crushed flat shortly after I purchased it, necessitating the addition of wooden blocks.

Putting on socks was a daily struggle. I couldn't just reach down and slide them on the way any other person would. While sitting on the bed, I had to put the sock on my hand, spread my fingers far apart, and then try to reach my foot. It was a near impossible feat never accomplished on the first attempt, because lifting my foot while bending forward, I'd come against my large stomach, requiring that I rock back and forth to gain momentum while trying to hook my toes. Sometimes I'd hook the sock partway at the same time that my belly sprung me backward, and the sock would go flying.

I wore jogging pants because they were big enough to fit. My shirt size was five-x and very tight at that. The only reason I didn't wear size six-x was that I couldn't find clothes that large in our small town.

After breakfast one day, I decided to walk to my friend's house, hoping to clear my head while watching him work on a small engine repair. We had a nice talk because he knew the local gossip. Walking home afterward, the pain spiking up from the soles of my feet was more excruciating than usual. Thank God, it was only about two hundred feet from his place to mine. Once home, I dropped into my recliner, noticing that the pain in my feet and legs was worse than normal. Though standing after sitting was often painful enough to collapse me to my knees, that day, putting weight on my feet was like being barefoot on burning-hot gravel.

Poor blood circulation had long turned my legs brown from the knees down. My ankles and feet were always swollen so large I could only see half of my toes. Each passing day brought increased pain and swelling.

I knew that if I didn't soon start taking care of myself, I'd be permanently imprisoned in a wheelchair. Haunted by this sobering thought, I often stared at my reflection trying to shame myself into losing weight. But facing the giant mountain in the mirror only sobered me further. *How many years of nearly starving myself to death would it take for me to return to a healthy body weight? Could I muster the stamina and willpower to overcome my food cravings in exchange for life?*

Self-ridicule daunted me daily. Disgusted to my core, all I kept thinking was how in the world I'd allowed this to happen. I'd slid into a horrible dark and lonely place, with no idea how to climb out or where to turn for help. Angered by a 'me' I couldn't escape and a life that no longer seemed worth living, I ate.

Compounding my shame, in public, people looked at me with distain, some snickering and elbowing their buddies. Though out of ear range, I'd imagine them saying, *Look at that fat slob…what a mess.* If they could have only known how much it hurt to be trapped in a large body by an addiction I didn't understand. Sometimes I'd consider giving them a piece of my mind, only to realize that the world was full of judgmental people. It was a battle I'd never win.

Wishing I could hide in the house but forced into society, I sometimes hoped that my weight would just hurry up and kill me; perhaps, as a result of a massive heart attack…quick, fatal and freeing. My morbid ponderings mirrored what I saw in my sister's eyes every time she glanced my way. And being that she was a paramedic, her concern made me realize that my ghoulish contemplations were close to being fulfilled.

Considerations of whether it was fair to cheat the world of the fun in having me around, weighed heavily against the freedom I sought in death—no more suffering; no more tears. Finishing my life via binging seemed a perfect strategy, until I thought about my family. *How would my wife, son and daughter react to my just giving up? My problems would be over, but my legacy might just be beginning. Knowing that kids sometimes follow in a parent's footsteps, would the lives of my children carve a similar weight-gain or addiction path?*

With that thought, my blurred thinking became crystal clear—I was through with eating for comfort. My food addiction was no longer going to rule my existence. There was way too much ahead that I wasn't willing to miss; mainly, walking my daughter down the aisle and seeing my son buy his first sports car. By giving up on life I wouldn't be cheating the world, I would be cheating *myself.*

Armed with an action plan, I booked a check-up at our small rural hospital. If it was determined that there was no permanent damage to my vital organs, I'd fight for my life. If there were serious problems, I would simply allow myself to die.

"Doc," I said, not bothering to hide my anxious fears, "I think I might have ruined my body. I'm hoping you can prove me wrong."

The doctor's main concern was my heart. Likely spiked by anxiety, my blood pressure was near fatally high. After telling me that my heart was beating as though I'd just run a marathon, he did an EKG and then checked for fluid around my heart and lungs. A short while later, I left the doctor's office armed with pills and hope. My blood pressure was a problem, and the fluid around my heart and lungs a concern, but with proper care and the diligent taking of the prescriptions he'd given me, I had a chance to reclaim my health.

"I know why I've been so tired of late," I announced when I returned home.

"Uh-huh," my wife responded, moving about the kitchen, totally unaware that I'd gone for tests.

"I'm a ticking time bomb!" I said, repeating what the doc had told me. "I guess my sister was right!"

Her brow furrowed, she stared at me confusedly. "What are you talking about?"

"I went to see the doctor today!"

"And why would you do that?" my wife wanted to know, obviously thinking of how much I dreaded medical professionals. After all, my motto was that a trip to the doc every ten years was good enough.

"Cause there's a skinny guy inside of me just screaming to get out," I said, donning a smile as cheery and wide as a watermelon slice.

Seemingly needing time to digest what she was hearing, she simply stared at me.

"I'm going on a diet," I continued, already figuring a meal plan I could live with. "If I eat healthily ninety-five percent of the time, and allow myself whatever I feel like five percent of the time, or about one fun meal per week, I should be able to handle the cravings. But we'll have to get rid of all of the bad food in the house."

Knowing that moving forward required understanding *why*, at age forty, I suddenly turned to food for comfort, I began examining the past.

Since a small lad, I'd always wanted to move to Vancouver, British

Columbia. Although I loved living nearby my family and friends in Nova Scotia, overtime, the financial frustration of being economically married to the fishing industry had taken its toll. It seemed that each time I built a business to where I felt monetarily comfortable, the economy would nosedive and take my earnings with it.

As my wife didn't share my dream and resisted moving, year after year, I did what was necessary to survive. For over a decade, I worked in the fiberglass boat industry, which was hard on my body as the floating talcum-fine fibers caused numerous nosebleeds and affected my breathing.

After receiving a camera as a Christmas gift, I came up with the idea of selling fishermen enlarged photos of their boats navigating the ocean. Though it meant building another business from scratch, I would be working in the fresh air, away from the fiberglass slowly destroying my lungs. At that point, I'd already put on a few pounds, but wasn't worried, chalking it up to the middle-age spread most of my friends were also experiencing.

The fishing boat pictures business was an immediate success. However, within a year, I'd photographed all the boats close to home, requiring that I venture further and further. It wasn't long before the distance traveled necessitated my staying away from home most nights. Unable to afford both a hotel room and financial support for my family, I slept in my car. Although extremely uncomfortable, living in my vehicle six days a week was bearable during the non-winter months.

In the North Atlantic region, when winter descends it does so with bluster and fury, making keeping warm overnight in a car impossible. Unfortunately, since Nova Scotia lobster fishermen are busiest between December and June, with only a short break at the first of the year, I was stuck. What sold best were pictures of the boats in motion, which meant many cold days on the end of piers trying to snap just the right shot. At night, too cold to sleep, I ate. Unequipped to cook and fast-food the easiest and cheapest, my diet became filled with saturated fats.

Having somehow managed not to freeze to death over the winter, when the next onslaught of miserable weather hit, my wife and I exchanged vehicles. She took the car and I converted the minivan into a makeshift camper. It was a bit small to comfortably live in, but at least I was able to make a bed so I could lie down at night.

The third year on the road, depression hit me with a vengeance. Lonely and often unable to sleep, nightly I parked at the end of a pier and waited for the fishermen. Starved for a few minutes of company and conversation, when no one came in from the sea, I'd lie in my makeshift bunk and stare out at the houses, wishing I was inside one of them, laughing and having fun with the people who lived there. The more I hurt emotionally, the more I ate.

Once my weight ballooned, it seemed as if there was nothing I could do about it. Glimpsing my reflection depressed me further, sending me scurrying for my sole comfort source. It was a catch-twenty-two I couldn't win. The only thing that kept me going was that I needed to support my family.

One bitter night, a blustery wind blew the snow sideways and the temperature plummeted well below zero. Unable to safely drive home, I sought shelter behind a twenty-four-hour service station. My only hope of staying warm was a small propane heater I'd just purchased. Leaving two windows cracked, creating a cross-draft to draw out the fumes, I curled up in my sleeping bag and nodded off.

In the middle of the night the propane ran out. By the time I shivered awake, the van doors had frozen shut. Without any more propane, nearing hypothermia, the ignition barricaded behind my belongings and equipment, I set to kicking the doors. Once free, shaking violently, my toes and hands frostbitten, I headed inside the gas station. Having warmed up and purchased another cylinder of propane, returning to my van I wondered what the heck I was doing living like a gypsy. There had to be an easier way to support my family.

Hundreds of lonely freezing sleepless nights took their toll, driving my weight upward while sinking me further into depression. Unable to comfortably stretch out in the van, and having a weight problem that had me choking for air when I did fall asleep, staying awake during the daytime became a minute-by-minute struggle. Chatting with friends, I'd often fall asleep midsentence. During a longer drive, I'd need to pull off the road for a nap every five or ten miles. One day, while driving, my peripheral vision went black and my sight shrank into a steadily tapering tunnel. By the time I pulled to the roadside and jammed the van into park, my vision had narrowed to a pinhole. Then I went blind.

I must have passed out, so am uncertain as to how long it was before I came to, shaken and convinced I was dying. My wife insisted I go to the doctor, where I learned that my sky-high blood pressure was likely the cause of my blackout. Embarrassingly, he wasn't able to weigh me on his office scales. The only scale capable of reporting my ever-increasing weight was the digital one at the fish plant.

Attending my son's high school graduation was a totally humiliating experience. All the other teenagers' fathers were dressed in suits or pants with a jacket. I wore the nicest clothes that fit. Certain everyone's eyes were on the fat slob in tight black jogging pants and bulging out of a dark green golf shirt, walking through the gymnasium I shuddered and cringed. *What must my son be thinking and feeling?*

The worst part was when my son crossed the stage to receive his diploma. As the family photographer, it was up to me to get the shot. Aware of all eyes on me as I moved into position, it sickened me that I'd become an embarrassment to my family. I wanted to just disappear.

No one in my family ever said anything remotely insulting; however, I knew they daily prayed I would start taking better care of my body. Hating myself for burdening and embarrassing my loved ones, my son's graduation was the catalytic seed that motivated me to regain control over my weight—my life.

The winter following my son's graduation was when the doc gave me the great news that my vital organs had survived my weight gain. As the fluids drained from my heart and lungs, I started sleeping more deeply and longer. My energy level began to rise and I could stay awake for longer periods without needing a catnap. However, the most exciting change was that for the first time in many, many years the pounds started to come off.

Afraid I might jinx myself, at first, I didn't tell anyone about how diligently I was following my diet. Excited that *my eat well ninety-five percent of the time and whatever I desired five percent of the time* diet was working, especially that I was able to handle the cravings, after about three weeks, I started to talk about it with my family. Daring to remember the man I was before my weight increase, the joy was overwhelming. One day soon, I'd again participate in physical activities without being short of breath or crippled by pain.

The fact that my family was very supportive didn't stop me from wondering if they believed I could actually lose the two hundred pounds necessary for me to live healthily. After all, I'd failed at controlling my calorie intake many times before. Thankfully, my 95-5 diet *seemed* doable, which was half the battle.

Fueling my determination was a major shift in self-perspective—instead of hating the fat guy in the mirror, I concentrated on seeing the skinny person trying to escape from within the mountain of flesh. Along with shedding the weight, I shed my shame. Despite the fact that society ridicules people who medicate with food, self-hatred was no longer a coat I was willing to wear. Each pound lost, brought increased confidence—no matter what came my way in the future, good or bad, I'd get through it.

As the weeks turned into months, my weight loss became increasingly obvious. For the first time in years, I received compliments. People actually said I looked great. It blew my mind! Only an operation could have removed my smile.

Regardless of how great I felt, the problems with my life had to be addressed, or I'd surely backtrack down a road I knew led to death. Behind my eating disorder was an unfulfilled yearning to explore the world. Like it is for many people, life got in the way of my dreams. My wanderlust imaginings derailed when I married at twenty and had a family shortly thereafter. Loving my wife and kids wholeheartedly, there was no way I could abandon them in exchange for following my heart's aspirations.

Aware of my desire to travel since before we were married, my wife had once moved west with me, but couldn't stand to be that far away from family in Nova Scotia. So for the next decade we lived where she was most happy. However, I always knew that one day I'd return to British Columbia.

Our children grown and living on their own, and well aware that being true to myself required a residence change—even if I had to do it alone—I had an emotional and heart-wrenching talk with my wife. We agreed that the only way for both of us to be happy, was for her to stay put, and for me to move to Vancouver. Missing my family the second I drove out of the driveway, I headed west in June 2006, feeling both scared and excited

The journey across Canada was absolutely beautiful, amazing and freeing. With each mile, weight lifted from my shoulders as I wondered about what my new life would be like. Arriving in Vancouver on a gorgeous, sunny day, even though tired from a four-day drive which normally takes seven, I felt more alive than I had in decades. Not knowing what my next step would be seemed unimportant. I was finally home.

Within a short while, I was shopping for a size fifty-eight pair of dress-pants for my new sales job. It was a heady experience for a guy who'd been living in sweatpants to actually again be able to buy clothes off the rack! I'd lost one hundred pounds by then, making my goal to lose another hundred within the next two years attainable. Visualizing that my third year Decision Day—Live or Die anniversary would be celebrated in style and a much smaller go-to-town outfit, I swore never to abuse my body again. Additionally, while slowly losing weight, I'd exercise to regain a youthful shape to fill those new clothes.

Fueled by ironman willpower, daily I walked as far as possible, not only for the increased weight loss, but because it felt great to be able to exercise pain-free. A few months later, I also started dancing three or four nights per week, making new friends and having the time of my life. On high blood pressure medication, after getting the okay from my doc, I started going to the gym and fell in love with working out. Within weeks, I was doing two hundred sit-ups almost daily, followed by cardio and weight training. By my third anniversary I'd lost two hundred and ten pounds. I made it!

Six years after Decision Day, at fifty-two years of age, I continue to be in the best shape of my life, emotionally and physically. The key to my success was re-introducing the guy I'd become to the skinny guy buried beneath layers of sacrificed needs and wants, that in the mirror looked like fat. It wasn't fat—it was pain and suffering. I was trapped inside myself, and the only escape hatch was a mouth that I kept filling with comfort foods that were burying me.

Today, when asked to participate in something bodily challenging, I no longer make excuses to hide away free from ridicule and physical pain. I'm now the first to say, "Let's do it!" As a result, I've completed two ten-kilometer marathons, and I am about ready to enjoy another one. I've parasailed, zip-lined, swam in underground caves, and continue to do what my heart desires. No longer does weight hold me back from the pleasure of living fully and completely. But I'll never forget the first step of my journey, or the long haul back to total health. A trek I know many of my kindred brothers and sisters have still to face.

Excuse the pun, but none of it was a cakewalk. There were numerous days I'd have killed for a steak and baked potato stuffed with cheese, bacon, butter, and sour cream. Weeks when my limit of *five percent comfort food* diet begged revising or being totally forfeited. Days when I didn't want to do sit-ups, walk or dance. But I still did, because *I* was worth it!

No one is overweight by absolute choice, and not one larger-than-life person deserves to suffer at the hands, eyes and mouth of another. Looking back, *Walk a mile in my painful shoes* is the slogan I wish I'd imprinted on my tight-fitting, green golf shirt. Instead, like so many weight-sufferers, I took on the shame others dealt out like a child's card game. But I should never have owned that shame, for it truly belonged to the beholders of the judgment.

As a society, too many of us suffer at the disgraceful manipulation of profit-driven advertising hounds in search of a buck-at-any-cost, who daily bombard us with messages of *thin-is-better, balding is fatal* and *wrinkles are sinful.* Thin is healthier, yes! Thin is freer, yes! But I'm looking forward to living life long enough to lose my hair and see my face become crinkled with memories. Each day, I decide to live grateful and open to the inherent joy in being true to myself.

Although we are now divorced, I'm still in friendly communication with my ex-wife. She's the mother of my beautiful children, and for that I will be eternally grateful. My son now lives in Vancouver too. I still chuckle that the first time I visited Nova Scotia, my daughter commented that if she'd bumped into me on the street, if not for the tattoo on my arm, she'd likely have walked right by me—her own father!

Besides visiting loved ones, the highlight of that trip was running into friends and saying hello like a long-lost buddy only to have them stare at me bewilderedly. Losing half a person is definitely an eye-popping, rollicking good time.

Without debating statistics, it's safe to say that many North Americans suffer from the stigma created from being labeled overweight or obese. Don't listen to what's *wrong* with how you look or how much you should or shouldn't weigh—listen instead to how you feel inside. Hear your own voice. Maybe keep a journal where you write loving notes to yourself, slowly discovering what it is that *you need and want* to be healthy and fulfilled. Then design your own plan for slow and steady progress back to yourself and dreams. Hopefully, your life changes won't necessitate moving five thousand miles away from those you treasure; however, do what you need to do to *live*.

God loves to give second chances and will gladly provide a helping hand. Just listen to your inner voice, and you'll soon know the joy of forging an inspirational pathway for others to follow. People suffering from all kinds of addictions now hang on every word of my journey, which gives me immense pleasure. Each time I recount my self-saving voyage, I cross my fingers that something of what I'm sharing reaches that person's tender heart in a helpful and healing way. Then I thank him or her for listening, because telling my story continues to heal the skinny guy no longer confined within. God bless.

Fearless, No Matter What!

J. Dennis Robert

From an early age, my insatiable quest for the meaning of my life took root. I wasn't exactly clear on what I was looking for, but I knew I had to find it. Trouble followed me no matter what I thought, felt or did.

The judge's words resounded in my ears, "Against my better judgment, JR, I'm giving you a chance to redeem yourself. Take it or leave it. It's up to you."

Never in a million years did I think the army would become my new home. It was tough. Mornings were the worst: 05:30 roll call; 06:30 mess hall; 07:00 parade deck. *"You get what you deserve, JR,"* I mumbled as I rubbed the steam off the bathroom mirror. Now structured, my life would never be the same.

As a kid, endless days were spent daydreaming gazing out the French paned kitchen window. My worldly view consisted of the intersection of Knox Street and Livinia Avenue. Obstructed in the winter months by coats of ice, I entertained myself by placing my thumb on the pane long enough to melt a clear circle to the outside. On the days when the ice was too thick, I'd open the vent and peer out that way. Summers proved to be more eventful. The neighborhood kids gathered just below me, racing around on their fancy big-tired bikes, laughing and daring one another to races out to some hidden place near the old pond. I could only guess what magical adventures awaited the boys beyond my window. My imagination kept me company for a while, but the loneliness always returned.

One day as I looked out, Mrs. Gallard, our English neighbor, stood at her back door staring bewilderedly at the rain barrel. Smiling, I recalled my escapade of two days earlier. At first, I'd just played with the water bugs; but after a while, it made more sense to join them. As I watched, Mrs. Gallard suddenly threw her arms up in the air, and then dumped the water. Luckily, later that day, the rain came down hard and refilled the barrel. I figured I should check for water skaters once more.

"What's your name, little boy?"

Startled, I sheepishly blurted out "Joey!" which is short for my first name, Joseph. I could have chosen a different name to tell her, because I have three given names. Dennis is my second name, and I think is the one my mom liked the most because she personally picked it for my baptism. My third name was once my grandpa's—Stanislaus. Nobody ever called me that.

"Do you know what the water in the barrel is for?" Mrs. Gallard asked.

"No," I tentatively voiced.

Mrs. Gallard explained that she liked to use the soft rain water for her laundry instead of the harsh water from the tap. *That made sense.* It was a good thing she didn't have any soft water for laundry that day. She didn't know it, but I'd set mink traps under the clothesline to catch some rats that lived near the compost pile by the old Silver Dairies milk wagon out back. She might have stepped on one. *What would have happened then?*

I accepted her invitation for tea; although, surely she must have known that it was me who had ruined her water.

For a small house, the rooms seemed big. As I started wandering about the badly lit rooms, I could make out a big gray model airplane covered in stickers, which was suspended from the ceiling on invisible string. There were more, eleven in total. From where I stood they almost looked real.

"My husband flew airplanes just like those. He was in the air force. It took him all over the world," Mrs. Gallard said as she caught me squinting to see if the planes were magically suspended, or if there were indeed strings attached to them.

A large world globe, with tiny colored flags sticking out of it, caught my eye as we entered the living room. It stood out against the solid wall of books as high as the ceiling. Pictures of varied people, some smiling, some not, hung on all four walls. The glass case protected a display of metal stars, commemorative ribbons, a two-edged knife, and even a box of bullets. There was no doubt in my mind that Mr. Gallard was a spy. No wonder he never came home. Maybe one day I would fly, I thought as she left me alone so I could gawk in private.

An overstuffed chair, carefully positioned toward the window, dominated the front room. *Odd place for a chair.* But stranger still, were the smelly slippers and old pipe. The pipe flew out of my hands when Mrs. Gallard surprised me with some biscuits and a hot cup of tea. We sat in silence as I wolfed down the treats and then let out a loud belch.

"That's a good one," Mrs. Gallard commented.

We both laughed about that before talking about everything and nothing. She lovingly picked up the old pipe, smelled it, and then gently placed it back in the ashtray. I asked her why the big chair was so close to the window. She just said it was a warm and comfortable place to be.

Our conversation covered many subjects—mostly with me asking questions and Mrs. Gallard answering. We were comfortable together. I hoped she would ask me to come again. Thankfully, she told me we were friends now and that I needed to "keep an eye on the water bugs." We hung out all summer. I helped her with outside chores, and she answered my questions. Once I made her laugh so hard, she started to cry. *Her husband had to be a spy.*

Fall arrived, and so did opportunity. Mr. Allan, who lived at the corner of Knox and Highway 1, was weeding his flower beds as I approached. Mr. Allan had the reputation for having the best yard in town. *It sure was nice.* After saying hello, he asked me if I wanted to make a few extra bucks.

"What for?" I asked.

"I've seen you work over at the Gallard's place. I thought maybe you'd like to help me out now that my son is away at university."

"Sure," I said. The next words out of my mouth shocked me, but there they were. "How much?"

"Five bucks," Mr. Allen shouted over the semitrailer trucks racing by.

Mad calculations occupied my mind. *How many quarters are there in five bucks?* I'd never even seen a five dollar bill! Before Mr. Allen could change his mind, I blurted out, "It's a deal!"

The next Saturday, I pulled a bunch of weeds out of his garden and turned over the planter soil. Sure enough, Mr. Allen kept his word and gave me my first five dollar bill. Not only that, he offered me his son's job of mowing the lawn once a week, starting next spring. I couldn't believe my luck! Five bucks a week was a fortune!

Winter at the kitchen window wasn't so bad that year. I knew exactly the bike I was going to get with my money. I picked it straight out of the Sears catalog. My Dad would be so proud when I surprised him with my earned purchase. I couldn't wait. The cold days flew by with me dreaming of playing, laughing and riding out to the pond with the boys. Surely my new bike would be my ticket into the gang. The taste of belonging was sweet. I owed it all to Mr. Allen.

After the first snow fall, I was out there with all the neighborhood kids offering to shovel people's driveways for a couple of bucks. I raced over to the Allen's. Theirs was the longest driveway which translated into three bucks. This time I did it for free. Mrs. Allen called me over to pay me and offered me a cup of hot cocoa. I took the cocoa, but not the money.

"Thank you, JR," Mrs. Allen said. "Your shoveling was just in time. Mr. Allen needs to drive to the doctor's office this morning. Come in and finish your drink. You don't mind me calling you JR, do you Joey?"

"I don't mind," I said. I liked being called by my initials.

"You remind me of my son Robert," she said, making me think that her son's first name was the same as my last name. *Huh.*

I was happy to get out of the cold. We had a nice time together. Mrs. Allen happened to be a champion checkers player. By the end of winter, I had mastered the game. She taught me well.

True to his word, Mr. Allen paid me the agreed upon rate for jobs well done. By summer, I'd saved up every penny earned and excitedly waited for the Sears delivery truck. As the back door of the truck went up, the sun lit the chrome on the front wheel of my brand spanking new bike. It almost blinded me. My heart pounded with pride and joy. I almost spilled the beans at dinner time; but, no, I wanted my surprise to be just right. It was so clear in my mind's eye. I could hardly wait to see my dad smiling from ear to ear, so proud of his son. *Tomorrow when he came home from work would be the perfect time.*

The first thing the next morning, I managed to sneak out unseen and rode to the golf course. I was the first caddy there, and got called up by Mr. Everbach right away. He was a good tipper. I knew I could count on at least two bucks for the eighteen holes. That would be enough to cool off at the swimming pool at Bison Park after the long day.

Imagine my absolute horror, when at the end of the day, I raced around the back of the caddy master's shack to pick up my bike and it wasn't there! Sweat poured down my back as I realized that in my eagerness to be the first caddy to arrive, I hadn't locked my bike. *How could I be so stupid?* Asking around, I found out that nobody noticed anyone odd lurking about, but it'd been a busy day at the golf course. Mr. Everbach was nice enough to give me a ride home. I guess he felt sorry for me. It was a quiet ride into town.

Tears streaming down my face, Dad listened intently as I blurted out the whole story. I told him: how disappointed I was that my surprise was ruined; how hard I had worked; how I thought he'd be so proud of me; and, how this bike was my 'in' with the boys. Kneeling in front of me, Dad looked me in the eye and consoled me by expressing how amazed he was that I had kept this a secret for so long. His arms felt good around me. But all I could think about was how I could get my bike back.

The following Sunday, Mom and Dad drove out to Granddad's farm and stayed all day. I watched them go from the kitchen window, feeling sad. *It was going to be another day without Dad.* He worked so hard and such long hours. We hardly saw him at all. The sting of losing my bike stayed with me all week long. I imagined the cops pounding on the door, my bike in hand. I dreamt about rushing back to the caddy's shack to find that it had been put back just where I left it. But then morning would come and still no bike.

"Wake up, JR. I have something to show you." Dad nudged me until I opened my eyes. "Come out to the garage."

I tripped over my pants while quickly trying to put them on so I could catch up to him. I ran outside and up the stairs to the garage. Mid-sprint, I came to a dead stop. There was my dad, smiling ear to ear, his hand on the handlebar of a red bike that had fat tires and wobbly fenders.

"It's for you, JR. I know it's not the best, but it works."

I looked up at my dad. Never had I been so proud. He had done all this for *me*. That's why he and Mom had gone to the farm. This was *his* old bike. He had fixed it and repainted it. "Thanks, Dad!" I said. "You're the best!"

You should have seen me riding around on my bike. My legs weren't quite long enough, so when I straddled the horizontal bar my feet barely reached the pedals. I had to sway from side-to-side in order to make the red beast go. What a sight! I was sure I was going to kill myself riding that thing. Determination is a good thing, so although it was difficult, I did it!

Later that day, I met up with the neighborhood boys. This was my chance. Beaming, I asked, "Hey, can we hang out together?" One look at my bike and they started to laugh.

"That bike is as ugly as you are!" And off they went.

I returned home, put the bike in the garage and took my usual place at the kitchen window. Ominous clouds started to form; some were in the sky too.

The suburb of St. Charles, just outside of Winnipeg, Manitoba, had only two schools—a public one and a Catholic one. Since our parents were of French descent, my siblings and I were placed in the Catholic school. We didn't care much for the uniforms with the school emblem embroidered on the front of the jacket. Plus, most of our friends were English speaking and went to the public school. My enrolment there was only for a short time, since I was a bit of a handful for the sisters. I loved the attention; especially, from Mother Superior, who tried to discipline me, often marching me off to her office while feigning annoyance. But I knew she had a soft spot for me. I was thrilled when my mom decided public school was a better fit.

I made friends with the Hartford girls right away. Amanda was tall, skinny, and her nose was always running. Christine, on the other hand, was short, normal weight and pale as a ghost. Both had long greasy hair. One couldn't help but notice them. On a number of occasions, Amanda was seen in the art room drinking the clear liquid from the blue glass bottles. Christine often ate the erasers from the tops of pencils. Fingers were always pointed in their direction whenever the lunch boxes were tampered with during a morning recess. I could feel those poor girls' embarrassment and remorse every time they were confronted by the teacher regarding their unusual habits.

One day, it occurred to me to bring bigger lunches and share them with the Hartford sisters during recess. Billy, Mr. Heatley's son, who worked at the local produce farm, took a liking to my sister and brought us extra fruits and vegetables, so we had some to share. The transformation of the girls was almost instant. Not only did Amanda and Christine look better, their test scores improved, and they started to behave differently. *What magic a little kindness could do.*

To everyone's astonishment, one day, Amanda and Christine arrived at school looking clean and smelling like soap. We were told that a man from the city had repaired their family's hot water tank. We later learned that an Al-Anon representative had stopped by to check on their dad's sobriety; afterward, he reported to the health authorities that the children had head lice. Our parents made sure we stayed clear of the Hartfords for a while. We succumbed to numerous baths that week and had our hair raked with a funny looking thin comb. We didn't mind too much, since we got lots of attention at home, which was something that didn't happen too often.

A school transfer was in the works once again. No sooner had I become accustomed to St. Charles, when the school district decided to build Buchanan Junior High. Gone were the days of the comfortable comings and goings of my familiar school. I didn't know what it was like to lose your freedom, until that new school opened. Endless rules and regulations greeted us in junior high; even the doors were locked when the bell rang. My classmates and I made the best of our new environment. But the locked doors made me uneasy.

Mr. Sparr, our geography teacher, was a big man and big on rules. Having obtained his teaching diploma in military school, and being six-foot-four and two hundred and twenty pounds, he was not a force to take lightly. I had trouble staying awake in his class. My friend, Darryl Thiessen, would often elbow me awake; however, sleepiness would once more take over and I'd nod off again. It was never long before Mr. Sparr noticed.

"Wake up, JR!" he'd holler from the front. I'd jump straight up in my seat, only to slump forward a couple of minutes later. Well, Mr. Sparr decided that he wasn't having any of that kind of behavior in his classroom. One day, wanting to make an example of me, he marched over to me and booted the underside of my desk hard enough that my head went flying up about a foot above it.

He saved his *favorite* reprimand for Darryl and me. Any chance he got, he'd grab one of us by the ears and practically lift us off the floor. Enduring Mr. Sparr's punishment was especially hard on us, as we both suffered from Horner syndrome and already had big ears. After a while, my friend and I really started to look like Dumbo. I always thought it was strange that Darryl and I, having each been diagnosed with the same rare disorder, ended up schoolmates. It was good that we had each other.

"Why are your ears so red, Son?" Dad asked from across the dinner table. Before I had a chance to open my mouth, my sister blurted out, "In geography class, when he does something wrong, Mr. Sparr pulls him up by the ears."

Well, that was the wrong thing to say! My father's face turned as red as my ears. If looks could kill, Mr. Sparr would have died on the spot. There was nothing my dad hated more than bullies. Mom called the school the very next day, and Dad took time off work to pay the principal a little visit. Darryl and I liked the substitute teacher much better.

It was great to have a friend like Darryl. We were inseparable that summer. Riding our bikes out to the swimming hole was the highlight of our day; especially, after caddying at the golf course. My parents liked him too, so he became a permanent fixture around the dinner table. He was there the night that I got a surprise that changed both our lives. Mr. Siffon, Dad's boss, had recently seen a picture of my family and noticed me. He recommended a couple of surgeons he knew that could help with my Horner's syndrome. My dad grumbled at the cost. Nevertheless, that year, I underwent three surgeries: one for my ears, another to lift my droopy eyelids, and a third to have my four wisdom and two impacted teeth pulled. Darryl's parents were so impressed with the miraculous transformation of my appearance, that they did the same for their son, thanks to the help of the bank. Darryl and I were twelve years old, going on thirteen and acting sixteen.

"Hurry up, Darryl! We have ten more hats to make tonight!" I just couldn't get Darryl to move fast enough. Our popularity soared after our surgeries. Everyone who was anyone wanted to join our group called the Black Hat Raiders. The fad we started caught on like wildfire! So much so, that at one point, our school principal had the hats banned. Regardless, things were happening! It was the best school year ever.

As my popularity rose, so did my entrepreneurial spirit and the trouble that always followed me. My aunt asked if I and a friend would be interested in helping out at our community club dances. "Of course, we would!" I answered, already imagining the scores of girls begging me to dance. (There was nothing wrong with my imagination.) I enlisted my Black Hat Raiders, added red-velvet jackets to our outfits, and we were in business. Betty was my favorite dance partner. Not that I wanted her to be; it just happened that she was the only one who would dance with me. The other girls thought I moved funny. In my humble opinion, I aced the twist.

The Christmas dance brought in enough cash to hire a professional DJ. We had a ball! Before that night, I hadn't realized dancing felt so good. The party went on into the wee hours of the morning.

Under the excellent guidance of my aunt, the Raiders and I soon added disk jockeying to our repertoire. The weekly dances were a hit! However, our thirst got the better of us. It was hard work—all that *DJ-ing*, dancing and helping out. So I took my Raiders hat off and put my thinking hat on. *All I needed was a straw and a bottle opener.* Conveniently, our community hall soda dispensing machine opened from the top and was just out of sight behind the canteen. *Open the lid of the dispenser, pop off the metal cap from a soda, insert straw, drink as fast as you can, and voila!* Thirst problem solved! All the flavors were available too. The tricky part about having a brilliant idea is that you are incapable of keeping it to yourself. The 'free drinks' opportunity swept through the neighborhood, and before we knew it, the soda company changed the machine to an auto-dispense model. No more could you just reach in and just drain what you wanted.

The hot Manitoba summers called me to the swimming hole every day. I'd even skip church and head out to visit and hang with friends. One Sunday, our neighbors, the Berniers, invited me to the lake. You didn't have to ask me twice. I was back with all my swimming gear in a split second.

I could see everything from the car window. The best view was from where I sat. Once in a while, a bumble bee would buzz in and we'd have to stop the car to shoo it out. The wind on my face felt like when I rode my bike, but even better. The long ride meant stopping halfway to wolf down a sandwich or two. Finally, with the lake in our eyes' view, we didn't wait for the car to make a full stop. Flinging the doors open, we raced toward the water, stumbling along as we exposed our swimming trunks. The cool lake water had a bite to it, but all you had to do to get used to it was keep moving around.

My friend's older brother, Raymond, was standing in the water letting the younger kids dive off his shoulders.

"Raymond, can I have a go at it?"

"Sure, you can, JD," he said, using my latest nickname. "But you gotta dive in at an angle."

Too excited to understand exactly what he meant, I dove straight in. I remember feeling something warm, someone pulling me out of the water, being placed on rocks and a cloth being put on my mouth.

"Are you all right? Does it hurt?"

It hurt all right, but thinking about the impending pain my parents would inflict upon me when I got home hurt even more. Apparently, I hit a rock diving straight into the water, knocking myself out and busting a few teeth. That ended my fun for the day. I sat on the shore until everyone was ready to leave and then slept all the way home.

Seeing my cut lip and bloody mouth, "Oh boy, JD!" was all my mom could utter over and over again. The memory of my recent expensive surgery and the fear of facing my father crept in.

Surprisingly enough, my father listened to my story before announcing that he would have dinner at home from now on, and that everyone needed to be present without exception.

A couple of days later, on his way to work, Dad dropped me off at his dentist's office. The walls in Dr. Goldberg's reception area were full of descriptive pictures of dental diseases and procedures. I was stealthily tiptoeing toward the exit, when a voice called out my name. I was then ushered into a dental chair. A nice lady introduced me to Dr. Goldberg, whose smile was like Fort Knox. They should've dropped the *berg* off his name. Dr. *Gold* would have suited him to a T. Right then and there, I knew I didn't want gold teeth! My friend Larry LaChance had a big silver front tooth; I wanted none of that either. My fears were assuaged when the dentist explained that, if needed, I would get new *white* teeth. The visit was endless. I couldn't help but fall asleep, even while having my fractured teeth extracted. Before leaving with beaver teeth (that's what they felt like), Dr. Goldberg explained that they were only temporary and he'd see me in a week. I couldn't wait.

The day came when my parents realized that their kids were growing up. They took us, one by one, into the bathroom and explained how the birds and the bees worked. It was about time, since we were all between the ages of thirteen and nineteen. Plus, my brother Arnold was spending way too much time at Elaine's house. As far as I was concerned, this new found knowledge was the beginning of my real adventures.

By the time I hit Taylor High School, my reputation preceded me. It turned out that I was famous. The minute I walked through the doors, I had a following. It certainly didn't help that my brothers had gone to the same school before me. The Robert boys were well-known. As soon as I walked into Miss Klausen's Grade 10 English Literature class, she singled me out. From that day forward, I couldn't stop the events that unfolded.

My healthy entrepreneurial spirit earned me a car, an old car, but still a car. This naturally added to my popularity. Along with the staff and other students, I parked my car in the school lot. It just so happened, from time to time, car parts from the newer models went missing. One day, I arrived late to Miss Klausen's class. She listened to my explanation and allowed me to come in.

"Dennis Robert, would you please immediately come to the principal's office!" was the announcement over the PA system that same afternoon. When I got there, Miss Klausen was sitting in the principal's office. She accused me of stealing the taillights and side mirrors from her car.

"Miss Klausen is certain that you stole parts from her car this morning, and this is why you were late for school," pronounced the principal.

"Who else could have done it?" blurted the teacher.

I denied any wrong doing. To this day, I have no idea who did the deed. Unfortunately, it was her word against mine. The one positive outcome of the unpleasant ordeal was that I was moved to another literature class. Everyone wanted to know what happened and how I managed to get out of Miss Klausen's class. (She wasn't a very popular teacher.) However, her harassment didn't stop there. She shared her suspicions with the local police. First chance they got, the cops pulled me over and interrogated me. I couldn't supply any more information than what I had given the principal, so they let me go. That was my first encounter with the police, but not the last.

Fast cars, parties, girls, mid-night street racing, speeding tickets, and getting chased by the police occupied my time for the next couple of years. *Fearless* became my second name. No one was going to tell me what to do or how to behave. I did what I pleased and enjoyed myself to the fullest. I didn't intentionally invite trouble in, but it followed me anyway. The police and the boys—we danced a well-choreographed number. They were always nearby, but kept their distance unless pushed too far.

My Honda 750 Super Sport was black, had lots of chrome and was very fast. Lightning speed was what I was after. It helped to clear my head. Always testing the limits of my new acquisition, I looked forward to my Sunday rides. This one particular day, I spotted the cops just ahead and suspected they were handing out speeding tickets. Something made me not want to stop. I slowed down, waved at them, and then gunned it down Portage Avenue. The chase was on.

Eluding one cruiser after another, I kept going: across the bridge, through the park, and back onto Portage Avenue. Having taken every back alley I could think of, I thought I'd lost them; but, no—four cruisers were waiting for me at the end of the street. I hopped the curb, two-wheeled it through an apartment underground parking lot, screeched out the side exit, and back onto the street. Bang! Out of nowhere, a police cruiser stopped right in front of me. With no time to brake, I slammed into the cruiser's driver-side door. Right then and there, they cuffed me, picked me up and threw me in the back of the cruiser. Three weeks later, still healing from my two fractured legs, I found myself in front of the judge. *My life was never the same.*

Early in my military career, I realized that I had a choice: I could continue along with my well-worn shenanigans or decide to make something of myself. Even though trouble still followed me into my new life, I was determined to prove my worth.

The competition for the base's Fastest Field Runner was announced. The master sergeant laid out the grueling four-week training schedule: five and then ten mile runs in full combat gear; hurdles and belly crawling through the mud; and, weapon assembly while blindfolded. Speed and accuracy were paramount. *This was my chance!* I threw myself into the training. Up every morning at the crack of dawn, I trained. Every chance I got, I trained. Weekends, my buddies rested their weary bones at the base's canteen. Not me! I felt my speed improving and could picture the win—it was right at my fingertips. I was focused.

Race day came. The competition was fierce. Never before had the stopwatches clocked such speed. The race course was brutal—through bushes and mud ponds, across swinging rope bridges, and finally a river crossing—all of which led up to the last task, rifle assembly. Sweating uncontrollably, red-faced and near exhaustion, I could hear my comrades cheering me on. "Way to go, JD!" they hollered. Any doubt of not making it to the finish line vanished. As I assembled the rifle in total darkness, I knew the win was mine!

"Trooper JD, front and center," the master sergeant hollered from the parade deck. I lifted my eyes, stood up tall, and began my walk to greatness. You could hear a pin drop as I made my way to the front. Standing at attention, I saluted and then accepted the trophy—a symbol of the possibilities that lay before me. It was a defining moment. I realized that my will to change was greater than the sum of all my fears—known and unknown.

After travelling fourteen hours by train from the military base, I entered my childhood home. I placed my *only* prized possession on the mantel. The hard-earned trophy stood tall among our framed family pictures. As I showered, thoughts of the future clouded my mind. I had five months and two days to go before I'd be free of the legal system and the army. *Then what? Was army life all that was open to me?* The judge had given me a chance to redeem myself. The army promised to make a new man out of me. It wasn't till I caught a glimpse of myself in the steamy bathroom mirror that I saw someone different being reflected back. I *had* changed, and I owed it all to the judge. Not that I'd ever tell him so.

I still live life by the motto: Fearless, no matter what! However, I now do it in a way that doesn't invite quite so much trouble.

Lonely Choices

Roswyn Nelson

"I've sold my place up country and I'm moving in!" Bags and baggage in hand, my ex-husband of fifty years announced we were going to be roommates.

Unbelievable? Yes!

Unavoidable? That too!

Unbearable? That comes later!

Why and *how*, you may ask, does someone find herself in a situation where she has seemingly no choice but to accept her ex-husband as a fulltime housemate? Well, let me tell you about it.

Once upon a time, in the land of rolling prairie plains, on a beautiful starry night under a magical harvest moon, boy meets girl and the story begins.

The local Saturday night dance was underway—music booming through the open doors; people arriving alone, in couples or groups; and, everybody wearing their best go-to-town outfits.

In those far away 'back then' days, dance halls were set with chairs around the perimeter of a huge rectangular hardwood floor. The girls sat and chatted while waiting for the next eligible fellow to come and sweep one of them off of her feet for a lively heel-toe polka, a rollicking schottische or a dreamy cheek-to-cheek waltz.

I was talking with friends, when a cute fresh-faced stranger, his twill pants tucked into a pair of worn 49er boots, asked me to dance. "Hi, I'm Pat. What's your name, address and telephone number?"

I wasn't very popular, and upon hearing those words I was smitten. It wasn't until our second date that he confessed his name wasn't *Pat*, it was Harvey. He'd utilized the safety-net singles use when unsure as to whether to date someone—wrong name, rank and serial number.

Harvey worked on the oil rigs and was what the locals called an *oil boy*. There was a certain romance, as well as prestige, in dating one. With the advent of the oil boom in Western Canada, things had changed in dusty, drowsy little farming towns. All over Saskatchewan and Alberta, dozens of oil companies were hiring young prairie farm lads who were dying to spread their wings and taste adventure. It was the first generation of girls marrying guys from other areas, instead of boys from next door. So it was with me.

We married in 1955 when I was seventeen. My cute, fresh-faced stranger was a dreamer, always chasing that proverbial pot of gold. He just *knew* that there was excitement and something fantastic and different beyond each curve of the highway.

Harvey was a nice guy—he didn't drink, gamble, cheat, or beat me. However, he never seemed to know what time it was. It was as if *I* was always catching up, just as *he* was moving on. There were fifteen moves in seven years, new jobs, new cities and sometimes new addresses within those cities, new dreams, new ideas, and a new baby every thirteen months.

The first time I was left behind happened in the summer of 1956. We lived in Calgary, Alberta and Harvey was hired as a time-keeper with a construction company located in Uranium City, Saskatchewan. I was expecting our first child in September. Because he was a new employee, Harvey's Saskatchewan medical insurance wouldn't be in effect soon enough to cover my maternity expenses. Until our baby was born and I could travel, moving to my parents place in Pinoka, Alberta seemed the logical thing to do. It wasn't much fun being without Harvey at a time like that, but there was no choice.

As it turned out, Harvey was transferred back to Alberta in time for the momentous event. Soon afterward, we moved back to Calgary. The next two years saw the arrival of two more little ones, making our lives busy, hectic, stressful, and rewarding.

Shortly after we were married, Harvey got his flying license and bought a plane. He thrived in the wild blue yonder, finding freedom in the skies. He was in heaven skimming over the hills and valleys, doing loops and spirals, and practicing takeoffs and landings. When he was flying, time became a mere triviality.

Seduced by tales of lost goldmines boasting veins of quartz shot with gold, and unsolved mysteries of miners and prospectors disappearing never to be heard from again, Harvey took up prospecting. Stories about the Lost Lemon Mine were adventurous enough to capture my imagination, so we spent the winter researching historical newspaper articles and interviewing old sourdoughs, diligently recording, charting and mapping our way to the legendary mother lode. Occasionally, we splurged on babysitters and went prospecting together. We trekked through slush and snow in the mountains in early spring, freezing at night as we lay in our sleeping bags beside the rushing Kananaskis River. I still treasure memories of our shared prospecting trips, occasionally re-reading old notes and smiling over the worn yellowed pages of our journal.

1960 was a year of unemployment and recession. Jobs were scarce in our city, and Harvey was among the unemployed. After selling our furniture, and storing what was left of our worldly possessions in my parents' garage, we headed for my sister's place in Edmonton. The plan was for me to stay with family, freeing Harvey to seek work anywhere they were hiring. Once again I was left behind, this time with three little ones and another on the way.

My sister and her husband also had three children, so our arrival put a huge strain on them. Feeling hopeful and optimistic, we settled into my sister's home for what I believed would be a short stay. When weeks went by without a word from my husband, I grew increasingly scared and discouraged. Every day, I stood at the window waiting for the mailman to arrive, praying to hear something…anything. I didn't know if Harvey was dead or alive. *Where was he? How could he do this to me? How could he do this to his kids? Why didn't he call?* I felt abandoned, and in a sense we had been abandoned—not one word, phone call or letter. *Was he ever coming back? If Harvey didn't return, what were we going to do? Where would my kids and I go? Where would we all end up?*

With each passing day, it seemed the house shrank smaller and tempers grew shorter. It was certain we could no longer stay and be a burden on my sister and her family. They were struggling to get by and couldn't be expected to feed and shelter us much longer.

As Christmas grew near, panic shadowed my anger and shame. My heart was so broken, I wasn't appreciative of the fact that we'd been taken in, loved, sheltered, and cared for. I was simply angry that *they* were a family and *we* were alone. The ice in the pit of my stomach felt as big as the berg that sank the Titanic. Unfortunately, that feeling would become increasingly familiar.

Christmas Eve dinner was over, carols were playing on the radio, and the kids—all six of them—were barely able to contain their excitement. It was just one more sleep until they could open their presents. Suddenly, we heard a car door slam. Then footsteps bounding up the back stairs, followed by a knock on the door—and there he was. Arms loaded with presents, a big happy grin on his face, Harvey announced, "I'm back!"

He'd found a job as an electronic technician, six hundred miles away in Cranbrook, British Columbia. As Harvey explained his absence, I understood that he'd suffered too. In the weeks he'd been away, he had driven many miles, stopped in numerous towns, and sought work in dozens of establishments. For much of his journey, he'd been weary, discouraged and disillusioned. It was probable he became more depressed with each mile that rolled by without him finding work. By today's standards, like me, he was still a kid with a huge responsibility on his young shoulders.

His new job was to start on the second of January, and he'd taken an advance on his wages in order to come back and get us. We left Edmonton early on December 26. It was a spectacular prairie winter day, so cold that frost crystals formed around your mouth, and breathing left a vapor trail. The highway was a solid slithery sheet of ice. Driving was a heart-in-your-throat, never-to-be-repeated exercise in sheer terror. Thank God, around midnight, we finally arrived at our new home. What was normally an eight hour trip had taken fifteen hours.

They were building a pipeline through Cranbrook and the downtown housing situation was hopeless. Fortunately, Harvey was able to rent a unit at the Hiawatha Motel, which was several miles out of town and part of a year-round campsite. Other families lived there too, so we were able to quickly make new friends. It was really pretty there—tall pines sighing in the breeze, the Moyie River roaring by, and majestic mountains standing like sentinels over the valley.

Three months later, our fourth child was born. The moves, the worry, and the responsibility had taken its toll; I was down to one hundred and eighteen pounds. Too skinny for my five-foot-seven-inch frame, you could almost hear my bones rattle. On many mornings, I was simply too tired to get out of bed.

One day, Harvey came home from work to find a soaking wet and squalling infant in bed with his sleeping mom. Aware that his brother, Kenneth, needed to be breast fed, earlier in the day, five-year-old Brian had pushed a chair over to the bassinet, climbed up, very carefully lifted his baby brother out and transported him to my bed. That done, he and his other two siblings, Rhonda and David, proceeded to build sandcastles on the floor in the living room. Apparently, the kids had hauled buckets of sand into the house for their special project because they needed to stay inside to look after mommy! They had also proudly fixed their own lunch that day, evident by the crackers and cheese, globs of peanut butter, cookie crumbs, and milk spilled everywhere.

Extremely upset, Harvey announced that he'd come home from work at noon the next day to take me to the doctor. "You'd bloody well better be sick!" was his comment.

"Don't you know what's wrong with you?" the doctor asked when we walked into his office.

Bewildered by a question he thought held an obvious answer, all I could mutter was, "What?"

"Just look at your arms," he said.

I looked. My arms were changing color right in front of my eyes. "Oh, good grief, I have yellow jaundice!" Turning to face Harvey, I asked, "Well, am I sick enough for you?"

Later, peering into a mirror, I noticed the whites of my eyes were also becoming a bright yellow. No wonder I had no energy and was so very tired. Thus began seven days of isolation, plus another three weeks of bed rest in our local hospital. Thankfully, my mom came and took care of the kids.

We left the motel later that fall and moved into a huge clapboard ramshackle haunted house in the ghost town of Moyie. The deal was that we could have three months free rent, provided we cleaned and fixed up the place. Since we needed a bigger place, we took it.

The advent of cable television was in its infancy, and several young local entrepreneurial individuals, including Harvey, started their own cable companies. Again, his work became his excuse for disappearing for days at a time.

Things didn't change much in the ensuing year. Harvey was still looking for that pot of gold. Actually, in fact, he was still looking for the rainbow. As time marched on, I no longer worried when he didn't show up for days.

Our big old house was right on the main highway between Cranbrook and Vancouver. Every day, numerous transients hitchhiked along that route. The house was tinder-dry, so there was a ladder up to the window in case of fire, and a gun under my pillow in case someone decided to come up the ladder.

It was summertime—warm sunny days, bees buzzing, the scent of clover, and long lazy hours spent on the sandy beaches of the lake. One Sunday morning, I received a call from a lady in Calgary whose son, Terry, was working on the cable system with Harvey. She was worried because the guys were to have been in Calgary on Tuesday, and here it was Sunday, and she hadn't heard from them. I panicked. Even for Harvey, five days overdue was unusual.

I was the only one who knew the general location of where they were working high in the mountains in grizzly country. Upon checking, I discovered that Harvey's guns were all at home. I called the Cranbrook RCMP to place a missing persons report and discovered that I had to go to the office to file one. Great! It was Sunday morning, I had four kids to worry about, lived twenty miles in the country, was without a car, and it was a long weekend. I had little choice but to throw myself on the mercies of a neighbor I barely knew, asking her to look after my children while I hitchhiked into town.

The RCMP jumped into action when they heard my story, immediately contacting the forest rangers in the Invermere search area. Since I had the best knowledge of where to look, the rangers insisted I go with them. They also told me I would have to make arrangements for someone to look after my kids, because it was likely we'd be gone for at least three days. Everyone I knew personally was away for the long weekend, so I had to ask the same neighbor to stay with the kids until I returned. *There was that ice in the pit of my stomach again.*

We were in the police car headed out of town when something told me to call Calgary one more time. I telephoned Terry's mom, only to have her say, "Oh, my dear, the boys arrived just after I called you this morning, and they're just fine." *Why had no one had bothered to call me?*

Seeing my fear turn to hurt, anger and frustration, even though it was out of their jurisdiction, the officers kindly drove me home.

Built at the turn of the century in the hey-day of silver mining, its weathered boards silvered with age, the big old mausoleum we lived in was a firetrap. As often happens, when the mine eventually died so did the town, and a lot of the big fancy houses were derelict and abandoned. Many homes, including ours, were reported to be haunted. It wasn't uncommon to hear bumps and thumps in the night.

Heating with oil in the wintertime was expensive, and we could only afford a few gallons at a time. The fuel truck came once a week, and if you ran out before they got there, so be it. One bitterly cold, bone-snapping, frost-on-your-breath morning, I awoke to find the heater had gone out during the night. The tank was empty! We had absolutely no fuel, and it would be days before the oil truck arrived. *What to do?* "I know," I said, talking to myself, "I'll go down to Ford's store, borrow a gallon of oil, pour it into the front of the stove, and light it. That will at least take the chill off."

Well, it certainly did that! I went to the store, borrowed the oil, poured it into the front of the stove, and lit it. KABOOM! Fire flared up the wall as the chimney pans blew off the stove pipes, spewing soot all over the house. The baby upstairs howled in fright as the other three tumbled down the steps to get out of the house. My eyelashes singed, I flew upstairs, grabbed the baby, and taking three steps at a time, escaped to safety. Fortunately, the small amount of oil didn't ignite the walls. There was just a quick flash that quickly went out.

Our guardian angels were definitely watching over us that day. Harvey was in Calgary again, so I asked the same neighbor to come to my rescue, while I thumbed a ride into Cranbrook to look for somewhere else to live. I was lucky and found a place. We moved in the very next day.

Settling down, life continued. However, all the incidents where I'd felt abandoned, ignored and treated as though I was insignificant, triggered a deep depression.

To help with finances I worked in the cafe of a local hotel. One Saturday night in March, Harvey picked me up after my shift, and along with another couple and a girl friend of theirs, full of high spirits and expectations, we headed for a St. Patrick's Day dance being held in the nearby town of Yahk. Little did we know, there had been a snow melt, followed by a sudden freeze when the sun went down behind the mountains. When we hit black ice on the S-curve just outside of Moyie, we skidded out of control, and the roadside guardrail slashed through the middle of our vehicle like a giant can opener held in the hand of a hungry ice God.

Although a 1952 Buick Skylark was built like a Sherman tank, ours folded up like a two-passenger Chevy coupe. When it came to rest, there were only two things left in the vehicle—the steering wheel, and sadly, the body of Maureen, the friend of the couple with us. She was killed on impact. The rest of us were thrown out as the car tobogganed down an embankment and out of sight.

It was an absolute miracle we were found. Two guys came around the curve, and as their headlights swept through the darkness, they witnessed in disbelief a lone wheel spinning down the center of the highway. Naturally, they stopped to investigate. But not for their actions, there would have been five fatalities that cold March 17th. Our guardian angels were working overtime that night.

Screaming sirens and flashing lights split the silence and lit up the darkness. The subdued voices of RCMP officers, medics, and passersby echoed as though in a cavern. The next thing I remember was being in an ambulance and momentarily seeing a doctor who appeared as if behind a misty gauze curtain. Then there was nothing but blackness for many hours.

The men had concussions. The other woman was hospitalized for over a year. I had a broken back and wrist, and my legs and arms were gashed. My head looked as though I'd gone down the embankment face first. I also had multiple other bruises, scrapes, and deep cuts that took many stitches to close. Once again, my family stepped in to help. They came from Edmonton, picked up the kids and kept them for the next three months, while I learned to look after myself wearing a full body cast.

The separate incidents—numerous moves, illness, babies, financial strain, and the car accident—took a toll on our marriage. We may have been able to survive some of them, one at a time. But there were too many, too fast. On the verge of a complete mental breakdown, and needing to heal, Harvey found someone to take care of the kids while I went away.

Flying into Vancouver on a beautiful sun-drenched September day, sparked my lifelong love affair with the city. The ocean was as clear as glass, and the snowcapped North Shore Mountains stood proud against a bright blue sky. However, having only twenty dollars in my pocket and no job was daunting. Fortunately, there were friends I could bunk with temporarily. Shaughnessy Golf and Country Club was hiring, so within a couple of days of arriving, I managed to find a job and a room to rent. The club quickly became my family, sanity and stability, and would remain so until I was well enough to go home.

Working at the club was an education. I learned to use a salad fork, discovered that sour cream was not just for baking, and that people actually ate things like escargot and lobster tails. Never having seen a live lobster up close, one day when a shipment arrived, I leaned over the open crate, fascinated by the pinchers of a dozen weird sea creatures waving wildly. Amused by my enthralled curiosity, one of the chefs, Tom, was standing beside me. Suddenly, he reached into the container and pulled out a huge writhing, squirming specimen and pretended to hand it to me. Unfortunately, he was standing too close and the lobster's flailing claws hooked the neck of my uniform.

Screaming and frantically trying to dislodge the unwanted passenger, I stumbled backward across the length of the kitchen as Tom tried to retrieve the offending beast. With the staff watching in open-mouthed amazement, he finally tackled me and removed the attack monster. By this point, I was teetering dangerously over the railing of a thirty-foot drop. As things quieted down and sanity returned, imagine our consternation when we discovered that the dining room lunch patrons had crowded into the kitchen to see what all the screeching and shrieking was about. Poor Tom nearly got fired that day.

The following May, recovered, rested and ready to give it another try, I returned home. *Oh-oh, I was just catching up as Harvey was moving on again.* He was going to Drayton Valley, Alberta to partner with his brother in an electronic shop. Pleased that I'd come home in time to look after the kids, we made plans that he'd come back for us in July. Before he left, he handed me a hundred dollars for groceries to tide us over until he could send more.

We were living in the area where the Sons of Freedom, a religion-based breakaway sect of the Doukabour population, were actively bombing and burning. They dynamited power lines, set fires to purify evil, and publically stripped off their clothes in protest against what they perceived to be government interference. They believed in 'Fire in the Name of God' and felt it was their right to do such things.

The morning after Harvey left, we were without electricity. Assuming the local power lines had been blown up again, I didn't pay too much attention. Later in the day, I called hydro and found out the lights were out because the bill hadn't been paid for several months. There were people in town who owed Harvey money, so I started making the rounds to collect. The electricity was restored before the hydro office closed that evening. There was, however, very little money left for food. *There was that ice in the pit of my stomach again.*

Still planning the move to Drayton Valley in July, the long weekend came, and so did Harvey. However, he arrived without a trailer to haul our belongings, even though I'd called to let him know all the rental places would be closed over the holiday. As we packed the few clothes and toys that would fit into the station wagon or could be tied onto the roof, my stomach turned upside down and inside out. I wasn't going with them.

The decision not to go with them was made during what was a long and sleepless night, which was triggered when I learned that Harvey hadn't even arranged a place for us to live in Drayton Valley. There had been too many disappointments, too much worry, and too many times when I'd been ignored and my concerns discounted. The idea of us continuing our marriage was in the final throes of defeat. My feelings of anger, sadness and futility were devastating. There was nothing I could do to change what had become unbearable circumstances, except start over without Harvey. Spending my life feeling unimportant, second class, and as if I was only along for the ride, had finally become more than I could endure.

Tears poured down my face as I stood alone early on that July morning, while four pairs of big sad eyes looked back at me through the rear window. Shattered, broken and defeated, I watched as their father drove away with them, down the driveway, around the corner and out of sight. I wasn't in a financial position to do anything about it right then. Leaving a houseful of furniture behind, I returned to Vancouver the very next day. It was time to make plans on how to get my kids back.

Holidays, especially birthdays and Christmas, were soul-searing lonely. It was a difficult time for everybody because the kids weren't even living together. Finding reliable help was impossible, so Harvey farmed them out to various homes. It was two years before I could afford to bring the youngest ones back to live with me. And then another long year before the eldest two joined us. My kids were ages nine, eight, seven, and five before we were all together again.

Life as a single mom was a challenge. Luckily, I loved waitressing. The tips allowed me to provide a decent life for my kids—if it was a good day we ate well; if not, there was always a can of pork and beans. We had some great times and not so great times. We had love, laughter, tears, and built a ton of memories. Over the years, many people, some who are still valued friends, stepped up to help in times of crisis. Deep abiding faith, instilled in me by my praying mother, carried us through some trying times. I'm certain our survival was largely due to her many prayers.

Our home was a hub of activity, with the neighborhood kids always congregating at our house. Parents never worried about where their kids were—they were at the Nelson's! There were adventures, as well as mishaps and emergencies. The kids were inventive about finding ways to earn money. There were the usual paper routes, babysitting, and collecting pop bottles.

One day, the owner of the local cookie factory came knocking on our door to report that they'd discarded several pounds of peanut brittle, and someone had seen my kids taking it. Well, they had. Realizing that the candy had been thrown away, they thought it would be okay to take it. Dividing it into little paper bags, they went around the block selling it door-to-door for a nickel each. It wasn't very funny when we found out that there were maggots hatching in the candy, which was why it had been thrown out. How embarrassed my kids were when they had to retrace their steps, get all the peanut brittle back, return their hard-earned money, and apologize. When one little old lady said, "Oh, I ate it all right away, and it was delicious!" the kids decided silence was the better part of valor.

Even with a houseful of kids, at times, being a single parent was pretty lonely. When there was bad news or emergencies, there was no one to hold me while I cried. There was no one to console me when— Ken was hospitalized with meningitis; Dave and Ken were hit by a car; Rhonda had a thyroid operation; or, when Brian had surgery on his foot to remove the hunk of shoe rubber embedded when he stepped on a rusty spike. On the flip side, there was no one to laugh or celebrate with when my kids made me proud or did something hilarious.

On top of it all, I was in another near-fatal car crash that left me unconscious for several days, and was followed by months of recovery, then years of back pain. Knowing the kids were alone, as soon as it happened, thankfully, someone called Family Services. A caregiver was promptly placed in our home. No one could pronounce her name, so she was simply called Mrs. T.

After I regained consciousness, Mrs. T. brought the kids to the hospital for a visit. They were dressed like little street urchins in mismatched ill-fitting clothes. She'd obviously scrambled the laundry, as each of my kids was wearing something belonging to someone else. Hearing their stories brought sunshine back into my life, until Mrs. T. dropped the bomb!

Beaming with delight, she proudly said, "The boys just loved your little ones and so enjoyed their visit."

Apprehensively, I asked, "Which boys? What visit? Where did you take them?"

She chuckled as she replied, "Oh, on Sunday, I took them for a free lunch at the Harbor Light Mission."

Immediately imagining what sort of desperate souls might gather for a free meal at the Salvation Army on skid row, my mother-bear instincts jumped to attention. Mrs. T. was very lucky I was flat on my back and unable to move—I wouldn't have been held responsible for my actions. Fortunately, my mother arrived the next day and took charge. I'm sorry that I wasn't home to see my pint-sized mom putting the run on Mrs. T. with the business end of a broom. It must have been quite a sight.

With the insurance money from that accident, I was able to buy the house we were renting. However, the neighborhood was becoming more transient and many families were moving away. The decision to move our family out of the area happened when I came home from work and found the kids sitting on the steps of the house next door, pot smoke swirling around their young impressionable heads. It put a whole new meaning to 'having their heads in the clouds.' I sold our city home, bought a townhouse in the suburb of Port Coquitlam, and quickly relocated.

One by one, the kids graduated from high school and began their own lives. Life was good—until I found a lump in my breast. The next year was a dark, scary time, as I underwent a radical mastectomy, followed by chemo and radiation. The kids were all supportive, caring and attentive. Through it all, I knew that dying wasn't an option—there was too much living left to do! Besides, I promised my eldest grandchild, Stephanie, that I'd be around to see her grow up, get married and have her own babies.

My kids have made great life choices. All of them are married with children, live in beautiful homes and are successful business owners. They are truly wonderful, productive human beings whose life values and family ties are strengthened by memories of their early formative years. My pride in my children, grandchildren and great grandchildren knows no bounds. My daughter told me that her brother once said, "We never ever felt poor." It was a compliment that I will forever cherish.

Our greatest glory is not in never falling
but in rising every time we fallfall. —Confucius

Having built a suite for me over the office of a family-owned business, my kids suggested a couple rooms be set aside for their dad to stay when he came to visit from where he lived near Kamloops, B.C. Knowing how much he disliked the traffic, noise and pollution of the lower mainland, I was okay with their suggestion because Harvey would NEVER come to stay permanently.

Never say never! There came a day when he arrived, bag and baggage in hand, and said, "I've sold my place up country and I'm moving in!"

The next couple of years were almost unbearable. I did not want or need a roommate. I was angry, hurt and disillusioned. Once again, I felt insignificant and unimportant. Moreover, and more importantly, I felt betrayed by my children. It was I who had raised them, struggling singlehandedly with no financial support from Harvey over all those long hard years.

Then one day—an epiphany! It was as though a veil lifted, allowing me to appreciate what my kids had done. Stepping up and taking care of both their parents was hugely monumental. I realized that my anger was not only hurting me, it was making my family uncomfortable. My complaining had even alienated a few of them. Harvey was, after all, their dad. I understood it was just circumstances, and above all, there was a choice—I was free to leave.

Recently, I moved to beautiful White Rock, B.C. where I have an apartment close to the ocean, trees and walking trails. My neighbors are great and there are friends living nearby. A sliding glass door opens onto a small deck where I sometimes sit soaking up the sunshine and ocean breeze, while reading a great novel, or enjoying a morning cup of coffee or evening glass of wine. Hobbies such as writing, watercolor painting, and genealogy fill my spare time.

Several years ago, I fell in love with the network marketing industry. To me, it's business 101, where everyone benefits from guidance, support and community. It's in my blood, and offers me the opportunity to help people with their health and finances. It also affords me the luxury of travel. My life is full and my heart sings—*the ice has melted.*

---And everyone lived happily ever after.---

Excerpt from a poem I wrote over 40 years ago.

One day, they are babies
Next day, they're half-grown
Tomorrow, I'll wonder
Where the time has flown

Social Laryngitis

Marcus Dwayne Harris

"Do you want to live with me or your Dad?" Mom asked, stroking my six-year-old directionless mop of black hair that she teased had a mind of its own.

Whenever she said it, I always wondered what my hair was thinking. Maybe it could help me make a decision today. Maybe hair was smart.

"Think about it while you eat your breakfast," she said, giving up on getting an immediate answer out of me.

She was used to me taking time to consult my hair before I answered. But even my hair wasn't smart enough to figure out how to make Mom and Dad get along. Eyes wide to the ceiling and the blankets tucked tight to my neck, fight-after-fight, I'd heard her threats to leave him. But in the morning, with my father off to work, there was always sugared porridge and reassuring smiles. Today there was Cornflakes served atop a makeshift cardboard table that was the caboose to dozens of boxes forming a trackless train. Some were double-deckers, others stacked so high they begged to be climbed. *Maybe from the top I could see into my friend's house.*

"Marcus, have you decided?" Mom wanted to know, not even noticing that my cereal was soggy. I wasn't hungry.

Trying not to cry was making my throat hurt like bees had flown in while I was sleeping, and they'd just woken up. *Would they build a nest and choke me to death?*

Scrunching down so that our faces were so close it was as though I were peering into a mirror, she smiled in an I've-got-a-secret kind of way. I knew she was going to tell me something good, but all I could think was that everyone said I had her eyes, but hers were prettier.

"I promise to stop at every McDonald's on the way."

"*Every* McDonald's?!" I double-checked as my ears sprung open. Still, I was torn. Dad was grumpy almost always. Mom was nice most always. But I worried about my father living by himself in our big lonely house. *With no one to yell at, would he cry all the time?* No, he wouldn't cry. He's too grumpy to cry.

"Yes, every McDonald's," Mom said, smiling really wide cause she knew she'd outsmarted Dad.

It was an impressionable lesson. *Nice* Mom *left* grumpy Dad. *Survival of the nicest* was not only logical, it was paramount. When you habitually please people, life is full of warmth and love. When you're demanding and grumpy, you get left behind and alone with no one caring if you bellowed until the sky collapsed.

In grade school, dubbed the teacher's pet, muffled whispers of protest rumbled about my noggin in silent confusion. *Why is being nice and helping others wrong? Mom's nice. I must be missing something.* There forward, silence became my favored defense, driving me inward and mute. Though too young to coin a phrase that encapsulated my suffering, elementary school was the beginning of my *Social Laryngitis.*

My self-imposed wordlessness served me well in high school. Basically left to suffer in silence, my grades soared, earning me a full college scholarship. Too afraid to ask a girl for a date or to dare step foot in a nightclub, Social Laryngitis ended up being the perfect recipe for an après college job. Unfortunately, I was missing an essential ingredient—social readiness. *Why is it that what's really important is always in the fine print that I never read?*

Imagined repercussions for voicing an opinion, want or desire rendered me speechless, making any sense of self-fulfillment impossible. The older I became, the more acute my Social Laryngitis. At work, my sole intention was to please my employer, no matter the cost—professionally or personally. Whatever the boss wanted, I did to perfection, constantly striving to be valued as an employee and as a person. All while being buried beneath a relentless fear of being fired. My motto: Work hard, keep your mouth shut, and do what you're told better and faster than anyone else. Personal powerlessness actually became a sought-after attribute.

There was one wonderful stretch working for IBM, when I actually dared to allow delight to feather my ego and happiness to enter my heart. Three college buddies also migrated from Florida to the eastern part of North Carolina, where the blend of corporate and college life seemed a heaven-inspired mecca. My starting salary was the highest among us four, presenting me with bragging rights and my first taste of true pride.

The initial year at IBM was a hot-air balloon ride, fueled higher by a year-end review that resulted in a five-thousand-dollar bonus and a four-thousand-dollar pay raise. I was on a natural high where each pat-on-the-back added comfort to my elevated altitude and attitude. Working for a corporate superstar was truly an adventure into exotic territories and cherished explorations.

Within months, I married, and my pleasing mission expanded to include keeping my wife happy. From my humble roots came the obvious vehicle—money talks, buy her things! Overspending on cars and entertainment, I rationalized that a raise would soon come through and fix everything.

Most people make conscious choices. Me? I physically follow my brain's meanderings. My current job assignment at IBM easy, unchallenging and boring, my thoughts wandered and I went along for the ride, suddenly finding myself engulfed in bowling! Unable to speak up and request a more prominent role at work, I was easily seduced by the praise elicited from a superior aptitude for knocking pins over with a ball.

When employed, focus and determination are two of my strongest assets, so my bowling average quickly climbed along with my love of the game. Like me, half of the bowlers were under the age of thirty. Talking wasn't a prerequisite to becoming a great bowler or fitting in. Blasting music and the smell of chicken wings filled the building with a tantalizing ambience that drew me in like a lover's arms. Naively mesmerized by being welcomed where everyone is dressed-to-impress in two-hundred-dollar bowling shoes and three-hundred-dollar bowling balls, I was enthralled with the game where every spare and strike counted. Where I counted!

Most top bowlers have a five-step approach, mine was only three; however, bowling strike-after-strike, I was coached to stay with it. Each time up, I held the ball high, pushing it forward as I led with my left foot, back swinging on my right step, releasing the ball on the third step with a follow through swing as I slid on my left foot. Eyes glued on the lane guide-arrow, I never tired of watching the ball roll over it and down the lane to its intended target—strike!

Between the cash prize and my five side bets, there was over five-thousand tournament dollars at stake (a nice addition to the twelve thousand I'd already won that year) when something inside me changed—it suddenly no longer mattered that to win I had to defeat someone else's dream. More staggering yet, was that I could actually voice my intention to take the other team down. Winning took priority over being nice. Bowling took priority over work.

But as the bills for two vehicles, rent, food, and fun surmounted, the reality set in that I needed the financial security of the job that voiceless me was doing his best to escape. But it was nine months after 9/11 and the IT industry was suffering worldwide. When IBM began layoffs, I was one of the first dubbed expendable.

Surprise wasn't even in the equation; my layoff a mere final formality to a job emotionally abandoned months before. I'd spent too many lunch breaks bowling, had never introduced my wife to my boss, and had long stopped socializing with my coworkers—employment suicide that had obviously not gone unnoticed. Reality check: A large company doesn't suffer from Social Laryngitis—it has a commanding voice. Management's solution to having found a maimed voice among their ranks was to eject it.

Without an income, my entire life tumbled like the pins I could no longer afford to bowl over. Defeated and humiliated, I quit seven leagues, forcing each to scramble for my replacement. Acutely aware that *pleasing others* had morphed into *disappointing everyone*, like water doused on fire, my flame expired. Social Laryngitis had cost me my job, self-respect, and soon afterward, my marriage.

Heading back to Florida, wifeless and lifeless, the self-talk during that seven hour drive home was a rollercoaster ride. One mile, I relived the rush of being in total control while on the lanes and the thrill of being the number one bowler. (Doing the math, thirty-six lanes, four people on a team—I'd outperformed one hundred and forty-four people.) Over the next several dozen miles, fear and shame ganged together. I'd let down my boss, workmates, bowling friends, wife, and self. Knowing that it was my inability to voice my needs and desires that had taken me down, did nothing to squelch my shame or the fiery anger that struck inward and outward. If only I'd spoken up and asked for a more challenging position at work. If only corporate America had a heart. Couldn't people *see* how badly I wanted to do a great job?

Didn't they know how desperately I yearned to please everyone? Why couldn't my boss *see* that I needed more challenge? Did people actually have to *hear* what should have been obvious? Did I have to *hear* that I was as disposable as a restaurant doggy bag before I got the message? Why couldn't I *see* the course I'd set when I mentally checked out of work? Was I as blind as I was mute?

Plagued by an affliction my faltering words couldn't explain *and* a black mark on my resume that couldn't be explained, finding another job was impossible. Wordless and jobless, for the next five months I taught myself everything there was to know about web and graphic design. However, it wasn't my idea. Of course not! I had Social Laryngitis. Where my brain wandered, I followed. My best friend suggested an income source, and I instantly embraced *his* idea to sell profile designs on social media and dating websites.

To reboot my confidence, I continued bowling. My average climbed to 215, positioning me about six months away from joining the Professional Bowling Association, when ambling desires once again nixed my career, but with a more pleasant impetus.

From three thousand miles away in Vancouver, British Columbia, a pretty woman named Shabena popped into my email. Her picture drew me in like a crescent moon on a still summer night. Perfectly arched brows above almond shaped eyes. Long brown hair feathered about cheeks heightened by a wide luscious smile which seemed natural, not posed. Reading her profile, I learned that family was her top priority, followed by adventure and laughter. She liked cooking, camping, dancing, hiking, and biking. She was writing for help crafting a bio that would lead her to a kindred soul who shared her values and vision of the perfect life. Unbeknown to her, she'd just met him!

After many days filled with endless hours of engaging conversation and silly texting, I flew to Vancouver to meet her in person. Cliché, or not, it was truly love at first sight. She was even prettier in person. When we exchanged cautious first kisses and hugs, I detected the soft scent of the Glow perfume she'd told me always topped her Christmas list. Two months later, I moved to Vancouver. Three months later, we were married.

Though it all happened pretty quickly, moving to Vancouver and marrying Shabena was the beginning of my taking a lead role in my own life. I was actually *choosing* instead of wandering aimlessly at the suggestions of others and happenstance. Though not in complete remission, Social Laryngitis no longer had me stifled in 'whatever' muteness. Determined not to mess with my second chance at love and family, although the high of the game beckoned, I *decided* to leave my professional bowling dreams behind. Marriage was serious business, and safeguarding it and supporting my family financially were assigned utmost dual priority—priorities chosen to please myself as well as those I loved.

Never wanting to again subject my career to the whims of some numbers-driven corporate giant, I continued on with my small website design business. Four years later, tired of the ceaseless struggle for a buck, but still leery of exchanging the freedom of self-employment for a job, I decided to search for contract work. Adding web design and Internet programming to a resume that already boasted a Bachelor of Arts in Computer Programming and a minor in Business, I secured a two-month contract designing duplicated websites and back-office systems for a network marketing company.

Needing to end our family money struggles, I somewhat begrudgingly signed the paper giving away the rights to everything I was about to design, before it was even created. My employment again dependent on pleasing the boss, Social Laryngitis commanded my existence. Beginning on Christmas Eve, for six weeks I put in countless hours to meet the aggressive timeline set by my boss. Because I was coding from scratch, his expectations of me, one man, would have been challenging for an entire programming team. But I did it!

Unquestionably impressed, my contract was extended indefinitely, and I slid into position as the boss's right-hand-man. *The work was right up my alley!* All I had to do was whatever he asked; which, of course, was my specialty.

Nagged by an earlier vow never to hold another corporate position, I rationalized that 'technically' I was a self-employed contractor. However, back on the please-for-pay treadmill, the reality was that I was merely an employee on contract. Regardless of my personal or family needs, what the boss wanted, the boss got. Once again, I was lost in the Social Laryngitis mantra: Don't complain, work hard, and do what you're told. You need this job.

In record time, the company expanded into fifteen countries in fifteen months, and pleasing the boss ballooned into a one-hundred-hour workweek! My exit from IBM daunting me like a toothache, I trudged through days of anxious exhaustion, determined to never again be axed from a job. But history repeated itself, anyway.

Finances were still a struggle, and Shabena rightfully complained about feeling neglected. To soothe what ached but couldn't be expressed, I sought an emotional escape that would also produce more income. Bowling wasn't an option, so I turned to the obvious—network marketing for the very company where I worked. *Brilliant!* The boss would definitely be pleased that I was involved in every area of the business. From motivational conference calls and events, to team building and training, I'd be there! Plus, I'd have a side-business that would help with the bills at home, which would please my wife. *Both at home and work, what could better demonstrate that I was indeed an all-in team player?*

Within weeks, my boss became my network marketing mentor and personal friend. When asked to host conference calls and run training classes for recruits, my confidence soared. I'd found my niche! Or so I thought.

A few months later, completely out of the blue, my friend/mentor announced that he didn't think network marketing was for me, further recommending that I just stick with computer programming. His words smacked and dazed me with the force of an unexpectedly deployed automobile airbag. *What was he talking about?* Networking marketing was exactly for me!

I was happy speaking up instead of shutting down; thrilled to be leading a team of people who looked up to me. And there wasn't a cap on my income! Day and night, I imagined building my business into an empire where I'd be the boss! *How could network marketing not be for me?* It offered everything I wanted—actually *wanted*. But I couldn't disagree with him and risk losing my job. Mumbling, "I know I'm a programmer," I let the matter and my dream drop.

Shortly afterward, too many months of working long hours having totally disconnected us as husband and wife, Shabena and I regretfully and miserably decided to separate. Our marriage was simply unable to survive the unfairness of one partner always working, leaving the other left to pick up the slack everywhere else. Coincidentally, the boss had decided to move to San Diego. Numb with sadness, I followed the paycheck back to the United States, leaving my heart behind in Vancouver where it belonged.

Miles from the wife and family I loved, needed and desperately wanted, pleasing the boss lost priority. I did what was expected of me, and his new business venture progressed as planned. But while packing for the move, there was a secret I'd kept to myself. One I hadn't even shared with Shabena or our kids. I'd find my way back to them and do whatever it took to repair our family.

Not a minute of the workday passed without envisioning at least one of their smiles. At night in my hotel, my eyes stared blankly at the television, while my mind's eye envisioned my family. Constantly I saw them laughing, playing tricks on one another, the kids making messes and Shabena cajoling them into cleaning it up. Sure to make me smile through the ruthless loneliness, was remembering the instant computer messages and cell phone texts my quick-witted beautiful wife and I'd exchanged when we first met. My favorite was our poking fun at various colloquial expressions that didn't make sense to us.

Six months blurred by with me staring in the rearview mirror. Slower than stalled, time reversed until there was no future. Constantly, I strategized about how to solve my family's Rubik's Cube. We were meant to line up, colorful characters side-by-side, strong in our solidarity. White, yellow, red, orange, and green would never align without blue me, far away in San Diego. It wasn't possible, because I wouldn't allow it. I was moving closer to home.

Convincing my boss to hire someone to help out in San Diego, I agreed to continue my web programming contract, but long-distance and part-time. I soon found myself living in Seattle, a mere two-and-a-half-hour drive away from my family in Vancouver. A short while later, realizing that the closer physical distance did absolutely nothing for the emotional distance, Shabena came to Seattle. Together, we drove home.

"Are we there yet?" I asked Shabena on the long drive home, desperate to again firmly plant my feet on Vancouver soil, and not entirely sure I'd made the right decision. *Why was it that I constantly felt forced to choose between love and money? What wasn't I seeing? How did other people do it?* Raising kids came with a mountain of bills I had no idea how to pay—especially, when my paycheck was torn in two, like me. *Would I forever live with one metaphorical foot pointed regretfully southward to the job I'd forfeited, the other northbound and eagerly anticipating the long awaited joyful chaos of family?*

"I know! I can't wait to get home either!" Shabena cheerfully responded from the passenger seat, completely unaware of the fear gripping my vocal cords.

There was so much I couldn't share without risking hurting her feelings or reversing the recent repair of our marriage. A different emotion seemed to win the battle every other minute—relief, anxiety, happiness, anger, sorrow, excitement, anticipation, then back to fear as though it were a magnet in a brain wrought with iron filings. Five miles down the road, I asked again, "Are we there yet?"

"You're just being silly," Shabena said, laughing as she flicked her hair back and the radio on.

"Maybe," I uttered too low for her to hear. It was terror talking, not silliness. Six long months of agonizing loneliness and heartache—was it over, or was I just bobbing for apples in a bucketful of oranges and vinegar? Surely, I'd have to top up my part-time income with more contract work or a job. *Would we soon again find ourselves at loggerheads over bills and long hours spent working?*

But this time, history didn't repeat itself. Within the accepting arms of my family, my voice grew stronger. Albeit, shaky at times, I increasingly became confident in my 'right' to make decisions and to seek what I needed and wanted. There was just one more step: severing the final tie with what was holding me back—fear.

Henry Ford has a wonderful quote that encapsulates it all: "Obstacles are those frightful things you see when you take your eyes off of your goal." It was time to put my eyes on the road ahead, and be the forefront explorer of my own frontier. A month after I returned to Vancouver, I quit my part-time contract, started another network marketing business, and went back to freelancing websites. The latter not being a heartfelt choice, but a mere means to an end—we needed food on the table.

With fear held at bay, another equally formidable feeling came to the forefront—anger. Years of cumulated fury and ignored disappointment had compacted like trash in my gut, occasionally firing up through my throat with volcanic fury. Festering for years, my words weren't always kind, sometimes spewing out thoughtlessly and woundingly.

Recognizing that a world of ire would soon cripple both me and my family, I sought ways to feel peaceful. I learned how to meditate and to actually ask for help—sometimes from the angels above; sometimes from my angel on earth.

"Marcus, you're not listening to me," is Shabena's kind expression that helps me to check my kneejerk reactions and erroneous assumptions. She's my barometer. When I hear those words, I stop, think, get a grip, and smile. The entire world no longer rests on my shoulders. Assistance and guidance are available anytime I choose to seek them.

Living my life of *choice* necessitates and commands balance: spiritually, personally and professionally. I know this now and seek it daily. I pursue dreams that align with my *heartmind*, and pursue social *interaction* rather than social *acceptance*. I live *with* my family, not *for* my family. I trust my gut instincts and whatever magic is paving the way for remarkable me.

Finding the way to the genuine Marcus was a long, winding and complicated journey, but I'm home now. There have been consequences along the way, such as losing my friend and mentor when I quit my contract in San Diego. But rather than resent that loss, I accept that when people change, some friends get misplaced along the way. Although most of my warts and pimples are still healing, I also accept my mistakes and misgivings as part of what makes me who I am— strong, capable and loving. I no longer float through life as a severed iceberg, cut-off from parts of me denied through fear or mired in anger. Happy and at peace, I stand tall in wisdoms gained.

Today, all areas of my life are balanced. We're not rich monetarily, but we're a wealthy family that sings a song for which the lyrics are continually changing. We laugh and we struggle. We pray and we hope. Together the colors of our lives align and march forward in love. As Dr. Wayne Dyer so wisely said, "There is no way to prosperity, prosperity is the way." One only needs to know what the word 'prosperity' truly means to have a fulfilling and rewarding life.

> "Do not go where the path may lead, go instead
> where there is no path and leave a trail."
> —Ralph Waldo Emerson

Divine
Connection

www.kindnessiskey.com

Born To Be Weird!

Karie-Anne Hawthorne

Gratefully, about age twenty-nine, I learned that Grandma, who continuously visited me from Heaven, had been intrigued by the occult and paranormal. Ironically, for many years, fearing what my parents might think, I'd kept my own 'weird' interests to myself. It was enlightening for me to realize that if I'd mentioned my curiosity about the supernatural sooner, Grandma's past would have been talked about sooner. But then, all things happen at the *right* time.

Apparently, for Christmas, Grandma once bought my dad and his brothers a Ouija board. Although *all-the-fad* back then, she kept it hidden from her husband, only bringing it out for the boys to play with when their father went bowling. She'd also sought out mediums in hopes of communicating with her deceased father. At first, I thought it was because she missed him terribly, only to learn seconds later that she'd really been in pursuit of her father's savings, which mysteriously vanished when he passed. Though his surviving relatives went as far as to dig up the property around my great-grandfather's house, the cache was never found.

Another hitherto well-kept family secret was that Grandma taught her impressionable children telekinesis—the technique of moving objects with one's mind. When he was a teenager, my father actually telekinetically moved a glass across the kitchen table. He and his brothers also levitated a coffee table by simply placing their hands on top of it! All of them more spooked than impressed, when the table proceeded to attack Dad's youngest brother, the 'game' was never again played.

"Mom, why was I born on June 15th?"

"I don't know," she replied, her mind on whatever preoccupied grownups, which, at that moment, was clearly not my six-year-old ominous ponderings.

"Why was I named Karie-Anne?"

"What do you think we should have named you?" she asked,

seemingly becoming flustered as she stirred something in a big yellow bowl that always reminded me of mustard and made me want hotdogs.

"Sally," I replied with limited conviction, the name having just popped to mind.

"Why Sally?" she asked, again making me do the answering.

"I don't know, I just like that name," I said, standing tiptoe so I could see what was in the bowl that was distracting Mom. "How come you changed my birthday?"

"What are you talking about?" Mom asked, wiping her hands on her apron and smearing chocolate all over the red and white checks.

"How come my birthday party is on June 6th and not on the 15th?" *Did parents have some special power to change their child's birthdate without even asking if it was okay?*

"I'm still not sure what you're asking," Mom said, her eyes scrunched up as though she were doing her best to read my mind.

"Well," I said, catching a whiff of the chocolate mix, "does that mean my birthday has changed forever?" It worried me that they might change the day every year. *How would I know which day to be excited and which day to get older?*

Mom laughed, so I knew something was funny. "Your actual birthday hasn't changed, Karie-Anne. You won't actually turn six until June 15th. The party is on the 6th because that's when everyone can come and help celebrate."

Dissatisfied with her answer, I wandered off to my room. Whatever Mom or Dad said was always the way things went, which didn't seem entirely right, but what was I to do? Besides, there was a lot in life to wonder about, even if my parents didn't have all the answers. For instance, why I was born on such a special day? June 15th was smack-in-the-middle of three hundred and sixty five days. June was in the middle of the year, and I was in the middle between my older brother and younger sister. Being in the middle of so many things couldn't be coincidental—it had to mean something. Could it be that I was supposed to be some kind of middleman when I grew up? But I was a girl. Could a girl become a middle*man*? Maybe I'd become a *medium*! I wasn't entirely sure what mediums did, but I'd seen one on television who found someone. Finding people seemed the perfect job for a middle girl child.

Turning to my stuffed animal kingdom, imagining Tiger to be a policeman, I said, "Hello, my name is Karie-Anne. I'm a medium and I find lost children."

Yap! It sounded and felt good!

"No, don't cry," I continued, soothingly patting my Lion's mane. "I will find little Tommy. He's probably just fallen into a hole and can't climb out by himself." *Why did male lions have manes, while female lions were bald as babies?* Girls have long hair. Female lions should have long hair too.

"Mr. Dragon, don't you agree that there is so much about life that doesn't make sense? For instance, changing someone's birthday just because of a party? And why did I get named Karie-Anne? Why not just Karie? Or just Anne? Why couldn't my name be Sally?" I rambled on, checking to see if my purple Raptor Dinosaur knew the answers. He didn't. None of my four friends had any *really good* answers.

I decided to ask again the next day, after they had time to think about it.

One day, after watching a video during a visit with my grandparents, someone said, "Oh, such great memories!" I was a little shocked because the moving images of our camping trip didn't match my memories of our family getaway. Since he was the cameraman, the video was from Grandpa's perspective. It was then that I realized that nobody in the world knew what the camping trip was like from my viewpoint. It also struck me that, unless they told me, I would never know what memories the rest of my family had of our trip or anything else. Memories seemed awfully important. *How many memories could one head hold?* Probably not many or we wouldn't need home videos. It was then that I knew everyone got to do and see different things— that was what made each of us different! *Different must be good!* It was great fun to think my memories made me different. Although, I didn't really like the idea that I couldn't know everyone's memories or how someone else saw the world. But it was the way it had to be if *I* was going to be different!

Throughout most of my young life, whenever I finally figured things out, people kept doing and saying things that made it necessary to think more about what I thought I knew was right!

"They're twins, so how can you tell Mary-Kate and Ashley Olsen apart?" I asked my friend Megan as we sat at her dining room table having lunch. She loved Mary-Kate and Ashley Olsen. And she had all their videos!

"Well," she answered, pondering the idea. "Mary-Kate has a small birthmark on her face and Ashley doesn't."

"I see," I said, losing interest in the Olsen twins and remembering that I hadn't read my horoscope that day, which I tried to remember to do every day, right after I read the comics. Horoscopes were related to birthdays, and birthdays were important. Originally, I hoped reading about the planets would tell me if it was legal to change someone's birthday for the convenience of a party. But I didn't find that out. I did, however, learn that some days and some numbers were lucky. Lucky days were my specialty, and whenever I was supposed to have one, I always did! "Let's read our horoscopes," I suggested, while trying to remember which day was Megan's birthday.

"No, you will not!" Megan's mom hollered from the kitchen, startling my skin so much the hair on my arms woke up. Had she read something bad in today's horoscope that she thought might scare us? I liked my friend's tiny sweet mom who always thought to make enough lunch for me too.

"Why not?" I asked, looking up at Megan's mom, who'd come to snatch the paper right off the table.

"Because we don't believe in horoscopes. Our lives are in God's hands."

"Weren't horoscopes also in God's hands? God created the planets, didn't He?" I wondered, thinking of what I'd learned in bible school while trying not to kick my feet back so high under my seat that they made banging noises, which in turn made the minister make harrumphing sounds. Mom usually helped me with that embarrassing conundrum by placing her hand on my knee when we weren't praying or singing. "*Yes, God made the planets!*" I distinctly remembered that, so I did some more thinking: "If God created the planets, then why couldn't they influence us? Maybe He planned it that way. Besides, how could anything on earth *not be* created by God?"

Leaving Megan's, I vowed to pay better attention in church. I was fairly certain we only went to church to avoid hell, and so that we'd feel guilty for doing or saying anything Mom and Dad didn't want done or said. But maybe with all the antsy fidgeting my Mom kept telling me to stop, I had missed something the priest said. *Oh, next Sunday was going to be the longest hour yet.* The only thing good about going to church was that all of my sins for that week were forgiven so I could get into Heaven. *Who wouldn't want to go to Heaven?* Personally, I thought it best to be good all the time because God might be watching.

But maybe some people just couldn't stop themselves from doing unkind things. Like the time when my brother Andrew pretended not to be able to see or hear me, so I kicked his shins over and over. I even told him, "Andrew, I'm bugging you!" But even that didn't spark a *stop it* from him. He just looked far away, as though I was just some itsy-bitsy fly that wasn't even worth swatting.

My grandma passed away when I was eight. She lived in Victoria, which could only be reached by ferry and was far away from each home we moved to throughout British Columbia. This was why I didn't see her often; until, she died and came to tea parties in my bedroom.

When she died, Dad was the saddest of all because she was his mom. Mom was also sad, which made me sad. However, it didn't make sense that we were all sad that Grandma had gone to Heaven. *Wasn't that where we all wanted to go and why we went to boring church?*

I asked Grandma about this conundrum one day while she and I were having tea with Tiger and the rest of my animal friends. She didn't answer. Some things about Heaven and death must be secrets God likes to keep to himself until you arrive on His doorstep. Like memories, you can't know every little thing, or every secret, until your life gets you there. I wasn't in any real hurry to know *everything*. I was happy just 'using my imagination' like Mom said I was doing whenever she heard me talking to my animals.

I don't know if my parents knew that Grandma visited me. But if they did, they kept it their secret, like God sometimes did.

The older I became, the more the possibility of going to hell worried me. I felt guilty almost always. *Was I being good enough to get into*

Heaven? Were my school grades high enough for God to want me? Having kicked poor Andrew's shins blue and black, had God already decided that He *didn't* want me?

What helped to ease my troubles was deciding that Jesus must be a medium too. He could talk to his father in Heaven, just like I could talk to Grandma. Megan's mom's reaction to reading horoscopes forever fresh, I didn't dare tell anyone about my delightful deduction.

Being different was sometimes hard on me, but became less so, when my best friend and I decided that we *weren't strange* we were 'weirdanators.' Of course, we were extremely proud of our carefully chosen title that celebrated our uniqueness. *Weird* was a compliment. *Strange* was an insult.

As a preteen, I could no longer accept the conflicting messages that God loved everyone, however, would sentence an unlucky person to hell for a minimum of ten documented indiscretions. Nor could I buy that we were all born with 'original sin.'

Despite questioning these beliefs, I still truly admired the priests because they were inspiring, funny, masterly, and eloquent. Noting that everyone else also admired the priests, I wanted to become one. It annoyed me to no end that because I was female, I'd likely have to settle for becoming a nun like my great-aunt Sister Columba. Additionally, it struck me as overly prudish that priests and nuns had to be celibate. I wanted to be everything—wife, mother and priest! *Why was our religion so dogmatically narrow-minded when others weren't?*

All my fretting about what I could or couldn't *be* or *do* didn't stop me from having fun and making pockets of *chosen* sister-friends, mostly ones who shared my preoccupation with religion. Drawn to less stringent spiritual beliefs, in grade eight I became friends with a girl who was Wiccan. Fascinated by her stories of modern-day paganism, I cautiously learned a few 'protection' spells, which I was fairly certain would be okay with God.

One spell involved choosing a rock to which I felt drawn, holding it in my hand until I could feel its heartbeat, and reciting an incantation (much like a positive affirmation) designed to protect family and friends or valued possessions. Uncertain as to whether it would actually work, but with nothing to lose, I recited an incantation to protect my backpack and everything inside of it. One day, after walking home from school, I noticed that my wallet was missing from my backpack. I immediately assumed that the spellbound rock hadn't worked; until, I realized the rock had also gone missing. *Had both coveted items fallen out of my backpack at the same time because the rock was actually protecting my wallet?* Luckily, my wallet was returned by a Good Samaritan.

Sometimes, for fun, my friends and I would test our psychic abilities. Our clairvoyant talents never astoundingly proven, that bit of experimenting didn't hold our interest for long. We also tried our hand at visualization. One of us would visualize an object, and the rest of us would try to identify the envisioned item. I don't remember any of us being overly successful at that either, however, it did open my mind to the wonderful concept of one's intuitive *third eye*.

At camp one summer we delighted in the scaring the pants off of each other with ghost tales about an unfortunate soul who'd been murdered in the dark and quiet forest, just inches from where we lay tucked in sleeping bags. We never tired of that bit of silliness. Scaring each other was truly invigorating.

Forever on a quest for answers, when my Wiccan sister-friend moved away, I made friends with some teenage Mennonites. My new chosen sisters believed in Jesus and God, and we regularly attended Youth Group and a few evening and weekend bible studies. However, for my liking, there was still far too much salvation and righteous-living rhetoric in their religion. My search for God continued; thankfully, leading me toward an important truth.

Through writing a grade-eleven humanities class essay, I discovered that there are numerous similarities between *how* and *what* Christians and Pagans celebrate. *All Hallows' Eve,* which is now called Halloween and embraced by many Christians, actually began as a Pagan autumnal equinox harvest festival. Christmas was originally a Germanic Pagan festival called *Yule* or *Yuletide.* Even the decorating of eggs and the blessing of food at Easter dates back to Pagan times. Learning all of this blew me away. *Did Christians steal Christmas from the Pagans?* It also made me wonder, "What could possibly be 'wrong' with a rural-based ancient religion that believed in many Gods, instead of just one?"

Around nineteen, partying temporarily took priority over further exploring my spiritual pathway. Albeit, not for long, as coming-of-age afforded me the additional freedom I needed to seriously investigate my psychic and mediumistic abilities. What being an adult *didn't* immediately present was a tutor to help me understand and decipher premonitions gleaned through dreams and knowings.

So I bought a deck of 'fairy' tarot cards. One evening, I meditated using the 'mermaid card' as my guide. The next morning there was a pencil sketch of a mermaid—with her face crossed out—on the wall above my bed. I hadn't drawn it, and interpreted the 'X' as meaning that mermaids should remain faceless. It was too weird an experience to completely fathom, even for me, so I shared what had happened with my friends. No one was fazed, because nobody believed that the drawing had mysteriously materialized during the night. Not long afterward, my friends grew tired of listening to me talk about all things supernatural, conducted an intervention, and advised, "Your imagination is greater than your ability to reason. Let it go."

How old did I have to be before people would start to understand, instead of doubt me? *Where could I find friends with similar experiences and answers to questions I just couldn't figure out? Was anyone on the entire planet like me?* Needing acceptance as much as answers, I became a chameleon, resignedly blending into a society that didn't understand me. Not wanting *others* to feel uncomfortable, *I* was the one who was uncomfortable as my inner *weirdanator* became silent, lost and lonely. Despite keeping quiet about further unexplainable occurrences and psychic knowings, premonitions continued to enter my dreams.

After graduating from high school, I worked as a cashier at a local grocery store. One night, I dreamed of being in a car accident and dying. In the dream, I saw my funeral, followed by a celebration of my life held at my parents' house. The next day, a lady wearing a sweatshirt emblazoned with 'Karie Young Soccer Tournament' came to my cashier's till. *Karie* was spelled exactly like my first name, which, at the time, was considered an unusual spelling. My maiden surname was Young. Intrigued by the similarities of our names, I enquired about the tournament. It was in honor of Karie Young, one of the woman's soccer teammates who'd died in a car accident. Clammy, trembling and as white as the ghost who had somehow entered my dream, I asked my manager for a work break.

On another occasion, I dreamt that a close girlfriend was pregnant. Amused, the next day, I sent her a text about my dream. She received my text while at the doctor's with her boyfriend where it was confirmed that she was indeed pregnant. *Why had the news come to me via a dream?*

In 2004, Nana, my mom's mother, was diagnosed with brain cancer. She died within a year of finding out. The night before her passing, I dreamt of a bright white light often described by those who've experienced near-death, accompanied by the message—*You'll find out on the 20th.* Nana passed over during the night of July 19th. I received the news the next morning via a message my dad left on my answering machine.

Another night, I dreamed of two babies, a boy and a girl, being born within days of each other. Throughout the following week, my husband and I learned that three different females in our inner circle were pregnant. Suddenly frightened for our close friends, I confessed my dream and fear to my husband—only two babies would actually be born. Events unfolded with the birth of a baby boy and girl. The third woman miscarried.

Having dreamt the night before of receiving a psychic reading by candlelight in a room filled with pillows, the following day at Astral Connections (a combination metaphysical store and Internet café) the lights went out, and my reading was indeed conducted under the soft light of a burning candle.

After a bit of searching, I discovered three churches in my area that I thought might offer the type of ministry for which I longed. After retiring to bed, I asked for divine guidance as to which one I should attend. My dream that night was of winter and a desperate need to buy flowers. In the dream, I drove around, eventually coming across a florist shop located in a house with an 'open' sign. Two women greeted me, escorted me around back, and there among the snow covered ground was a beautiful flourishing garden.

I interpreted the dream to mean that I should attend The Inner Garden Chapel in Surrey, British Columbia near where I lived. Sunday morning at the chapel, I was greeted by two women, each with the name Lynne.

I felt I'd arrived home from the first day I listened to the spiritualist teachings of the Inner Garden Chapel. No longer was I alone in deciphering my psychic dreams. Within a month, I attended a Connecting with your Spirit Guides class, followed by an Introduction to Mediumship course where I discovered that what I originally thought was my imagination was actually *clairvoyance*. All those long years ago, I hadn't just imagined I was speaking with Grandma over tea.

During weekly mediumship circles, I learned how to connect with my spirit guides, and various techniques for communing with totem animals, angels and the ascended masters. Within a short while, I blossomed as a medium. Particularly thrilling for me, was mastering one teacher's healing exercise series known as GAPP: Grounding, Ascending, Protection, and Prayer.

Grounding involves imagining your feet are roots that extend to the earth's center, while breathing into and through the connection, and sending love to and expressing your gratitude for Mother Earth's bountiful provisions. *Ascending* is much the same, but your connection is with Father God and your gratitude is for all of your blessings. *Protection* involves asking negative energy to be directed and absorbed by the 'white light' where it will be transformed into positive energy. *Praying* is the final step, during which you set your 'intentions' for the day, stating them as if they have already happened. The entire four-step spiritual exercise was easy to learn and remarkably healing.

Excited to my soul, within a year, I was giving psychic readings, providing spiritual guidance and chairing chapel services. A little further down my path, acting on a message from my higher guidance, I developed a boot-camp for *intuitives, psychics and mediums*. Watching boot-camp attendees blossom and grow warmed me to the core.

During an 'automatic writing' session I was gifted with the following message: *The essence of confidence is that you don't need outside acknowledgement, because you know that you are the perfect version of you. You are not better or worse than anyone. The only person that can tell you that you're wrong in your beliefs, pursuits or knowings is yourself. Good times and bad times walk through this world hand-in-hand—it is up to you to decide how to interpret and respond to each. Be a child of learning, not of hiding or denying. Change is desirable as it represents growth and newly opened doors. Always be open to the universe's welcoming arms of love and guidance. If for some reason you are not happy with the way you are, you always have tomorrow to fix it. Love yourself and the skin you are in. Don't care what people think, but care for other people. Stay connected with yourself as an essential ingredient in our web of absolute love.*

Finding like-minded worshipers and mentors helped me to reach for what I believe is life's most precious gift—connecting with others, on earth and above. If only we all followed our heart-emanating desires and inner knowing, what a glorious universe this would truly become. Instead, too often we're distracted or knocked off-course by naysayers and those bent on maintaining the status quo. My wish is for every person to free his or her fears and self-doubt to the wind (or white light) in celebration of our differences and the fact we are all God's children.

Now a minister-in-training at the Inner Garden Chapel, I sometimes chuckle when I think back to how frightened I once was to share my extrasensory abilities with family and friends; especially, my mom, who is a devout follower of a traditional religion. My family may still sometimes view me as a *weirdanator*—not strange, but different. I've come to accept the varying ways others may perceive me, and no longer shrink away to avoid scrutiny. Today, I truly rejoice in my uniqueness. When all else fails, I talk with Grandma and together we try to figure out what happened to my great-grandfather's fortune.

God gave you gifts to graciously and trustingly utilize. My seasoned advice: identify what makes your heart sing, and then just do it! Namaste.

> "What we are is God's gift to us.
> What we become is our gift to God."
> —Eleanor Powell

Eternally High

Bill Streng

"Best acid in town—pure windowpane," Mike announced, while holding a plastic sandwich bag containing about a dozen tiny silver squares. His skinny chest inflating like an emergency life-jacket, he continued, "The dealer's a friend of mine. Said he tried a hit last night and had his best trip ever."

"You gonna trust a dealer's testimony," I retorted. Ribbing Mike was a favorite pastime.

"Trust him! If it's as good as he says it is, I'm gonna marry the son of a gun."

A couple of gulps of beer later, he dropped a tiny tinfoil package into my palm, as he cautioned, "Be careful. It's that tiny little clear spec, and it's pretty potent stuff. Drop it on the floor and the cat'll be the only one getting stoned."

"Uh-huh." Mike's word was about as reliable as a coastal weather forecast. Just the same, I took my time gingerly unwrapping the quarter-inch-square of tinfoil. "Where the hell is it? You sure you put it in here?"

"It's in there," Mike said, sauntering to my side and peering into the shiny silver paper. "See!" He pointed at a nearly invisible speck-sized clear square."

"That's gonna get me off?" I asked, narrowing my gaze at his gullibility, before licking the foil a few times.

"Higher than a kite, man," Mike chirped, too cheery to be believed. "And you owe me twenty bucks."

"We'll see." I sat at the head of the table and watched as the rest of our friends lapped at their tiny tinfoil squares. Then, turning toward the blond to my left, I asked, "You off yet?"

"Give it a chance," Mike interjected, taking my bait like a blind fish.

"How long did your friend say this hit was gonna take?" I goaded, pretty certain Mike had been had, and refusing to dig in my wallet until it was proven otherwise.

A half hour later, still straight and none too pleased, I bugged Mike, but this time I was serious. "You're not getting my twenty bucks. I'm half drunk, but I ain't stoned." Nods from my friends let me know they were still straight too.

"Drop another one," Mike suggested with a shrug. "It's your funeral, not mine."

"Hand it over," I said, thrusting my hand in his direction.

"You should give it a bit longer," he cautioned, but likely tired of my bitching, dumped another tiny square of tinfoil into my upturned palm.

Sometime later, contemplating heading to the kitchen to get another beer, I again turned toward the blond, thinking she might want one too. Astoundingly, she wasn't the only one directly to my left. Emanating from her body was a separate entity—a stunningly beautiful angel surrounded by a mist-like rainbow of pastels. The angel was breathtakingly gorgeous with abnormally bright eyes, alabaster skin and perfectly formed glossy lips. Blinking a couple of times, I stared at the angel, mesmerized not only by her unbridled beauty, but also by the absolute love that radiated from her and enveloped us both. Enmeshed in her wondrous aura, so awe-inspiring it defied anything worldly, I knew she'd been sent from Heaven to be with me. Folded within her love, I experienced a serene peaceful joy. For a long moment, I simply savored our heavenly spiritual oneness.

"Should we go, now?" she conveyed telepathically. Between us, words weren't necessary.

As her kind blue eyes glanced in the direction of the window and then back at me, I knew she wanted me to go with her to Heaven.

Wishing we could spend forever together, it dawned on me that if I didn't agree to go with her, she might just suddenly disappear. I definitely didn't want that!

"Watch with me, and I'll show you," she relayed, her halo expanding so that I was enshrouded within her bowed ribbons of soft pastels.

Together, our two minds seemingly becoming one, we envisioned our souls floating upward, out through the white-curtained open window and toward Heaven. Trusting and loving her, it seemed a beautiful idea.

"Should we go, now?" she silently communicated, extending her delicate hand.

"Absolutely!" I decided as my hand floated toward hers. I loved this angel and the feeling being with her elicited. Then I thought, "But what about my friends?"

"They're not ready," she calmly relayed amidst the seemingly distant whispers of my buddies.

Studying my companions, I knew the angel was right. None of my friends were ready to accompany us heavenward. And I wasn't wild about leaving without them.

"Should we go, now?" she again relayed, her love so pure, tranquil and inviting that I wanted to bask in it eternally.

"*Eternally!* Oh-oh," I thought, "I need to think about this." Torn between going and staying, I pondered my dilemma. In the midst of my go-or-stay conundrum, the spirit of Jesus appeared before me.

Breathlessly spellbound by the depth of Jesus's love, I barely smiled.

"Confess all of which you are not proud," Jesus wordlessly conveyed, His absolute compassion for and acceptance of me obvious.

"What exactly did Jesus want me to confess?" I wondered, aware of the beautiful angel still at my side, and knowing I could still leave with her. "What have I done that was so *wrong?*"

Enveloped in Jesus's sweet placid love, as though watching a movie, I saw my much younger self snatching my two-years-old cousin's yellow dump truck.

"That's not so bad. I was just a little kid," I inwardly rationalized. "Why must I die?!"

Still feeling His tremendous love, I was dumfounded as the movies of my misdeeds doubled to two, then four, then eight. Grouped and continually multiplying, my wrongdoings quickly became too plentiful to count. Weirdly, I was aware of them all simultaneously, recognizing every scene as being indiscretions committed by me—some more shaming than others. Yet, I didn't feel ashamed. I felt absolute love and an eager need to take responsibility for my past actions and become a better person.

Overwhelmed by Jesus's love for me, and my love for Him, I

considered expressing my devotion, hesitating as I speculated about what my friends might think. I was fairly certain they wouldn't understand my sudden love for Jesus.

"If love is in your heart, then speak of Me and say what you feel."

Struggling between my surreal moments with Jesus and my imaginings of what would happen in my real life should I suddenly declare my love for Him aloud, I said nothing.

"Bear witness for what you feel," Jesus encouraged.

The intensity of His urgings swelling within—mind, heart and soul—I realized that Jesus was right, and I must declare my love for Him. Still, I remained mute.

"Bear witness for what you feel," Jesus silently emboldened, spreading his arms as though welcoming me to His flock.

Fevered, frenzied and prepared to do so at the top of my voice, I shouted, "I love Jesus!" But my words came out in a much quieter voice than intended.

Exactly as I'd anticipated, my friends' jaws dropped in shock. Then Mike said, "Okay, that's it. Willy's cracked-up. I've got to make some phone calls. Nobody's gonna believe this."

I'm not certain why it was a trigger, but seeing and hearing my friends' responses, I suddenly knew that it was now or never. If I was going to accept my wrongdoings, I had to dive right into them and accept my fate—even if it meant that I must die.

Agitated, I jumped up from the table. Consumed with intense, erratic emotions, my head felt like it was going to explode. It was as though there was a readied shotgun next to my skull. "I have got to get out of here," I said aloud, while inwardly knowing there was no way to escape—I had to dive into my past indiscretions and die.

But dying wasn't a fate I was prepared to accept, not even with Jesus's blessings. *No, way!* I had to at least *try* to escape. Pushing back the nagging inner voice repeatedly echoing, "You can't escape from who you are and what you've done," I attempted to move toward the door. But making headway was nearly impossible. Held back by some imperceptible imprisoning force, my heart thudded both from fear and the effortful physical strain it took to move. My body, especially my legs, felt heavy and no longer subject to my control. *Was the weight of my error-speckled past holding me back?*

There was no actual gale pushing back as I pushed forward, but the dynamics were similar. Head down, I struggled against my invisible potent opponent. It took forever to reach the door. Once there, my hands and arms eerily weightless and seemingly detached from the rest of me, I slothfully reached for the handle. It wouldn't twist open. I tried again and again, until finally successful. Stepping over the threshold was mountain-climb taxing. Navigating the lawn, then the curb, and eventually getting into my car required triathlon endurance.

Feeling imprisoned seated behind the wheel of my 1964 Pontiac convertible, keys in hand, I considered going back into the house to face my past. But as an icy chill edged toe and fingernail upward, risking death quickly became a non-option. *I was stoned, not stupid.* Life still in slow motion, I finally started my car and just sat there fearing there was no escape. Still, I had to try. Desperate and scared, I headed down King Edward Street, and then east on Kingsway. *How far did I need to drive to escape? Could I escape?*

Car after car passed by, making me realize that I was driving well below the speed limit. *Did my fellow motorists have me pegged as crazy? Was I crazy to think I could travel out of the inevitable return to my own destiny? I'd best go back.*

"Do you believe?" commanded a voice I immediately recognized as being God's.

"Yes!" I hollered without hesitation, as a luminous beam of God's eternal promise shone down from the sky, filling my car with its blinding brilliance. Amazingly, it soothed, rather than stung my eyes. No sides or dimension, His everlasting light of love completely encased me in spiritual power of unimaginable clarity. Without warning and at quantum speed, I was abruptly scooped out of my car and lifted heavenward. Suspended in the universe, I gasped and gawked in wonder, not fear. There was absolutely nothing to see, yet I was seeing everything there was to see—absolute love. A love so intensively beautiful, that if you were to recall the most wonderful and peaceful moment of your life and multiply it by a million, you might begin to know the magnitude of universal love emanating everywhere.

Still, although I was immensely enjoying the magnificent feeling of God's heavenly love, I wondered, "Do I believe?"

Swoosh. I was seated back in my car, my world again in slow motion as I drove along Kingsway. Wanting to go back to Heaven, I hollered, "Yes! Yes! I believe!" But nothing happened. Desperate and confused, I tried to decide if I did indeed believe in God. After some time, I decided, "I DO BELIEVE!" *Swoosh*. I was back amidst God's love and light.

Again my ponderings turned to doubt. *Swoosh*. I was back driving my car. I must be a slow learner, because it took a few more trips between Heaven and Earth, until God asked, "Do you have faith?"

"Yes!" came my heart-emanating answer.

"Bill," God said, catching my attention with His use of my name. "You're going the wrong way. I want you to make an immediate left turn, followed by a right at the corner. From there proceed to Willingdon Avenue, where you will make a right turn and then stop."

"Okay," I responded, eager to please Him.

"Now, close your eyes."

Close my eyes! Was He kidding?

"If you believe, then you will drive your car safely, coming to a stop at an intersection, and the light will be red."

Trusting His word, I followed God's instructions and drove His suggested route with my eyes closed. Spiritually guided, though only a short distance, what seemed like an eternity and a zillion heart thumps later, I arrived at my destination safe and sound. Opening my eyes, I noted that the light was indeed red. I was a believer! I'd experienced omnipotent and omnipresent love. Stunned and in total awe, I wondered what would happen next.

In the blink of an eye, the light turned green. *Swoosh*. I was down from both my spiritual high and acid trip, and suddenly completely sober. Relief swept over me like a spring breeze—I'd been given a second chance to right my ways. Humbled and grateful, I drove home, feeling smaller but wiser. Mind, heart and soul, I knew I'd forever be a better person.

From that day forward, I never touched another illicit drug. For a short while, I started going to church with a girl I met at Kitsilano Beach a few days after my spiritual awakening. She confessed that she had also been into drugs before she found God. Unfortunately, rather than recognizing my divine experience for what it was, members of her church tried to convince me I'd been visited by the devil. I didn't buy it, and walked away from organized religion, but not Jesus, God or spirituality.

A few months later, my brother Gerry came for a visit. Gerry is a retired RCMP officer. At the time, he lived in Winnipeg, Manitoba which is a few thousand miles from my home in Vancouver, British Columbia. Sometime during our reminiscing and catching up, he told me that one night while lying in his bed and wide awake, my face appeared to him. He said that he could see and hear me pleading, "God, help me. I am going to die, and I don't want to go." Deeply disturbed, but living far away from me, there was little he could do, except respond as he did, "Bill, just hang in there." Understandably, although he'd wanted to telephone me about his vision, he didn't for fear that I'd think he was crazy. When my brother didn't receive word of my death, he simply forgot about his bedtime visitation from what must have been my soul.

After listening, I told him about my life-changing high. He couldn't be certain, but most likely at the same time as I was visited by the beautiful angel, then Jesus and God, Gerry had experienced his vision of my troubled spirit.

I now have three grown children that I treasure above all else— Chereen and David and my stepson Brendan. I remain very spiritual and know that God exists, by whatever name one chooses to worship Him. In the sixties, like me, many young people were influenced by a subset of the Hippy Movement and adherents of Timothy Leary who championed LSD and espoused nonsensical philosophies such as "turn on, tune in, and drop out." Life is so wonderful, I now wonder, "Why would anyone want to turn on, tune in and drop out? *Why did I want to do that?*"

Perhaps, it's the superman complex of youth—a belief in being invincible that leads certain subgroups of every generation to experiment with drugs, alcohol and/or pedal-to-the-metal driving. Fueling such erroneous thinking is the innocent desire of young people to act differently and separate from their parents' generation. Knowing about this naïve exuberance is how Hitler was so successfully able to recruit for his Youth Movement. No matter how far you reach into history, youth have always sought to be different from the society in which they are being raised. Even Jesus was a rebel, but with the greater cause of saving humanity.

Wanting to be different isn't inherently wrong. However, fortunately or unfortunately, the *choices* you make in your teenage years, can greatly affect your adult life—whether you earn your keep doing something you love or hate; whom you marry or don't marry; whether or not you have children; whether you enjoy life or worry and regret incessantly; and, whether you can afford to take vacations and live in the house of your dreams. At any point in time, the circumstances of each of our lives are largely a direct result of our unique choices. Like pieces of a puzzle, big and small, individual choices come together to form the entire picture of one's life.

Albeit, some of us begin life with more advantages or disadvantages than others. Perhaps, it is simply a matter of luck that some people are born healthy and into emotionally-supportive and financially-advantaged families, while others are not. Perhaps, there is a divine purpose for each of our birth circumstances, such as being positioned where we can do the most earthly good. One thing is for certain: when you waste your life worrying about unchangeable circumstances and/or blaming mistakes on lost opportunities or your parents, you also unwittingly forfeit control of your life. My father was a self-proclaimed atheist; yet, I found my way to my own spiritual path.

I know of a middle-aged mother with two Ecstasy-addicted adult children. Her son still dips into the drug underworld, disappearing for months. Her daughter calls about once a year to report that her own kids are in foster care because she has relapsed and is again admitting herself to a drug rehabilitation facility. I feel for this woman who endures countless hours worrying about her drug-addicted offspring. Besides being there when one of them needs her, there is little she can do to help either stay straight. *Is she responsible for how her children turned out?* No, she's not. She didn't once contemplate how she could ruin her kids' lives. As the saying goes, she did the best she could with what she knew. Undoubtedly, she made mistakes; however, it was never, never, with the intention of harming her offspring.

Unlike Timothy Leary (whose death in 1996 wasn't drug related), I *do not* recommend illicit drug use. I was incredibly lucky despite my youthful stupidity. Many of my friends didn't make it, some overdosing alone on a misbegotten quest for peer acceptance, a temporary escape from reality or a fun time. Daily, all over the globe, young people die from truly preventable acts whose potential disastrous consequences are well-publicized.

Overcoming drug or alcohol addiction is a tricky business because the addict must reach for soberness via a damaged mind. Those of us who aren't addicted to mind-altering substances, often miss this crucial piece of the puzzle. What youth too often miss is that addiction is a sneaky and invisible opponent that never announces its pending arrival. Parasitical in nature, addiction just moves into your brain, and then clings on, takes charge, and stays put. Beware: Whatever substance you choose for self-medicating or fun, might one day become a compulsion that controls you—mind, body and soul—until you either die, or claw your way back to your youthful vision of how you dreamed your life would be.

My final bit of wisdom: If you never try cigarettes, drugs, alcohol, or killer-speed road racing, you are infinitely less likely to unwittingly destroy your life. Stay in control of *you*, and who knows what miracles your life might unfold.

Lessons from an Uninvited Houseguest

Elin Nash

Is the girl living in my home a manifestation of my grief and quest for answers, or was she always there and unhappy to have a stranger moving into *her* space? Did she come to me as a spiritual guide, or did I come to her?

After reading my story, I invite you to share your insights and spiritual experiences on my *Heartmind Wisdom* blog. Perhaps by working together, we will better understand why some beings exist in the dual dimensions of life and death.

Anita's Passing

On June 22nd, 2008, my sister, confidant and the one person in my life that truly was of kindred spirit, passed away at age fifty-seven. Anita was a mainstay in my life: she was my labor coach when I delivered my youngest child, Kristen; was the one who continually helped me calm my anxious Snoopy, a dachshund-terrier cross which I adopted from the SPCA; and, childless herself, a valued respite mom to my children. We were sisters and friends by birth and choice. Committed to upholding each other through thick and thin, we relished in unconventional humor others missed, and often spontaneously danced to Rhythm and Blues. Oh, how I miss her warm hugs, quick laugh, and often whispered, "*I love you, Elin.*"

June 27, 2008

Scheduled for surgery that couldn't be postponed, five days after Anita's passing, my mother and I drove to Seattle. On the way, my mother advised, "Your phone is playing music. Answer it."

Reaching for my phone, I said, "That's weird, I've had this phone for a year, and it doesn't play music." Upon answering it, there was no one on the line.

On the way back, the tune played again; still, no one answered my bewildered hello. *Had Anita found a way to let me know that she was watching over me?*

July 6, 2008 – Anita's Memorial

My daughter Lexia and her baby, Rory, came from Edmonton for Anita's memorial and stayed with me for a couple of weeks. Late one evening, entering my room with the lights off, I knocked over my purse. Simultaneously, I heard a loud racket outside my bedroom door and a distinct *scchh-scchh-scchh* sound, followed by a storybook style *hee-hee-hee*, then a shrill voice announcing, "There's ice cream in the fridge!"

I threw open my door, expecting to see my daughter. The hall was empty. Perplexed, I rounded the corner toward the living room and spotted Lexia standing in front of the picture window. "Is everything, okay?" I asked, realizing it was physically impossible that she'd been the one at my bedroom door.

"Is everything okay with *you?*" she returned, appearing equally spooked and puzzled.

"So you heard it too?"

Lexia nodded, her pretty green eyes glistening in fear as she sought a reasonable explanation for the childlike voice proclaiming that there was ice cream in the refrigerator.

"Oh, it was probably a neighbor playing a joke in the outside hallway," I reassured her, ignoring the chills playing along my spine like a maestro on a keyboard.

"Yeah, probably," Lexia agreed in a quivering voice, fright etched in her forehead.

"Come on, let's take a look," I protectively suggested, already on my way to the kitchen, uncertain as to whether I wanted to actually find ice cream in the fridge.

Digging through mountains of leftovers in assorted plastic containers, ice trays, Popsicles, and frozen vegetables, I spotted it. Crammed way at the back was a long forgotten box of vanilla ice cream. After yanking it out as one would a rotten tooth, I traipsed over to the sink and ran hot water over the near-empty box of frostbitten creamy muck. "No more ice cream! Now we can relax," I announced with semi-conviction.

"Sure, we can," Lexia said, on her way to check on Rory, who was still fast asleep.

"Sure," I mimicked, knowing that I would be spending the night with one eye and two ears open. The strange *scchh* sound, the *hee-hee-hee* witchlike laughter and eerie voice had definitely come from the *inside* apartment hallway.

In the morning, both exhausted and still unnerved, we sought a logical explanation, repeatedly asking each other, "You're sure it wasn't you playing a joke on me?" After several dozen reassurances later, I was convinced that I had a houseguest from another dimension. Vanilla was Anita's favorite ice cream flavor. Was my sister trying to communicate from the other side? *But why would Anita want to scare us like that?* My sister was kind and compassionate. She would never deliberately frighten us. So why did the voice we heard mimic both Anita's and mine? And if the voice wasn't hers, why was another soul attempting to communicate with me?

Thankful to have a witness for what I might otherwise have believed was a hallucination, I dreaded the day Lexia and my grandson would return to their home in Alberta, leaving me and Snoopy alone—well, sort of.

Manifesting my Apartment—backtracking to a few years earlier.

Oscar Wilde said, "When the Gods wish to punish us they answer our prayers." Perhaps, he was right.

In February 2005, three years before Anita's passing, I realized that I had to move. My current residence was a dark, dank two-level apartment in North Vancouver, fronted by a sidewalk and blemished by an adjacent drab building and constant passers-by. To see the sky, I had to step outside onto my narrow patio and look straight up. Kitty-corner there was a liquor store. Drug dealers scattered the block, the sweet-and-sour icky smell of crack cocaine often wafted my way. On weekends, my yard-sale-fanatic neighbors set up chairs and 'items for sale' along the green space adjacent to the sidewalk—three feet from my front window! Constantly, I thought, "I'm in a zoo and I don't like it!"

One morning during a leisurely stroll, my seven-year-old dachshund-terrier cross, Snoopy, pulled me toward *our* favorite store, Utopia. Warmed by the welcoming smell of sandalwood incense and soothing exotic music, I smiled as the familiar female clerk and my beloved pet exchanged greetings. With the clerk scratching behind his ear, Snoopy settled in for a visit as she looked at me and asked, "What's up?"

I# 140?

.ng for answers as to what I am meant to be doing with
.d, hopeful she could recommend a book to guide me. "I've
.nbo since 2001, and I'm not happy."

ow, great timing!" she exclaimed. "We shelved a book today that
) .night be for you." She then handed me Dr. Anne Marie Evers's
Affirmations: Your Passport to Happiness.

Nodding, I stared at the blue and green cover splashed with hopeful
words encased in bubbles: *Miracles...Happiness...Loveable...Healing...
Peace.* For me, they were the lyrics to the song I had yet to sing.

"It's a participatory workbook that helps a person define and
achieve what they want in life," the friendly clerk explained, enthusiasm
lighting her face.

She got a sale, and I got a new tool!

With manic vigilance, I delved into the healing exercises, and over
time, defined three or four realistic and attainable affirmations; one
being, if I am to remain living in North Vancouver, I must have the
view already saved on my computer under the title—MY VIEW.

Mid 2007, my affirmed move long overdue, I started seriously looking
for a new permanent home, only to be met with repeated rejections at my
answer to, "Oh, I forgot to ask if you have any pets?" Months of active
searching passed. Then like a slap in the face, a Craigslist ad jumped forefront:
'Small dogs accepted. Affordable rent. VIEW in North Vancouver.'

Snoopy tucked in my arms, off we went. The neighborhood felt
right, and when I walked through the front door there it was—MY
VIEW, including the *North Shore waterfront, Vancouver harbor,
downtown buildings and beyond, Stanley Park, the Lions Gate Bridge,
and a vast sky space.* Delight dancing internally, I knew to stay collected
as we moved from room to room. *Be cool. Don't let on how badly you
want this apartment, or what was advertised as 'affordable' might soon
be astronomical.* "It seems fine," I said, adjusting Snoopy on my hip.
"What's the procedure? Is there an application to fill out?"

January 1st, 2008, thrilled to the bone, we moved into our new
home with just me, Snoopy and the best TV channel going: MY VIEW.
Or so I thought, because euphoria aside, over the following few months,
I began to suspect there was more to my apartment than met the eye.

On a couple of nights when almost asleep, I sensed an uneasy
rustling energy low to the floor by my bed. Imagining snickering little

gremlins running about, I pulled the covers over my head and scolded myself for having such silly thoughts.

Sometimes when arriving home, like a parent happened upon misbehaving teenagers, walking through the front door I felt a peculiar energy. It was as if I'd interrupted a gathering, and upon my surprise arrival, everyone scattered into hiding. What unnerved me further, was that in contrast to our previous residence, Snoopy always seemed super anxious whenever he had to stay home alone.

One night, I heard the sound of crunching wood, alerting me to what I thought was someone forcing his way through my apartment neighbor's door. Alarmed and ready to call 911, I ran to look through my peephole. Unable to see anything, I cracked open the door. Dead silence. Opening the door further, I could see that there was no one in the hall, and my neighbor's door appeared intact. *Hmmm?*

Another time, startled by the sound of a loud BANG at my hallway closet, I found everything, including the rod, toppled on to the floor. At first, I thought it was the weight of the clothes that caused the rod to collapse. However, when I rehung my clothes, I discovered that the rod and brackets were sturdy. It seemed the only way this could have happened, would be if an upward force knocked the rod out of position. I pondered over this for some time, deciding to dismiss this abnormality as well.

While shopping, I fell in love with a children's wooden rocking chair and bought it. Visiting me sometime later, my mother asked, "Did you buy that for Rory?" Oddly, I had no plans to give the coveted two-foot-high carved rocker to my grandson. "No, I bought it for myself!" I answered, suddenly aware of how bizarre it was for me to have such an attachment to a piece of furniture that neither fit my apartment decor nor my taste.

In August 2008—two months after my sister's passing—Lexia and Rory came to visit again, this time with my son-in-law Mike. Our conversation once again turned to the bizarre incident after Anita's memorial, and for the umpteenth time we tried to make sense of what we'd heard. A few minutes later, while walking down the hall, I accidently brushed up against the beaded curtain hanging by my bedroom door, and heard the haunting *scchh* sound. Startled, I clanged the beads together hard, three times, hearing *scchh-scchh-scchh*. It was the exact sound we'd heard before the *hee-hee-hee* followed by, "There's ice cream in the fridge." Mystery semi-solved, all I could think was, "Oh, my God! The spirit sharing my apartment has the power to physically shake the curtains."

It was just after 2:30 a.m., November 26th, 2008 when another inexplicable incident triggered my decision to keep a 'strange happenings' journal. Awakened by the sound of Snoopy munching away on a bone, I patiently waited for him to stop, surprised when he switched to vigorously clawing the carpet. Unexpectedly, there were three distinct, loud raps on my *bedroom* door! Alarmed by the knock-knock-knock, barking viciously, Snoopy pivoted to face the door.

Equally terrified, I rocketed up, scooped him into my arms, and dived back into bed. *Cripes!* It was the dead quiet of the night, and I was unarmed, alone and petrified. This was the second strange happening at my bedroom door. *If a spirit could rattle the curtains and knock on my door, could it also open it? What else could it do? What else would it do? And, if it wasn't a spirit but a human at my bedroom, who was it and what was going to happen next?*

Snoopy clutched in my arms, my wide eyes staring at the door, I waited as each hour struck by. At 7:00 a.m. I started my journal. My imagination wasn't playing tricks on me. I would no longer just dismiss the flickering lights or the eerie coldness in the apartment. It was time to record, research and investigate the ghostly happenings in apartment #307.

"Did the fellow living in the apartment before me ever mention anything odd?" I casually asked the caretaker the next day. "Nope!" was his one-word, disinterested reply. So I asked some of the long term residents, "Have you witnessed or heard of any unusual goings-on in the building?" Receiving similar apathetic responses from them, three questions came to mind: Was I the only one living with a spirit? Were the other tenants aware of the spirit but afraid to admit it? Or was the spirit somehow attached to me?

Strange Happenings Journal Entries

December 25, 2008

It is six months since Anita passed away, and sadly, our first Christmas without her. Fussing about the kitchen today, I recalled past holidays and happy occasions, and how much Anita loved celebrations. Mostly, I think, my sister loved celebrating because it presented an opportunity for her to dress up in her unique, high-fashion glamorous style. In her younger days, it was usually something black with a low-cut back, accessorized with slinky over-the-elbow gloves, and a foot-long cigarette holder. She always hugged people and told them she loved them. The holidays will never be the same without her.

Atypical for North Vancouver, there was a foot of snow on the ground today; many family members invited for dinner were unable to make the drive. But my children did. My place decorated with everything Christmas, my grandson delighted in a windup snowman that moved and sang in an adorable kid's voice. It was fun watching Rory's young face lit brighter than the tree, as he marched the toy to-and-fro and sang his little heart out.

After dinner, full and happy and gathered in the living room, the unexpected sudden playing of an electronic Christmas tune caught my attention. *None of us had wound anything, so what was playing the tune?*

"Where's that music coming from?" I asked, as we all glanced around. Just as we determined that the sound was emanating from my immediate left, the music stopped. There weren't any musical ornaments or toys anywhere near my left-hand side, and none in the entire apartment programmed to play that particular tune!

Glancing at me, her expression puzzled, Lexia suggested the exact same explanation I was considering, when she asked, "Auntie Anita?"

Perplexed, we all simply looked at each other. *What or who else could it be?*

In retrospect, it's unfortunate that we didn't know what to do or how to respond. If the music was indeed Anita letting us know she was nearby, it would seem that we missed a wonderful opportunity to acknowledge her presence and to tell her how much we loved and missed her. Though, I'm certain that her coming through to this side was more about comforting us, than herself.

December 31, 2008 – New Year's Eve

This morning, while sharing the elevator with a neighbor, my phone again played a tune. As per usual, when I answered it, there was no one on the other end.

"I think you have a ghost latched to you," the woman offered matter-of-factly.

"I might," I agreed, realizing she was likely recalling our conversation from a few months earlier, when I'd asked if she'd noticed any odd occurrences in the apartment building.

March 10, 2009 – Audio Effects

Today, I have confirmed that the channel on my *old non-programmable*

TV is being changed when I'm not home! Every day before going to work, for Snoopy's sake, I tune the television to Channel 5, which has a lot of children's programs. Recently, there have been many days when I noticed the TV was on a different channel when I returned home, but simply assumed I'd forgotten to change the channel from whatever I was watching the night before. When it happened again a few weeks back, I decided to steadfastly check the television station each morning before leaving for work. I distinctly remember ensuring it was on Channel 5 this morning; yet, when I came home today, it was on a different channel!

April 3, 2009 – 8:00 a.m.

My cell phone rang a tune again, and it was one that I didn't recognize as having ever heard before. Am I having a *The God's Must Be Crazy* moment and simply don't know that my phone can play tunes? I'll check. But even if my cell does indeed have the capability of playing tunes, why is there never anyone on the other end? Why did it start playing tunes just after Anita died? Why does it happen sporadically and infrequently, sometimes months apart?

April 6, 2009

Last night, I was awoken by my cell phone ringing at 2:00 a.m. Since the on-call staff has called me in error before, not wanting to deal with a work issue, I ignored it. It rang again a while later, then once more after that. Having left the phone on the hallway table, I was awakened each time, wondering if it might be someone other than a staff member calling. In the morning, checking the call log, I discovered that my phone wasn't even switched *on* and remained turned *off*! Remembering having turned it off before going to bed, the hairs on my neck, arms and legs jumped to attention. *How had it managed to ring?* According to earthly physics, it couldn't have.

When I returned from work tonight, the television was switched from Channel 5—again!

Friday May 8, 2009 – Visit to a Spiritual Intuitive

I met with Diane Daniels today. She recently moved from New Westminster to a new commercial office space at a mini mall in Coquitlam. Upon complimenting her on the décor, Diane said she had her artistic daughter to thank for the interior design. Her office has wonderful, themed wall hangings and a variety of displays, including numerology posters, astrological charts, crystal balls, and several spiritual decks of cards. I discovered that we have a lot in common, including age and birth sign; she is one week younger than me.

Because I wanted the very last appointment on a Friday, I waited approximately six months for my meeting with Diane. It was so worth it! What was supposed to be a one hour session lasted approximately two and a half hours.

Diane is a highly-advanced intuitive who communicates with the eternal side via a spiritual guide. While we were talking, she frequently tossed her head backward, nodding and listening intently to her spirit guide. I am confident that she is a genuine spiritual intuitive. Many of the occurrences she relayed as proof that she was indeed communicating with my sister in Heaven, were happenings and circumstances that only Anita and I knew about. The messages about our family that Anita conveyed through the guide and then Diane were dead on.

Drawing on information that she gleaned via tarot cards, astrology, numerology, and her spirit guide, Diane presented an entire chart to me before saying, "Your apartment is highly charged. All the configurations around it, the location, the numbers, the history, and your own psychic abilities have made your specific apartment a receptor, or target, for extracurricular activity from the other side."

"What?!" I screeched, before calming enough to ask, "Wouldn't there be other people in the building experiencing similar things?"

"Yes, most likely. But this is not the kind of thing people tend to talk about."

"No, it isn't," I agreed, recalling the reactions of my skeptical neighbors when I'd made the rounds to see if anyone else was experiencing unusual happenings in his or her apartment.

"It's no wonder you don't sleep well, with all that activity going on," Diane continued. "A child spirit is responsible for the antics in your apartment, and is acting up because of your apparent lack of regard that he or she was there before you. You're viewed as an intruder—or an uninvited houseguest."

"*An uninvited houseguest,*" I repeated, trying to get my head around the idea.

"I've worked extensively with the First Nations chief in your area.

You're on reserve land, and a house had to be torn down to make room for your apartment building."

As Diane again studied her collection of telling paraphernalia, my rather conservative mind swung between *This is crazy!* rejection of her paranormal explanation and *Oh, my God. I'm living with a ghost who hates me.*

"Regarding your rocking chair," she continued, oblivious to my doubt and fear, "your *sub*conscious clued into your ghost before your conscious mind. You unwittingly bought that chair for the child spirit."

Momentarily comforted that the poltergeist shenanigans weren't Anita's doing, I breathed a sigh of relief.

"The mysterious Christmas tune that emanated out of thin air, and your cell phone ringing even though it was switched off—those incidents were gratis of Anita."

I could live with my departed sister announcing her presence via sound. After all, we both loved music and often talked on the phone.

"What you thought sounded like someone hacking into your apartment neighbor's door, was actually a breaking and entering taking place nearby where you live. If you'd read or heard the local news the next day, you might have been able to connect the dots. The hacking was real, but it was your psychic sense, *not* your ears that picked up on the noise."

Before I had time to fully digest what she was telling me, frowning, Diane went on to say, "This isn't good. The numbers in your address represent *endings* or *death.*"

"I love my apartment. Are you insinuating I should move?" I asked, doing my utmost to ignore my *doubt* versus *fear* dueling thoughts.

"I'll check." Diane closed her eyes, again tuning into her mystic guide. "No, you don't have to move. I'm told that you can alter the energy by adding the letter 'D' next to the numbers on your unit door. It will take some time, but the energy will change. You will also need to *smudge*, and while doing so, ask for the child's permission to be in the apartment. Remember, you are the one who *invaded* the spirit's space, not the other way around."

"*Smudge* my apartment." Nodding, I tried to recall where I had placed the smudging wand I'd purchased after learning that Native Americans and some religious sects burn a bouquet of sage herbs to clear spirits. My understanding of the practice of smudging was that any *negative* energy in my apartment would attach itself onto the smoke, disappear into space when the smoke cleared, where it would be transformed into *positive* energy.

Somewhat disoriented and still unsure whether to believe *everything*

Diane said, but figuring that there was little to lose, after leaving her office I went shopping for a stick-on letter. Arriving home, I stuck the 'D' on my unit door. Locating and lighting my sage wand, I walked from room to room smudging every corner of my apartment while repeatedly requesting permission to be in *this* space.

Now, there is little I can do, except wait to discover whether the child spirit will leave, or if I'll forever be *an uninvited houseguest.*

December 21 and 22, 2009 – Visual Effects

It's been eight months since I noticed anything out of the ordinary; however, last night I deliberately left the closet hallway light on—this morning, the dining room and main hallway lights were also on!

January 20, 2010

Strangely, a couple of times over the past few days, I experienced the sensation of a subliminal force restricting my movements. Although abrupt and brief, it was unnerving.

July 25, 2010 – 1:31 p.m.

Having enjoyed six months of normalcy, this afternoon, during my tri-weekly aerobic exercises, I was startled by a teddy bear sitting on the table in the middle of the blue-framed mirror in front of me. Placing it back on its usual perch atop the stereo speaker, I wondered if it might have toppled off during the night. *But then, why was it sitting upright as though purposely positioned where I'd notice it? And why, four or five days ago when I got up in the morning, was my daughter Kristen's super-creepy-looking mannequin head on top of the table by the window, instead of covered and stuffed in the cabinet where I wouldn't accidently see the ugly thing?* It would appear that my little child spirit is acting up again—this time, relocating items at whim, seemingly to deliberately taunt me.

November 14, 2010 – 7:00 p.m.

This evening, I heard a loud CRASH in the hallway that sounded like shattering glass on tile. My floor is carpeted! *Hmmm.* Checking everywhere, there was no broken glass to be found. Earlier today, I noticed my kitchen lights flickering.

August 26, 2011 – Solitaire

I've enjoyed nine months of relatively peaceful occupancy of my apartment. The only thing haunting me of late is my regret of being in denial of Anita's impending death. How I didn't—couldn't—respond with anything more than "Me, too," when she said, "I always thought we'd grow old together, Elin."

I think about my beloved sister every day. *Will we one day be reunited on the other side?* I hope so.

October 24, 2011 – Snoopy's passing

Snoopy, forever my #1 love, passed away at approximately 11:45 a.m. Fourteen, the poor little guy's heart simply couldn't beat any longer. This afternoon, my friend and neighbor, Sue, unexpectedly knocked on my door. Unaware that Snoopy had passed, she'd come straight from work and was holding a powder-blue gift bag.

Noticing my red eyes, she seemingly sensed what I was unable to say, and simply pressed the beautifully wrapped present into my hands. Inside, was a sparkling dog pendant on a silver chain.

"It looks exactly like Snoopy, don't you think?" she said, as her kind eyes locked with mine.

"It does," I agreed, hugging her and crying. "I'm going to miss him so very much."

"Snoopy's your special angel now and will always be with you," Sue soothed.

Comforted by her words, while putting on the necklace, it dawned on me that I'm no longer amazed by my own or another's inner knowing. Undoubtedly, Sue was spiritually nudged toward the sparkling Snoopy lookalike charm that I'll likely wear for a very long time. *Angels guide us all in mysterious and wondrous ways.*

October 28, 2011 – 10:17 p.m.

It has been four days since Snoopy died. When I removed my coat this evening, I felt a cold hard object against my chest. Glancing down, my cell phone brushed up and over my Snoopy charm, and then popped out of my sweater. *How did my phone get inside my sweater? And what caused it to suddenly pop out?* Checking and discovering the phone was off, I turned it on and glanced at the call log. No calls. Neither were there any messages, unless I counted the one my beloved Snoopy might have just sent.

January 23, 2012

After four unnerving years of complimentary audio and visual effects, I've enjoyed almost one year of peaceful occupancy of my home. I have no idea if my child spirit roommate has left, or has simply become quiet because Snoopy is now guarding over it with a menacing dog sneer. Not taking any chances, I daily say aloud, "Thank you for letting me *be* in this apartment." Regardless, I've resolved that in the event of any further paranormal activity, I possess the strength to deal with it.

I recently watched Oprah interviewing Tony Robbins. His profound advice about standing up to and conquering your fears still resonates with me, giving me the courage to stand up to *my* uninvited houseguest. Should the child spirit return, in a loud, strong voice, I'll banish it from my home! Unaccustomed to being that assertive, I've been practicing by sometimes hollering, "Go away and leave me alone!"

March 5, 2012

As I scrambled to finish this *Heartmind Wisdom* chapter draft to meet our printing deadline, guess what? This morning, there were hundreds of broken bits and pieces of glass all over my hallway carpet and no cover over the ceiling light! Cleaning up, I discovered the light fixture cap among the broken debris. It would have taken quite an explosion to knock it off. *What explosion?* The recommended sixty-watt bulb is still intact and in the socket! Perhaps, it was simply faulty glass. *But I'm not that sound a sleeper, so why didn't I hear the glass fixture breaking?* Looking back over my journal, I can't help but wonder, "Why did I hear the *sound* of the glass fixture breaking on November 14th, 2010, nearly a year and a half *before* it actually broke?!"

May 7, 2012

Though initially causing me to somewhat doubt my sanity, I'm now grateful for my uninvited houseguest. The spirit(s) in my apartment likely knew that the only way to catch my attention was through abrupt, consistent shenanigans. Shenanigans that gradually led me to embrace what I'd previously feared—an embracement that therapeutically transformed my fear into an exciting spiritual awakening.

"And then the day came when the risk to remain tight in a Bud was greater than the risk it took to bloom." — Anais Nin

Rainbows, Butterflies and other Miracles

Joyce M. Ross

When I was nine, my financially struggling parents moved all six of us, two adults and four children, into a two-bedroom shack smack in the middle of the boondocks. Too poor to afford twenty-four hours of heat, our barely-functional oil furnace was nightly turned off. Getting dressed for school in the morning took place under the covers. During one heavy rainfall season our dugout dirt-floor basement flooded six feet deep. It was the only occasion presented where I could boast that our family had an indoor pool.

When a spine injury landed my father on his back for months and unable to work, Mom took a job for fifty-five cents an hour, and I became Super Daughter while Super Mom worked all day long and then went to night school. In those days, we all did what we could to help our family survive financially. My contribution included washing our family's clothes in the bathtub, grape-stomping style and wringing them out by hand until my purple-red appendages bled.

Born with a Cinderella complex, with the aim of reducing Mom's burden, after feigning some minor illness to get out of going to school, I'd spend the day cleaning our cluttered and tiny home. On one particularly brain-dead day, in the midst of ironing a thousand shirts and blouses, I decided to switch tasks. Knowing I'd have to later finish the wrinkled heap in the clothesbasket, I had a proverbial stroke of genius. Why bother with folding and unfolding the rickety old ironing board? Why not lift it onto the faded, yellow arborite kitchen table, still upright and ready to continue with ironing? It seemed to be a great plan and would escape the possibility of the board's clumsy metal folding mechanism again pinching, indenting, purpling, and rendering my poor index finger useless. Remarkably proud of my bright move, I yanked on the table leg so I could wash up the crumbs and gobs speckling our floor, sending the ironing board crashing through the kitchen window.

With a sudden appreciation for Robbie Burn's poem (written for mice) about men's schemes going awry, I telephoned Mom at her workplace with the not-so-great news. After her brief, "Uh-huh, so why did you really call?" interrogation, she accepted having given birth to the idiot-of-the-century and called our new neighbors, Glen and Edith Eby. Glen replaced our window that afternoon. Following that incident we were all lifelong friends, until Mr. and Mrs. Eby took turns dying. They were good people, so maybe the ironing-board-on-the-table trick was a good thing.

As far back as the sixties, worldwide, mothers constantly warned their children about STRANGERS. Not that any of us totally understood what dangers lurked in the minds and actions of strangers, or even who or what they were. Connie, my younger sibling by six years, obviously didn't, and when we moved into our boondock shack, she quickly made friends with an elderly gentleman who lived in a bullet-shaped silver trailer next door to our backyard. When Mom discovered Connie and the silver-bullet-trailer-man talking, she descended upon my poor little sister like a mother bird swooping up a fledgling prematurely knocked from the nest. "Didn't I tell you not to talk to strangers?" she implored, marching my young sibling back to our shack. "He's not a stranger," Connie reasoned. "How do you know that?" my rather stressed mother demanded to know. "Because I asked him if he was a stranger, and he said he wasn't."

All four of us kids were clever, ingenious actually. One evening while our parents were out, we entertained ourselves with our customary après dinner potato fight. As was usually the case, some coward (could have been me) globed mashed potatoes into another sibling's hair, then dashed for the bathroom, locked the door and refused to come out. Never ones to easily give up, the rest of us banged on the door, goading, "You gotta come out some time, you cowardly moron." One of us, (could have been me) with shoulders braced against the bathroom door and a foot on the adjacent hallway wall, after grunting several times, shot his/her foot clear through the Gyproc. *Yikes*, or some other utterance, accompanied our mirrored astonished concern. But as stated earlier, we were a pretty ingenious bunch, so together we fashioned a patch made of watercolors on paper, and adhered it to the wall via glue made from mixing water and flour. Perhaps our parents were upset when they returned to find the dishes still in the sink and a foot-sized hole in the wall. We'll never know for certain, though, because they both took one look at our patch-job and burst into laughter.

We were animal lovers, my three ingenious siblings and I. But money was tight and the house small, so a dog was out of the question. Fortunately, a neighbor-chauffeured trip to Mattick's Farm (and petting zoo) quickly changed our no-pets family status. "Do you think Mom and Dad will let us have a Guinea Pig?" my slightly-older-than-me sister Alaura asked. (You might better appreciate this story if I share with you that my then twelve-year-old sister, is now a lawyer.) "Why don't you call and see?" our neighbor and outing driver suggested. "Good idea," my sister responded. Of course, under the scrutiny of a good friend and neighbor, my parents caved and gave permission for us to adopt *one* Guinea Pig. "Are you sure it's pregnant?" Alaura asked, holding up and inspecting a plump, squiggling squealer. "Oh, I'm sure!" our neighbor exclaimed, a grin splitting his face so wide it must have hurt.

Young, and rightfully never satisfied, our brood decided we needed more pets. Obligingly, the area rabbits provided numerous offspring that would surely fill the bottom half of the pen we'd successfully bid on at a local auction and housed our six-count—food-color dyed into various muted shades for easy identification—Guinea Pig family. "Dad, if we can catch the baby rabbits, can we keep them?" my gangly, extraordinarily tall younger brother Terry asked. "Sure!" was our father's naïve reply. Apparently, he doubted our ability to actually capture the rabbits.

Trusting the word of our father and somewhat godlike parent, we set about catching the baby rabbits. Thanks to another ingenious plan that involved a cardboard box, string and countless carrots, one-by-one we captured and caged four little bunnies. With only the mother rabbit still running wild, and her babes desperately missing her, we employed Dad's soon-to-be-torn-to-shreds fishing net, and after a half-dozen, or so, failed attempts Mother Rabbit was frantically trying to jump her way out of our bathtub. The very next day, Dad donated the works of them, Mom Rabbit and all four of her babies, to Mattick's farm. Not that his fishing net was totally useless; it could still hold really big fish. And isn't it every fisherman's dream to catch the big one?

For a sixties' mom, our mother was fairly liberal, seldom chastising us for speaking our minds, or disagreeing with her. Looking back, I've decided she's a better woman than I'll ever be, for there were many times when our whiny tantrums, in front of her women friends, were darn right rude. The upside is that we are now adults who liberally express our ideas and opinions. The downside is that we sometimes don't know when to shut up.

One day—Dad having survived two spine operations and thankfully back at work, and Mom still employed for fifty-five cents an hour at the weekly newspaper housed in the onetime duplex at the top of the hill above the boondocks where we still lived—I decided to skip school. Backtracking home and spotting Mom's purse on her bed, I became a wee bit concerned. Surmising that she'd forgotten it, I flipped on the television in preparation for a lazy day. Within minutes, I heard Mom cough. (Thank God she smoked, or I'd have had absolutely no warning that she would momentarily swing open the kitchen door and catch me goofing off.) Forever ingenious, I ran to her bedroom and dove under the bed.

If you grew up poor, you already know that far-from-rich people have small bedrooms. Mom and Dad's bedroom wasn't any bigger than their non-existent closet should have been. The space between the bed and walls was under a foot, which was about the depth of dust under their bed. Lo and behold, and strike me dead if you don't believe me, Mom not only came home unexpectedly, she decided to clean out her purse—on top of her bed! Buried in dust-fluff, I started choking. At first she ignored my wheezes and wee coughs, thinking that our cat, Dumb-Dumb, was under her bed and coughing up a fur ball. All seemed well, except for the fact that I was trapped and nearly choking to death, until the phone rang.

"Are you saying that she never arrived at your place?" my mother asked, panic hedging her displeased tone. "She left here with her brother this morning."

"Darn that stupid Crystal!" I thought, totally dismissing my error in not notifying my close friend that I was playing hooky and wouldn't need a ride to school.

"Thanks for letting me know," my mother said, hanging up the phone and starting to dial another number.

Figuring she was calling my school, between coughs and snorts, I bellowed, "Mom, I'm in here!"

"Here, where?" she asked, replacing the phone receiver on its base.

"Under your bed," I confessed, readying for the inevitable and rightfully deserved chastisement, while fruitlessly trying to dislodge my five-foot-nine plump body from where I was trapped beneath her nine-inch-high bedframe. Mom laughed so hard, I never did get punished for skipping school that day.

Nor did I get punished for removing the mouthpiece from the telephone, so that she couldn't answer the phone on my many more skipped school days. I didn't get punished, because she never knew *why* the phone was often out of order between eight and four, and miraculously working again by five. She does now, and laughs about the numerous times she complained to various B.C. telephone company employees, who likely thought she was wacko.

Mom also laughs about the time I was arrested for drinking underage when my sister Alaura, Mom and I were visiting with cousins in Ontario. Having to appear in court, my fifteen-year-old self managed to finagle her way out of a probation charge by telling the judge that my mother wasn't in court, because if I was "old enough to get myself into trouble, I should be old enough to get myself out of trouble." But then, my people skills can be directly traced back to the advice I received from her when I came home from the corner grocery store in tears.

I'll never forget the day, or the lesson. Mrs. Somebody, who was the post office lady, but whose actual name I no longer remember, was darn right mean to me, for some reason I can no longer remember. However, whatever she said sent me scurrying home to the sanctity of my mother's arms. When I arrived, puffing and red-faced from the two-block dash, I recounted the incident to my mother, expecting to be coddled and soothed with *Oh, my poor baby* exclamations, followed by a comforting hug. Confusingly, Mom was non-perplexed by my horror story as she retrieved two apple pies from our outdated gas oven. Wide-eyed and bewildered, I gaped in disbelief as she said, "You never know what another person is going through. Take Mrs. So-and-So this apple pie and she'll be your friend forever."

Taking a pie to the post-office lady, who likely commuted to work via her witch's broom, wasn't an inviting idea at all—it was terrifying. But after much consoling and cajoling on my mother's part, and a dozen or more muffled obscenities on my part, I did as Mom advised.

The post office lady demonstrated her gratitude that day and for many months, perhaps years, later. Just as Mom had promised, we were forever friends.

Growing up poor as dirt—which I've already told you was literally the substance flooring our basement—came with unexpected, and sometimes missed, generosity from neighbors and near strangers. An old soul from birth, I enjoyed the company of our adult neighbors more than that of kids my own age. Quite often I'd visit Mr. and Mrs. Kind-Hearted-Souls who lived in the teal trailer, next to the silver-bullet that bordered our backyard. Both members of this kindly couple were likely in their fifties, although at the time, I assumed they were near centenarians. They were delightful people and always gleefully rejoiced in stories about my family, including recounts of my father's philosophy that earth is merely stopgap housing for souls being studied by aliens. Surprisingly, about the time of a good friend's graduation and prom, Mrs. Kind-Hearted-Souls magically produced a sheepskin coat and a turquoise mini-dress. Amazingly, the coat precisely fit my then six-feet-tall, thirteen-year-old brother Terry. Equally amazing, the turquoise lace-over-satin dress precisely fit me. We were both ecstatic, and after hurriedly thanking them for their generous gifts, which were passed off as having been hanging in the back of their closet, we raced home to tell our parents about our cache. Terry's account was more amusing. He'd misheard their description of his coat and proudly announced that he'd been given a *cheap*skin coat.

It wasn't until a few years ago that I realized Mr. and Mrs. Kind-Hearted-Souls had provided our gifts out of the goodness of their hearts. There is no other reason for why two such thoughtful and wonderful gifts were hanging in the back of two rather conservative people's closet. I wish I could remember their names and wonder if they're still alive. Perhaps, they're spiritually still nearby and know how grateful I remain so many years later.

Brother Terry had a knack for using the wrong word. Returning from a visit with his best friend's hospitalized mother, in answer to our Mom's question, "How's your friend's mother?" he replied, "Oh, she's fine because they're keeping her heavily seduced."

My special knack was the proverbial foot-in-your-own-mouth trick. Self-conscious about my large feet, when needing shoes I'd scout local stores for styles I liked, and then send Terry to check for availability in my size. On one such shopping expedition, he returned with a pair of white, size-ten sneakers—one size larger than I generally required. "What do you think I have, elephant feet?" I screeched, not too pleased as I tried them on, and Terry grimaced. Well, they fit. You can guess what nickname followed me throughout high school.

As is often the case with siblings sparring for top pecking position, we frequently teased one another that he or she was adopted. Of course, doing so always elicited the desired response of a quick visit by that day's lowly rooster to Mom or Dad for reassurance that he or she was indeed a blood relative. Once teenagers, absolutely convinced that the two of us were superior to our family, my sister Alaura one day remarked, "Remember when we used to tease one another about being adopted? Don't you now wish that we actually were?"

In her third year of university, Alaura was also the brain who posed the question, "If ninety percent of society is dysfunctional, don't you think we should lower the norm?"

One day, I longingly stated, "I wish I could sing awfully bad." She retorted, "You do!"

When I was dating a Jewish man and learned that men of this faith don't often marry gentiles, I shared my concern with Alaura, telling her that I was going to confront my then boyfriend about this disturbing news. "Well, when you do," Alaura said with a snicker, "make certain you don't say genitals instead of gentiles." "Ha-ha," I replied, holding back credit for what was truly a quick play on words. You guessed it! There I was lying in my beloved's arms as I softly asked, "Is it true that Jewish men don't marry genitals?" My then boyfriend was very kind, becoming quiet for a moment before saying, "I'm sure you meant to say gentiles?"

As with many families, the years tumbled by, and though still close, as in you-make-me-so-mad-I-could-clobber-you, my intelligent, emotional and semi-judgmental siblings remain contact intact. What always harmoniously synchronizes our scatter-the-ice-is-breaking-up relationship, is a health crisis; especially, one threatening the life of one of our parents. Just such an incident happened recently, when our eight-five-year-old dad received news of a shadow on his right lung.

Being a little closer to Source than we'd like, all four of us kids worry about our aging father. First to rock our reality was his prostate cancer. Word-to-the-wise, should any one dear to you be diagnosed with this largely men's disease (I know, I know, just being cute.), and should you decide to research treatments on the Internet, you will very quickly become the shocked recipient of numerous penis-extension ads, that will be sandwiched between many rather explicit invitations from scantily dressed women willing to help you overcome your appendage shortfall. Apparently, the fact that my email address includes my first blatantly female name 'Joy' doesn't tweak these worldly women into realizing that I likely don't have an extension problem requiring their assistance.

Following his rather humiliating and slightly painful prostate biopsy, Dad and I were sitting in my van as he recounted the ordeal. "It sounds horrible," I offered. "I'm sorry you had to endure that." Of course, Dad being Dad, within minutes he was again his good-natured self, and switched to stories about how the nurses had fussed about, almost embarrassing him with their attentive care. Waiting for a punch line—and with Dad there is always a quick quip or punch line—I gazed out the windshield in time to glimpse a bright rainbow. Catching my smile, Dad's gaze followed mine. "When your Uncle Alex died, I saw a rainbow just like that one," he said, calm entering his soft-blue eyes. "Did you?" I commented, nodding that I understood, before adding, "Dad, I think that rainbow is meant for us, and is the universe's way of letting us know that you're going to be okay."

Dad's prostate cancer was treated with a series of radiation treatments, and four years later, he remains healthy prostate-wise. However, foretelling rainbows continue to coincide with bulletins about our father's health. When Connie, my younger sister and live-in caregiver to our father, called to say the doc had detected a spot on Dad's lung, I spent a sleepless night worrying. Serendipitously, the next day while driving, beautiful bowed ribbons of color caught my eye, and I knew he'd be okay.

It was a glorious, cloudless day and I was watering the garden when Connie called with the scheduled date for the surgical unclogging of Dad's left-side carotid artery. Aware of the risks in clearing plaque from a large vein that supplies blood to the head, I thought, "Oh, no, how can I see a rainbow today, tomorrow, or any day this week? It's summertime and not a raindrop in the forecast." Within seconds of my rainbow wish, an unusually vivid stream of pastels arched across the spray from the garden hose. Once again, I knew that the angels were nearby.

The clearing of Dad's carotid artery didn't happen scot-free of worry. The night before his operation, while asking for the angels to watch over him, I received a message: Following his operation, his blood pressure will drop significantly and will be difficult to regulate. But he will be fine.

I shared my angel-knowing with my *Kindness is Key* mission partner and longtime close friend, Patricia, before heading to Victoria, B.C. to be there for Dad's operation. It was a weird couple of days, sitting with my father, noting how healthy and vibrant he was, and knowing that a spot of cholesterol they were clearing from his artery could very well induce a stroke, maybe killing Dad. Our family lived fervently that day, sucking up our time together like teens on their first unchaperoned camping trip. We watched music-videos of Johnny Cash, Hank Williams, Connie Francis, and a dozen other country legends on YouTube. We played card games and recounted comical family history. And we worried and prayed.

An hour past the time the admitting nurse had promised to call Connie and me with news as to how Dad's operation had progressed, my sister and I went to what was supposed to be his room. *No Dad.* Enquiring about him at the nursing station, we learned that he was still in intensive care because they couldn't stabilize his blood pressure. "He just needs to see us," I said, recalling the angels' message, and suddenly somehow knowing that as soon as Dad set eyes on his middle and youngest girls, he'd be fine.

"Uh-huh," the desk nurse said, raising a brow in a way that let me know she'd flunked the nursing lesson: When a patient's crazy family makes crazy demands, remember, they are worried sick. Don't insult them or give any hint of your true feelings; just say something innocuous, so they'll leave you alone to get on with your work. "Visitors aren't permitted in Intensive Care," she said stiffly. "You'll have to wait."

I wasn't about to explain my message from the angels, because I was standing next to a sibling who occasionally doubted my sanity, which was a little daunting since she's a counselor trained to recognize psychotics.

"If we give you our cellphone number, will you call us the second you hear anything?" Connie asked, blubbering along with me.

"I will," a kind young male nurse interceded, smiling and handing us a pen and paper.

Grumbling, feeling hopeless and still crying, Connie and I went for lunch. Halfway through something neither of us could taste (thank goodness) we noticed that my sister's purse was missing. We backtracked to the restaurant; her purse wasn't there. We went to the security office; it was closed. Not knowing where else to look, we returned to Dad's room, thinking perhaps she'd left her handbag there.

"Oh, good, you're back," the male nurse exclaimed, smiling like he'd aced his *patient's family relations* course. "I was just going to call you. I cleared it with intensive care for you to visit with your dad for a few minutes."

"Really, that's great! You didn't happen to see my sister's purse?" I asked, as we hurried to Dad's side. Assured by the female nurse escorting us to intensive care that she would contact security regarding Connie's missing handbag, we approached our father's bedside, both of us scared, and me praying that my guardian angels were right.

Gently touching his arm, I said, "Hi, Dad. It's time to wake up."

Dad immediately opened his eyes, smiling as relief washed over his handsome face like midday summer sunshine.

Taking his extended hand, I quickly glanced at the blood pressure monitor, noting the machine's steady rise. Our father was coming back!

"Maybe, it's because he's talking," one nurse said to the other.

"Maybe," the other agreed, adjusting Dad's intravenous fluids before writing something on his chart.

We were allowed to visit for about five more minutes while they ensured our father was stabilizing. Then, informed that Dad would remain in intensive care for a few more hours and wouldn't be back in his room until at least ten that evening, my sister Connie and I headed home.

The next morning during a shared elevator ride, I thanked the nice male nurse for his kind actions, and told him about how our visit did indeed return Dad's blood pressure to normal. "It's not always about the medicine, is it?" said the nurse, nodding and likely thanking the angels he'd sent to my father's side.

"No, it isn't!" I agreed, smiling my gratitude to him and the angels. "When you pray from a place of absolute love and then listen with your heart open to the sky, everything becomes possible."

Dad's recovery went remarkably well, which I think was largely due to his rather bizarre sense of humor. Well, that...the angels, a tremendously skilled surgeon, and the constant fussing of four relieved middle-aged bratty kids. I think he was actually disappointed when his six-inch scar began to fade, weakening his joke about how the doc had tried to decapitate him.

About a week after his operation, Dad complained of being itchy and hating stubble, so I volunteered to shave his face and neck. Obviously unaware of the many scars running the length of my hairy legs, he eagerly accepted my offer. After hunting through no less than six dull razors, I located a new one in the back of his suitcase. Bowl of hot water on the bedside table, I removed the warm towel that had been softening his whiskers, and applied shaving cream. *God, don't let me send him back to the hospital for more stitches* I prayed, while practicing on his operation-free side. Slowly, my confidence increased and I shaved his face within an inch of his fresh scar.

What struck me most while shaving my father, was life's circle of care. I'm not suggesting that there is any correlation between Dad's face and my butt, but I pondered about the hundreds of diapers Mom had changed for all of her children. I thought about the numerous cuts she'd kissed, and hundreds of hugs she'd administered to her frightened, hurt or sad offspring. Affectionately, I recalled that as she turned off our bedroom light at night, Mom always cheerfully said, "Sleep tight; don't let the bedbugs bite." I also thought about Dad. Though his work as a boat builder at the HMC Dockyard just outside of Victoria must have been demanding, he never complained. He remains the most generous person I'll likely ever know. As the saying goes, Dad would literally give his shirt to anyone in need. It's through him that I learned, when all else fails, make a joke. If no one laughs with you, make a dumber joke. If they still don't laugh, the buggers have absolutely no sense of humor, and you might as well let them be miserable. He also advised: *Speak well of your enemies, you made them. When you seek revenge, dig two graves.* And our collective sibling favorite, *Water on wood, no good!*

Last summer, I spent a couple of weeks clearing two years' worth of rather militant blackberry bushes from Dad's property. Over morning coffee and afternoon lunch, we'd sit on his balcony looking out at the lake and gabbing about whatever. Of course, our conversations often included my spiritual beliefs about animal signs, rainbows and angel whispers. These days, Dad's quite spiritual too. One of his favorite transcendent stories is about when his mother's appendix burst, and he and his brother transported her to the hospital via sled. It took hours for them to mush across a frozen lake and then miles of head-high snow banks, before Grandma Ross was pronounced dead on arrival. The Ross's don't give up easily, and she was revived. When well enough to talk, she told all of her children, "Never worry about dying. It's so incredibly peaceful and beautiful that I didn't want to come back." Grandma saw her hundredth birthday before the angels escorted her return to the peace and beauty she so loved.

One day while chatting together on his balcony, which was abundant with flowers that attracted dozens of butterflies, I shared with Dad that some people believe butterflies are really angels letting you know they are nearby. Thereafter, whenever I was in the kitchen preparing a meal, each time he spotted one flittering by, Dad hollered, "Joy, your angels are back." It was such a loving gesture, I smiled each time he announced the angel-butterflies. Of course, I never did tell him that the way he dragged out the last word reminded me of *The Shining* when Jack Nicholson hollered "I'm baaack" as he axed through his victim's door.

The shadow on Dad's lung was treated with radiation, and he's still fervently alive, joking and doling out advice. Mom's in great health and remains full of laughter and wisdom. My three siblings—Alaura, Terry and Connie—wonderfully echo what our parents taught and demonstrated: *No matter what, love will always get you through.* When you listen to your guardian angels, stay grateful for your earth angels, and reach outward, inward and upward with love—rainbows and butterflies appear everywhere.

Healing from Loss

Alchemy of Grief

Shirley J. Bueckert

*The Alchemist outwardly is meant to mutate simple base
matter into Gold while inwardly unlocking the secret of Inner
Transformation and Creativity.* —Rachael Kohn

I cringe when I hear the saying *God only gives you what you can handle.*
Well, 'She' must have assumed I was Mother Teresa, Wonder Woman
and a female Dalai Lama all harmonized into one! In just over three
years I lost six beloved souls. A short year later, our family dog died.
A solid axis of love held my core firm—but only my core, as my world
lurched, teeter-tottered and reversed one hundred and eighty degrees.

I led a charmed life surrounded by affection. Adopted, my parents
continually stated and demonstrated that I was their chosen special gift. From
the moment we met, my husband Lou and I knew that destiny had brought
us together. I was enticed by his bull-like strength and teddy bear gentleness.
He was bewitched by my vivacious attitude and raucous laugh.

Lou stood six-feet-three-inches measured to my five-foot-nothing;
two hundred and fifty pounds weighted to my one hundred and ten.
Built like a linebacker, his arms hung away from his sides when he
walked. His legs were as thick as tree trunks, a physical tribute to his
grounded and stable manner.

We resided in Metro Vancouver, British Columbia, Canada, part
of the largest temperate rainforest on the planet. A daughter and son
completed our wedded bliss. Like a symmetrical hanging mobile, our
family swayed in life's wind, but always quickly came back to center.
Connected through strong yet flexible braiding, heart-crafted by
inherited traditions, each piece grew stronger by lovingly adjusting to
create balance for the whole.

A devoted daughter, wondrous wife, magnificent mother, perceptive
pet owner, enthusiastic employee, fabulous friend, and joyful jester—my
place on the earth was safe and sound—until EVERYTHING changed.

Disclaimer: I was not alone. The paths' of my son and daughter, now adults, are intertwined with mine on this journey. They are the purpose for my being. They have provided more lessons and guidance than can ever be put into words. The silver lining of having gone through this tragedy together is that their fortitude and honesty have added numerous layers of steel to the luminescent, fairy-winged umbilical cord that I share with each of them. It is not my place to assume that I know their stories. To assist in my healing, I can only lay bare my own inner emotions. This is *my* story.

After being hospitalized for a month and undergoing a myriad of painful tests, Lou was diagnosed with Non-Hodgkin's Lymphoma. It was the month of our daughter's grade-twelve graduation. On a day pass from the hospital, too weak to participate, peering through a friend's car window, my husband watched his daughter mature from princess to goddess as she entered the hotel for the grand march. Thus began my heart-stopping, mind-draining, running-on-sheer-air descent through multiple levels of loss.

Weeks of normalcy would pass, and then emergency room visits and hospital stays would overtake our lives. Planning was forbidden. At times, when Lou was enjoying a good day, we'd arrange a relaxing outing such as a much-deserved dinner with friends. We were careful to take our time getting ready so as not to exhaust his energy; but often, just as we were about to leave, the cancer demons would begin their havoc dance in his cells. Within seconds, 'feeling fine' twisted into violent vomiting. I hated having no control in these situations. Friends became distant. It took years for me to realize that their lives remained constant, while ours jerked and sputtered in the thrust of change.

Rufus, our twelve-year-old Labrador-terrier cross, was pleased to have Lou home twenty-four-seven. Well, at least in between hospital stays. He relished the additional time in bed and extra couch duty. Seemingly aware of his master's every need, Rufus sensed if Lou was readjusting because he was in pain or simply rolling over for comfort. It was a process that happened many, many times, with Rufus always knowing whether he should leap away or simply claim a new position. As they breathed together in synchronicity, each drawing a special comfort from the other's energy, I often wondered where the man/dog connection began and ended. Ironically, in my estimation, my husband began to age in dog years, seven-to-one, as the cancer progressed.

To add to my guilt and shame—I needed Mom and Dad, but they needed me! My parents in Saskatchewan, both eighty-six, were beginning to show their ages. As the primary caregiver through my mother's ill health, Dad's strong will was waning. My parents had created magical, invisible ancestral bonds that held us in close embrace. They had provided comfort, security, laughter, and wisdom with an innate knowledge of what I needed and when. Knowing, in linear earth time how old they were, it still shocked my overwhelmed system to finally realize it in a physical sense.

Dad called for my help. Mom had fallen, been hospitalized, and my father was told that he could not take her home. She needed to be placed in a long-term care facility with round-the-clock aid. Lou's health and spirit were also deteriorating. Due to weakening kidneys, he was retaining water. His legs began seeping, and then his skin literally split open. Chances of his wounds becoming infected were high, and his mobility was greatly reduced. Fearing my son would come home from school and find his father dead, I did the only thing I could think of—I called an ambulance and told them my husband was having problems breathing. Lou was hospitalized. I left for Saskatchewan.

Waiting for my next flight in Alberta, the midpoint of my continuous trips back and forth, was a lesson in patience. Instead of enjoying the time to sit, I worried about who needed me more. Although I'd passed through this airport countless times, now continually stressed and often befuddled, I found myself becoming confused as to which way I was headed. *Am I going to my childhood home or my marital home?* Whoever yelled the loudest, east or west, I would head in that direction. Thoughts of staying in Alberta whirled through my mind. *Could I save myself by abandoning them all?*

While Mom remained in the hospital awaiting placement at a Level 3 long-term care facility, I returned to British Columbia. My father faithfully visited Mom daily, assisting with meals and singing or reading to her. The only time he was not at her side was when he went home to shower and sleep.

Three months later, a bed became available. Mom now had a complete routine with specialized, caring staff and many activities. As difficult as it had been for Dad to go back and forth between his home and the hospital, he knew it was only a temporary situation. Once Mom was in the Level 3 care facility, I believe Dad realized that this was permanent. Although he could visit Mom daily, he came back to an empty home each night and woke up alone each morning. A proud and self-sufficient man who'd always taken loving care of his wife and others, he never questioned his purpose or felt lost—until now. It depleted him.

Dad's doctor summoned me to assist my father with establishing his own 'new' routine. This did not work out! He, too, needed to be in a long-term care facility; however, he only needed Level 1 care. My parents would not be together! *Are you kidding me? Dad would crawl from one end of town to the other, if that's what it took to be with the love of his life for over fifty years!* I surmised the levels had to do with incontinence. Stressed out, I offered to urinate on the floor, daily or hourly, if that would keep my parents together.

Saskatchewan was in the middle of a provincial election. I called the sitting Member of the Legislative Assembly, who unbeknownst to me, knew my father well. They had been teaching colleagues for many years. The wheels began to turn. The care facility admittance coordinator quickly devised a plan. They would admit my father at the same facility as Mom, under respite for thirty days. I was to sell their home so he would have nowhere to go and would have to stay another thirty days, and so on. What was originally planned as a four-day trip turned into a horrendous two week ordeal.

Tim, my sole sibling, had passed away nine years prior. Alone, I packed up fifty years of treasures and memories, placed my childhood home for sale, signed do not resuscitate orders, pre-planned funeral documents, and dealt with banking, legal and government forms—on of all days, my birthday. 'Devoted daughter' tasks completed for now, I put on my 'wondrous wife' hat and flew west to my ailing husband.

Dad passed away nineteen days later. Regrettably, I recalled our last visit. Handing me his house and car keys, he had a look of utter disbelief that I, his precious daughter, had stolen his last bastions of manhood. The care facility staff, mainly unaware of my circumstances, detailed the toll caregiving takes on one's health, explaining that often it is the caregiver that tires out first.

Envisioning a late fall return to the prairies, barren, cold and empty, I shivered. Overwhelmed by hopelessness, in my mind's eye

I saw a roof, heavily laden with snow, cave in as the main beam gave way. Dad was gone.

Leaving my teenage son to care for his father, I took my daughter for moral support and flew east to bury my father. Even though it wasn't his fault, I was infuriated that my husband was not able to support me through this dire time.

When one member falls ill, the rest of the family stumbles too. My nineteen-year-old daughter was attending university. She tried crystal meth *once* and was hooked. One more lance stabbed into my heart. The 'magnificent mother'—sleep-deprived, gasping for breath, functioning on frayed nerves, and burnt-out—had missed all the warning signs.

To afford the drugs she couldn't live without, and likely in a bid for help I was too raw to understand, she started blatantly stealing from us. As well, she became increasingly belligerent. After one hair-raising violent episode, I finally realized the extent of her addiction. As my heart broke into a zillion pieces, the police removed my child from our home. The daughter that had previously known my thoughts and finished my sentences was out on the streets—penniless! For the next few months, every ring of the phone sent my organs and muscles into spasm. *Would this be the call that announced my daughter's death?* I was unglued.

As the business manager at an auto dealership, I worked six days a week, often ten hours a day. 'Enthusiastic employee' be damned—I operated by mechanical repetition. I was scared to leave the house in case something happened, and scared to return home in case something had. Exhausted physically and spiritually, to survive the drive to and from work, the music blared. I didn't want to hear myself think. One day, an ambulance almost rear-ended my car. I had not seen the flashing lights or heard the siren. I knew nothing of the term 'self-care.' There was no time left in a day to worry about me. I existed solely through the primitive response of fight or flight—scream or detach.

Forced to mature quickly, my son's teenage years were hijacked. At sixteen, instead of his father teaching him to drive, he was pulling his father off the toilet. Instead of learning to fish, he was cooking our daily dinners. Instead of receiving lectures on the dangers of drugs, he was dispensing his dad's medical marijuana. He was also the one attempting to maintain some resemblance of order in our household. Everything was mixed up!

Part of Lou's daily medical regime included taking an average of thirty pills. There were pills for pain that would upset his stomach... so there was a pill for that...but it would bother his kidneys...so there was a pill to stop that...but it would upset his bowels...so there was a pill to soften that—and round and round it went. There were times he couldn't eat and times he wouldn't eat. There were days he wouldn't know us, and days he was so medicated he didn't care if he knew us. When he reduced his prescription meds, and began smoking or vaporizing marijuana, and/or ingesting *cannabutter* cookies or brownies—he was himself again. His eyes cleared and we could see the 'real' Lou behind their hazel hue. His pain would decrease, his appetite would increase, and most of his body would function normally, albeit slowly. Lou battled his disease with dignity and patience, seldom getting irritable or demanding. He calmly adapted to continual life-altering shifts and new realities. Not me. I was always the one freaking out.

Every night that our daughter was gone, in my heartmind, I lit a candle in the window, trusting the light would illuminate her way through the shadows. When my daughter returned, I was thrilled to have her home where she belonged; yet, I wondered, "Could I keep the family fire burning brightly?" Fear, my constant companion, threatened that we might all just smolder away in a puff of black smoke. At the time, our home was more apt to breed illness than offer a place of solace where our daughter could heal. However, with dogged determination, in a few months, she was working and had returned to university. Gratefully, 'learning' became her drug of choice.

Other than very close friends, no one had a clue about the craziness that illness and death brought into our home. Perhaps not wanting to burden others, or make them feel uncomfortable, we sheltered ourselves from the world. No one seemed to know what to say or how to act around us anymore, and vice versa. Everyday conversation paled against what we daily faced.

My lifeline was Pam, a kindred girlfriend for over thirty years. Although she lived almost halfway across Canada, in my hometown, she provided the safety and comfort of familiarity. She knew my parents, had attended our wedding, and through visits had watched our children grow. As per luck or fate (there are no coincidences) her husband Ken was also ill. Years earlier, he was diagnosed with a terminal genetic lung disorder. Pam was convinced that if she 'ran hard enough and fast enough' she could outrun the truth. For years, it worked. Ken outlived all odds. However, his quality of life, and subsequently hers, diminished.

A nineteen hour car ride apart, as if sitting face-to-face on a comfy couch, on Friday nights we would lock ourselves in our respective rooms and talk sister-to-sister, caregiver-to-caregiver and soul-to-soul. No one, husband or child, dared enter our sanctuary or call out for us. Our conversations ran the gamut from the surreal to the sublime. We solved the world's problems, yet could not quite get a handle on our own.

We talked about driving off bridges, meeting in Heaven, and having volunteers feed us grapes as we lounged on puffy cushions of air. We talked about having the rest of the world drive off bridges and leaving us with the peace and quiet for which we longed. I told Pam things that I hadn't even told myself. Left other things unsaid; I knew she knew. For these few hours each week, time and distance were neutralized. Across the miles we had our own little party. To this day, we have admitted to no one else, the amount of empty beer cans we later recycled. Sharing our vulnerabilities kept us sane. We now laugh and ask each other, *"Did it work?"*

My yearning for an energy-renewing sunny summer didn't make it happen; instead, Ken died. Stunned, anxious and dreading another trip east, I packed a variety of medications long ago prescribed by my doctor. I took the high blood pressure pill daily, but the anti-depressants and sleeping aids were reserved for emergencies. Feeling Pam's pain as my own, and knowing I had to somehow deliver Ken's eulogy, this qualified as an emergency! Jittery the morning of the funeral, I popped a pill. Trying to cope with our shared heavy sadness made breathing nearly impossible, so I downed another. Having volunteered to meet Ken's body, and feeling no effect from the meds, driving to the church, I gulped one more. My husband hadn't been diagnosed as terminally ill, but this sorrowful day provided an ominous glimpse into my family's future. I gobbled another.

The next year, my precious mother with the sparkling blue Irish-eyes departed to join my father. In the last few years of her life, Mom was afflicted with dementia. Visiting with her, she'd often fade in and out, sometimes recognizing me, other times confusing me with her sister. She had been an inquisitive lifelong learner and teacher. Though her *mind* and *body* had unfairly betrayed her, our soul-to-soul connection was a comfort. Losing Mom was heart-wrenching, however, she departed as she had lived—graciously and gently, which made it easier for me to prepare intellectually and emotionally. I think she deliberately held on to ease me into the idea of life without her. She died while Lou was cresting his rollercoaster ride of health highs and lows. Thankfully, he was able to accompany me to Mom's funeral.

Lou's cancer was in remission, but we were told to prepare for the eventuality that he would require kidney dialysis. We carried on with our family's 'normal' routine. When Lou began experiencing another bout of flu-like symptoms, accustomed to his health downswings, we weren't overly concerned. He had a doctor's appointment in a few days, and the usual course of action involved a change of medication or a brief hospital stay until he was stabilized.

Lou then weighed one hundred and eighty pounds, but at six-foot-three he was skinny as a rake. Sleeping in the spare bedroom gave me an occasional refuge from his tossing and turning. That Saturday, I awoke to an eerie calmness. Over the course of breakfast and a pleasant chat with my daughter, an oddly delayed, uneasy thought struck me: "Where's Lou?" Even ill, he was always up early. Heart pounding, I walked down the hall and opened our bedroom door. He wasn't in bed! I looked back up the hall, wondering how he could have gotten past me. *Where was he?* Intuitively, I realized he'd fallen out of the far side of the bed. An ethereal hand guided me across the room. Lou was lying face down on the carpet.

"Lou! Lou!" I shrieked.

My daughter and son bolted into the bedroom. All I can remember is seeing their bright blue eyes, as reality faded. Somehow, I dialed 911. As the emergency dispatcher began asking baneful questions, my knees buckled as I seemingly floated skyward. Disconnected from my body and shocked numb, I observed the scene below. In slowed motion, my children and I were mercury-like silver balls, with trails of gray light following us as we attempted to maneuver alternately through black smoke and red heat, then silver snow and blue ice.

"Mom!" our daughter screeched, sparking something deep within.

Taking charge of the 911 call, she snatched the phone from my hand. Her touch triggered my spirit to fall, full-force, back into my body with a discombobulated whoosh!

My daughter frantic, her voice cracking as she tried to stay in control, repeated the 911 dispatcher's questions. "Does he have a pulse?"

"I'll find one!" our son said, pressing his fingers on his dad's wrists, then his neck. After numerous attempts, in desperate resignation, he admitted, "I can't find one."

"Is he breathing?"

Each holding our breath, my son and I took turns leaning over the face we so loved—listening...praying...that we'd hear Lou breathing.

"I can't tell!" our son cried out.

A steady stream of emergency personnel flowed into our home. Politely and professionally, they ushered me away from my husband's side. Over and over, almost as though they were interrogating us, the emergency workers asked the same questions repeatedly. A while later Lou was placed on a stretcher. Unable to watch him taken from our family home for the last and final time, I faced the wall.

Finally and kindly, one of them asked if there was a friend they could call to come over. Strangely, the phone was no longer working. Science has proven that all things consist of energy. *Was it divine correlation that the line went dead as my soul mate returned to pure love?*

My beloved Lou died on a blustery winter day. Years of caregiving and Lou's unexpected death splayed me wide open. Sorrow oozed from my wounds, and festering anger welled within. *How could mankind carry on its normal pace? Did people not realize what I'd been through?* Of course, they didn't.

However, when someone did know, it was worse. Awkward silence, an obligatory hug, and sympathetic words were often followed by well-intended advice. Although what some said didn't necessarily help, maybe even hurt, I numbly listened. These encounters either sent me rushing for home before the endless tears welled up, or 'pissed me off' for days. All I wanted was companionship, not hugs and advice.

Tickets purchased well in advance of Lou's death, four weeks after he passed, my daughter and I flew to Germany. She had been accepted into a Study Abroad Program and could not forfeit this opportunity. For the first few days, we met up with her fellow international students in the heart of Munich, Marienplatz Square. Together we'd walk to outdoor markets and ancient cathedrals while listening to the chiming of the glockenspiel's bells. I was incredibly grateful for the optimism and energy I felt while participating in their grand adventures.

I could sense Lou's presence as we knocked items off *his* bucket list: driving the autobahn; eating fresh-baked pretzels for breakfast; and, drinking a Maas (one liter stein) of beer at the most famous pub in the world, the Hofbräuhaus am Platzl.

Once my daughter was settled, I encouraged her to spend time with her new friends, leaving me to explore on my own. The German people did not see the 'black veil' I wore, nor did it seem unusual that I was unaccompanied. Whenever I entered a restaurant or pub, I was immediately seated with English speaking businessmen or families. No one dined alone. No one knew my story.

Returning to a spouseless house also returned me to my mourning. When I ventured out in public, it felt as though my forehead was emblazoned with a bright flashing neon sign that read: WIDOW. I hated that word. It conjured up images of a hook-nosed, dried-up, dressed-in-black, misery-ridden creature—a sorry soul that I feared becoming! While filling out a form that required selecting Mrs., Ms. or Miss, I wondered, *"Who am I?"* My identity as wife, confidant, cheerleader, dream weaver, and lover extraordinaire (no one left to dispute this fact), were all cruelly stripped away. Grief became my identity.

Though no longer married, I felt married. *Was I expected to take off my wedding rings?* There was no instruction book to tell me when was the correct time to stop wearing my rings—a token which I'd worn continuously for over twenty-eight years. It was as much a part of my finger as the skin that had softened under it, creating the perfect niche to hold it in place. My wedding ring was a badge of honor; to take it off would feel like betrayal.

Nine months after Lou's death, on my birthday, I was back in my hometown attending my mother-in-law's funeral. For forty years, she had fought and won numerous battles with cancer. As diseased portions of her bladder and colon had been removed, she had a colostomy and a urostomy. Over twenty years had passed since she was given five years to live as a double ostomy patient. She told me that her will to live was born of a desire to watch our kids grow up. On dialysis for four years, after her 'baby's' death, she gave up the fight.

My father-in-law and I were the best of friends. Although he was raised in a generation when men didn't show feelings, he'd phone and we would openly share our loneliness. I was surprised that he was reaching out and honored to be entrusted with his emotions. Two months later he died. I could not bear to attend another funeral. My son went to represent our family.

Beaten by loss after loss, I had the sensation of being placed in a gunnysack and hung on a lone creaky tree to swirl round and round, forever at the mercy of a looming, thunderous prairie hailstorm. At times, when the spinning stopped and I dared to peek out, the landscape was foreign. Mundane everyday chores were overwhelming, requiring more concentration than I could muster.

Despondent, food tasted and chewed like Styrofoam, making it difficult to swallow. Flowers had no scent. A few of my coupled and happily married friends included me in their ongoing Friday night dinners. Getting ready spanned the entire day because I wanted to look better than I felt. A huge part of me missing, it was hard to find my reflection in the mirror. *It was as if I didn't exist.* Chatting with Lou helped ease my anxiety; however, once in the company of others, my aloneness magnified. It was so much easier to feel him nearby when at home. *Why did you have to leave me?*

Having never witnessed cries of agony that violently shook the bed, my bawling sessions frightened our faithful old dog. *Poor thing.* Rufus was our sacred family icon—unconditionally available to welcome, soothe and heal. Sixteen, he was no longer able to navigate stairs or control his bodily functions. *Was he carrying all my pain?* What still sends shivers down my spine was his wolf-like howling in the corner of our yard. *Could he no longer find his way across the only yard he'd ever known? Or were his cataract-clouded eyes looking for his master?*

The day came when I knew it was time to let Rufus go. He appeared peacefully oblivious as the veterinarian calmly and skillfully administered the euthanasia medication, petted us both briefly, then left the room. Once again, I was alone to deal with death. As I looked into his dark chocolate-brown eyes, I envisioned the energized young puppy he had been. Hugging him, the tears pent up from six recent deaths cascaded down my face and onto his. I sensed that he didn't want to go. *Was he crying too?* "It's okay, Rufus, go to Daddy. I will be all right." Still, he didn't immediately pass. Perhaps he wanted to continue protecting me. For his sake, I commanded, "Go find Lou!" At last, he lay still.

Eventually, I found solace in the anonymity of travel. I was free to be whoever I chose. In Europe, I discovered that the people wove ancient mythology with modern culture, reassuring me that my story hadn't ended. I could move forward without abandoning my past. I didn't have to die with Lou, although he would be part of me forever.

Drawn to stories of powerful heroines etched in stone for eternity, my imagination flourished, uncovering a 'remembering' of my divine feminine wisdom. In Turkey, I envisioned being *Artemis*, the goddess of wild animals and protector of young girls. The steel drums of the Caribbean rhythmically enticed *Calypso* into my being. At a women's retreat in Hawaii, I connected with the fiery *Pele,* and bravely breezed through my first zip-line experience. In China, *Kwan Yin*, the goddess of motherly compassion, guided me to help a suffering co-traveler heal.

At home, I was called to gardening. A magical spot, between the roses and the lavender, activated imaginings of carefree dancing through a bonny flowering meadow adorned with butterflies and merrily chirping birds. The faeries, forever at work and play in my yard, protected me from stings and mischievously hid my tools. *What could be more perfect, on a June day, than eating strawberries fresh from the patch while watching hummingbirds drink from the honeysuckle vines?* Sitting on my deck, connected with nature, I found peace, and gratitude for the months of rain that enabled these miracles.

Needing a place to 'be and become,' I found a women's circle. *Or did it find me?* Their rituals created a 'safe container.' Sheltered within we shared our stories, without interruption or judgment, mindfully present, listening, and discovering. There was empathy, not necessarily agreement. We understood and nurtured one another's potential. We supported and challenged one another. A big hallelujah moment for me was—I'd always had the answers to living 'my' best life.

With motivation gained from this community, my spark relit! Jean Shinoda Bolen says in her book *The Millionth Circle*, "When a critical number of people change how they think and behave, the culture does also, and a new era begins." Within the circle, we found a culture of peace—inward and outward—forever rippling forward to our families, communities and the world.

My new era had finally begun! Attending workshops and retreats on a variety of spiritual modalities provided inspirational implements for my life-toolbox. A circle sister introduced me to the sensual rhythm of hand drumming that aroused a long forgotten path to the *sacred* within me. The exercises in a Pilates class that I'd *won* helped to release the heavy burdens of my heart and soul. *Had my guardian angel arranged my win?* Intensely aware of the involvement of my muscles, nerves and arteries, as I pushed and pulled against the machinery, I began to overcome long suppressed anguish. For the first time in years, I became aware of my soul's vessel—my body. Winning six months of sessions with a life coach whose motto was *Joy First*, taught me how to laugh out loud; surprisingly, with no guilt attached. *Thank you, again, guardian angel.*

Now also a proud dragon boater, a channel of the mighty Fraser River is my team's playground. Twenty-four members, hips to the gunnel, lean and rotate forward, slicing the surface with our paddles to find the 'hard water' below. We kick, pull our paddles, exit the water, and repeat, stroke after stroke. My favorite training exercise is one that involves closing our eyes to feel the thrust as we paddle and kick in unison. It is then that I feel the union between water, earth, air, and sun as we traverse this ancient route. We are a varied group in age and ability. Many of us joke that we are just in it for the burger and beer afterward—however, we all have our own reasons for being part of this amazing connection.

I still have 'off' days. Gentle cures are: releasing my need to be in control; allowing the miracles that surround me; being in gratitude; taking time for and care of myself; recognizing my less positive human traits; and, knowing that throughout my entire life, the perfect situation or person—including those I loved and still miss—have always entered with divine 'timing.' *Unfortunately, I was sometimes in a different 'time' zone.*

Most days: my eyes are wide open to new insights; beyond hearing I am listening; my grateful heart quells my mind's chatter; and, ego takes a back seat to intuition. I've learned to forgive, especially myself for not being able to be everything to all people at all times.

It is exciting to see what lies around each bend in the curves and spirals of life's labyrinth. My thoughts and the meaning I assign to events influence my experiences. I choose to have fun and be happy! I have peacefully accepted change as being a consistent natural occurrence. Protons and neutrons are the nucleus of life, but it is our stories that bind us together forever.

Now, I can imagine filling the deep trenches of my sorrow with an abundance of joy. There is comfort in remembering the 'gift of family' that my parents and husband so generously provided. There was *purpose* for us coming together. Forging the gold and diamonds from my parents' engagement ring with those of Lou's and my rings, combined our life forces into an intimate circle of never-ending past, present and future love. Transforming the rings into a treasured heirloom allowed me to embrace the torment of grief, enabling me to pass through it and carry our shared stories forward. I am empowered with love, light and laughter.

SPARKLE

A faerie tarnished her soul, living in grief and pain.

Wallowing in this fable became her bind.

Wilting in her dark valley, above she heard a whispering refrain.

Louder and LOUDER it echoed—

Relight your spark—

Find,

A new story, kindness, joy

and love you will gain.

Spread peace and laughter from your true heartmind.

—Shirley J. Bueckert

Til Death Do Us Part

Daisy Landrigan

Dedicated to Robbie Landrigan

Anybody can be a father, but it takes someone special to be a dad.

"I didn't get a chance to say good-bye," our youngest daughter shrieked, tears spilling from her pretty brown eyes as she spotted her father's family standing beside his hospital bed and crying.

I nodded, my lips pursed against grief too potent to process. She cradled against me and clung on. Guided by her aunt, our eldest hesitantly walked toward Robbie's bedside. His family stepped back. It was time for the girls and I to say goodbye to their dad.

Watching my eldest as she stood silently crying, I wondered if either of our children fully understood that their father had passed over to the eternal side. *Did I?* I'd never lost anyone that close before.

The stunned sadness that engulfed the room in an uneasy quiet was one that a child should never know. But our children now did. Would this moment forever taint our daughters' happy memories of their father? I hated that it probably would. Hated that there was nothing I could do to ease the loss of the man they thought had hung the moon in the sky to chase away the darkness.

Two days previously, all of us had gathered in a private family room at the hospital. Unable to deliver such devastating news, I'd hung back as their aunt and uncle told them that their dad wasn't going to make it. My youngest screamed, "NO!" My eldest looked to me for verification, crocodile tears pouring down her cheeks. Hugging them close, we wept. Afterward, we spent some time with their dad and his family before going home.

Later that evening, alone in my room, I wanted to sob; to just curl up with someone's arms around me while I cried like a little kid. But my days of being nurtured like a child were over. I was a mom—my beautiful baby girls' mom to whom they looked for guidance and strength.

The next day was Valentine's Day. Robbie's family brought us all cards and chocolates. The girls decorated their dad's room with valentines they'd made at school. Later in the evening while I was giving him a Reiki treatment, Robbie seemed particularly restless and in greater pain than usual. Knowing that his increased suffering was likely a sign that he was going to pass over, even though the plan was for the girls and I to stay with him overnight, I asked another family member to take our place. This wasn't how I wanted our children to remember their dad.

Sometime around 4:00 a.m. Robbie's family arrived at my house to take the girls and I back to the hospital. While his family was there, his eldest brother called from the hospital to say my husband was in horrendous pain even though the nurses had maximized his medication. The eerie sound of Robbie's moans cut into the phone like a siren. He couldn't hang on much longer. Willing myself calm, I was about to wake our children when the phone rang again. Their father was gone.

The adults grief-stricken and the girls still half asleep and unaware that their dad had passed, no one spoke during our twenty-minute drive to the hospital. In contrast to the daytime and evening busyness we were accustomed to, the palliative care ward was eerily silent.

Not knowing how any of us would respond to seeing Robbie's lifeless body, when we arrived at his room the girls and I stayed near the doorway. Our youngest was the first to realize and react to her father's passing.

Approaching his side, our eight-year-old still tucked under my arm, I noted how peaceful and young Robbie appeared. The pain that had wracked his body was gone. *How was it possible that he wasn't just sleeping? How was it possible that he was gone?*

Watching our daughters tearfully kissing their father's face for the very last time, my heart collapsed inward like an imploding star. Losing him was devastating for me, a grownup who'd known for a few years that this day might come. *How could their young minds and hearts endure such sorrow? How long would it take before they braved another laugh, or trusted that the world was a safe place to be?*

I touched his arm. He was still warm, making the idea of his passing even more surreal. Death was final...too final to truly comprehend. Wanting to protect my children from seeing their mother falling completely to pieces, distancing more than connecting, I stooped forward to kiss his forehead—his still warm forehead, that topped a face that would never again smile, frown or contort in awful pain. My children's father had bid the world farewell, and it was up to me to make certain his daughters would remember the light he shone into the world, not their sorrowful anguish at having to say goodbye to the man they loved with wholehearted awe.

Someone said, "There's nobody home. He's gone golfing." Another family member said, "He's not in pain anymore." The statements were intended to help the girls. Gratefully, whimsical imaginings of Robbie playing one of his favorite sports somewhere in the universe, peacefully happy and pain free, helped to soften my sorrow too.

His soul had left his body and it was time to take our girls home, so he could rest in peace and we could begin to heal. How I handled the sad days ahead would forever affect how our children viewed life and death. It was now up to me to hang the moon in the sky to chase away the darkness.

In 2005, when Robbie received news of his stage-three colon cancer, we were separated but still living in the same household. To minimize the impact of our breakup on our girls, when we decided to live separately, our homes were only a few blocks apart. We each had a key to the other's house and practiced an open-door policy. He was free to come and go at our place, and vice versa. The kids saw their father almost daily. Family remained our central focus. He sometimes came for dinner, joined us for holiday and birthday celebrations, and continued coaching our girls' ringette (a form of hockey played with straight sticks and a rubber ring) and soccer teams.

Because they were so very young, we didn't use the 'C' word around our girls or immediately share Robbie's dismal prognosis. Instead, we explained that their father had stomach problems, making it easier on the kids when he went in for surgery or underwent treatment. However, when our eldest child one day asked if her dad had cancer, though it broke my heart to confirm her deepest fears, I answered honestly.

Learning that Robbie had advanced colon cancer altered my perspective. Past hurts and seemingly insolvable marital issues took a backseat as we teamed together to beat his disease. He was my children's father, and I wanted him alive and well in this world. Above all, I wanted our kids to appreciate and experience more of who he was; especially, his zest for life.

What first attracted me to Robbie was his social ease. Naturally charming and caring, he made certain that others knew that what they thought and said was important. In his eyes, everyone was equal, regardless of race, social status or economic placement. Every Halloween he'd dress up in a costume he chose and I sewed. Somewhat a sports jock, it always amused me that he enjoyed being disguised as various female bombshells. He was equally at home dressed as Elvis or the yellow teletubby Laa-Laa. Much to our girls' chagrin, if Halloween was close to a sports practice, their father would attend in costume. The other kids and parents loved it. Our kids wished he'd just grow up and be a normal dad.

Even when the girls and I moved into our own place, Robbie often joined us for meals. Regardless if he lived to be one hundred— or died six months after his first set of chemotherapy as his specialist predicted he would—the two of us were determined that our kids were going to collect a treasure chest of happy times with their father and me.

We travelled to Disney World in Florida, Disneyland in California, and took a Disney Cruise to the Bahamas. In New York, the kids and their father visited the Empire State Building and rode dozens of rides at Six Flags Discovery Kingdom. When local medical professionals claimed there was nothing else they could do for him, the kids went with us while he underwent alternative treatment in Vermont. We celebrated Robbie turning forty-nine with his lifelong friends and family in Halifax, Nova Scotia. It was his last birthday.

Early after his diagnosis, we studied various books and considered different treatment and coping strategies suggested and given to us by friends and family. Though somewhat skeptical, Robbie agreed to help me explore alternative therapies and remedies. We attended a wellness clinic where we learned more about the importance of diet and nutrition. At the suggestion of friends, we took an introductory class in EFT (Emotional Freedom Techniques), which is based on acupuncture principles and involves 'tapping' on the body's energy meridians to stimulate healing. Impressed, we enrolled in a weekend seminar that included EFT and Neuro-Linguistic Programming. (NLP deals with the correlation and effects of thought and self-talk on the body.)

The more I learned, the more it perturbed me that none of his doctors suggested using alternative medicine in conjunction with conventional medical treatments. Equally disturbing was that they gave him a death sentence of just over six months. *Why not just push the man off a bridge and hope he could swim?*

Belief predetermines outcome—positively and negatively. Belief shored with hope and prayer produces miracles; especially, when sprinkled with 'Get well' cards made by your kids and 'I know you can beat this!' encouragement from others. My husband actually lived three years past his initial diagnosis—most of which he was well enough to enjoy.

During those three years, we and our kids built a lifetime's worth of cherished memories. Had my husband forfeited *hope* that he'd get better or at least live longer, he would likely have passed into the eternal side much sooner. Had I *not believed* in and sought alternative therapies that might help, maybe even miraculously cure his disease, he may not have maintained the quality of life that he did.

Some of the statements others made were a bit perplexing; one being, "Daisy, what you are doing is very noble. Most women would just walk away." Although hearing this usually caught me off guard, my response was always the same, "He's my children's father." What I didn't often share was a precious moment between Robbie and me that happened one evening when I was leaving the hospital.

As I always did after he walked me to the elevator, I turned around to say goodbye, expecting to see his familiar smile. But he wasn't smiling. Near tears, his sad, scared eyes pierced my heart, completely dismantling the self-preservation barrier I'd erected after our separation. It was in that moment, peering at him soul-to-soul, that the last remnants of my anger and hurt drained away. Hugging him, we reconnected as spiritual beings in human form—heart to heart, not mind-to-mind. No matter what had transpired between us as husband and wife, we were connected forever through our children and the universal love that connects all souls through all time. It was a very beautiful and freeing moment.

In my quest for knowledge and practices that might heal Robbie, I discovered an exciting array of teachers willingly sharing their formulas for a happy and healthy life. Dr. Wayne Dyer's *Power of Intention*, Greg Braden's *The Divine Matrix*, and a variety of Deepak Chopra's books were among my most enlightening and favorite information sources. Luckily, I was able to listen to all three of these gifted and wise men at an I Can Do It seminar in Las Vegas, which was put on by Hay House. Being among spiritually-centered speakers and an audience of hopeful people shored my belief in one's ability to sustain emotional and physical health, perhaps even eradicate disease.

Dr. Wayne Dyer advises that, "Intention is not something you do, but rather a force that exists in the universe as an invisible field of energy—a power that can carry us." What I gleaned from reading this bit of wisdom was that by becoming aware of one's heart-centered intuition, or divinely-inspired motivations, life naturally unfolds within the magic of universal intention. As a result, I no longer felt a need to control every situation. Instead, I began to view each challenge as my teacher, and each reward as a sign that I was living my life as universally intended.

I also read the *Dreamhealer: His name is Adam* and later attended a seminar with the author. World renowned as a distant healer, Adam demonstrated how positive intentions directly affect one's health. What he wrote, verbalized and demonstrated profoundly reinforced the importance of living with positive intention and staying connected to one's higher-self. Spiritual health directly correlates with physical and emotional health.

Colon cancer is mostly preventable. When caught early, it is largely a curable disease. Unfortunately, we and then the doctors missed many of the telltale symptoms. For years, Robbie's medical professionals ignored his complaints about intermittent stomach pains. The summer before he was diagnosed, his red blood cell count was low, which combined with his stomach symptoms should have twigged the doctors to the possibility of colon cancer. However, he wasn't sent for a colonoscopy until the early part of the following year.

Once diagnosed, our lives became a whirlwind of medical tests and chemo treatments, followed by a series of drug therapies. While he was alive, friends of ours included Robbie's frustration with the medical profession in an investigative documentary about Canada's pharmaceutical industry. The documentary 'Pills, Patients and Profits' didn't actually air until March 2010. Robbie passed over on February 15th, 2008. What my husband asked at the beginning of the W5 documentary (produced by CTV) was, "How much is my life worth?" He was frustrated because the drug he needed to slow his disease was extremely costly and not yet available through our universal health care system. Luckily, we were able to afford this medicine and have it administered at a local hospital. Typical of his caring and giving manner, Robbie agreed to the interview because he was concerned about those who weren't financially able to buy the drugs needed to save or extend their lives.

What Robbie endured, no being should ever suffer. Witnessing his agony was tough for me and the girls, particularly toward the end of his life, when there was nothing anyone could do to ease his pain. Hopefully, the frustrations and wisdom he shared on the W5 documentary will help to improve our imperfect medical and pharmaceutical systems. Perhaps reading this story will nudge others toward getting early diagnostic testing that will prevent a similar fate.

Although heartrending at times, sticking with Robbie throughout his illness allowed me to discover the true beauty within each of us. Compassion for and acceptance of others has become second nature to me and our children. The girls and I now live our lives full of gratitude for the many blessings each day unfolds.

I am thankful that my family was at our sides when we gathered to say 'so long' to Robbie. I'm also grateful his family visited often, accompanied us on our Disney vacations, and was by his side when he passed over. Robbie's emotional and physical responses to their steadfast devotion reinforced my knowing that 'being loved and loving' matters more than any other of life's many gifts.

Nobody can predict which will be his or her last day on earth. Be it right or wrong, our physical mortality is a conundrum most of us prefer not to consider. Better to busy ourselves with earning a living, owning and consuming. Better to fill our time with mindless activities than sit with a loved one and count our blessings. My husband and I were actually very lucky to have three extra years to be a family. The girls and I will forever cherish the wonderful times we spent swimming with the dolphins, exploring new lands, and laughing.

One memory that still makes us chuckle happened during our Disney Cruise when the girls and I came back to our cabin and caught Robbie stark-naked as he stood in the balcony doorway gazing out at the ocean. Quickly closing the door, the kids and I doubled over in laughter. Who'd have known catching a glimpse of their father's butt would become one of our most treasured memories.

'Never too old to have a happy childhood.'

Robbie, we love you always.

There is Always a Solution

Sudipta Banerjee

Oh, Bishu, it's been twenty-five years since we said goodbye on this earth. I am fortunate to be surrounded by many good friends who are very close to me. Let them be close, but you know the truth—in my heart, you are still closest to me.

"Tia, why don't you come to Kolkata with us for few months?" my mother suggested just one short week after the death of my dear husband Bishu.

For a long moment I didn't answer. I still couldn't believe Bishu was dead. It felt as though he was simply gone on a business trip and would be back any moment. *How was it that a dynamic young man could die at thirty-nine?* It didn't seem real or right. "Na, Ma, I'm not going anywhere," I finally answered, "I must think about my daughter's future. I can't afford to waste time relaxing or grieving."

There was also a promise I had to fulfill, but I didn't immediately share it with my mother.

"I knew you wouldn't listen to me, you never do!" Her hands flailing, Ma stormed out of the room mumbling, "Do whatever you want."

I watched her small frame disappear into the hallway. She didn't understand. No one understood what my life was like since the moment the doctor referred Bishu to a gastroenterologist. I was so naïve then, and asked the doctor, "What could be so wrong that he needs to see a specialist?" We didn't have medical insurance, and although the whites of my husband's eyes were turning yellow, he didn't seem that sick.

Rather than frighten us, our family doctor simply wrote a referral to Dr. Sama. "Let's wait and see," was his advice as we shook hands goodbye.

The next morning, Dr. Sama checked Bishu into a nursing home and ordered a number of medical tests. I wasn't worried because it didn't dawn on me that my husband might have cancer. As far as I was concerned he was suffering from jaundice, which I didn't believe

149

was a life threatening disease. But I was very wrong—jaundice can be life threatening. In fact, it not only threatened, it took Bishu's life. Bishu, my best friend and dear sweet husband, was gone within a few months.

Bishu and I met at a wedding ceremony and were instantly attracted to one another. How could I not be attracted to him? He had bright brown eyes and a soft genuine smile. I was going through a bad time and was kind of rude to everybody. I was not a 'bunch of roses' at that point of my life, rather more like a cactus plant. But Bishu was willing to decorate his home with cactus—in Japanese style!

Oh, how I miss him, even our many arguments that never lasted long.

"What! You've already made the decision?" I asked, shocked when Bishu casually announced he'd taken a well-paid job in New Delhi and we were all moving. My mind whirled with what to say to change his mind, but the best I could come up with was, "I am not moving to New Delhi. I am not going anywhere. We are so comfortable here in Kolkata, why would you make us move?!"

My mother-in-law quickly added her own whiny questions, "Why? Bishu, why? Aren't we all happy here?"

'Well," Bishu said, "someone is mad because she has to go away from her mother, and someone is unhappy because she has to go away from her daughter."

"How would you understand?" I argued, backing my question with a pout. "You are taking your mother and your daughter with you!"

When he wouldn't change his mind, frustrated and mad to the power of infinity, I threatened him. "I will leave you, and you will be alone with your good-paying job. What will you do then?"

Bishu wasn't amused and shouted, "You want a divorce? All right, let's go to the divorce office!"

I was stubborn like a rock, so we left our house to get a divorce. Riding on the back of his motorbike, I refused to hang on to my equally stubborn husband.

A few miles down the road, Bishu hollered over his shoulder, "Okay, okay. I haven't said you cannot hold me."

I said nothing.

We ended up at my favorite Chinese restaurant. Our disagreement was over.

When he was sick, Bishu wanted me by his bedside, so I quit my job. Both friends and family worriedly questioned my decision, many times asking, "What are you doing? Your husband has pancreatic cancer and will soon die. Is this the right time to quit your job?"

When someone is dying and wants you by his side, is that not the right time quit your job? My husband was dying—dying. He deserved quality time with me. *Couldn't they see that?*

But when my sweet Bishu did die, I had to think about getting a job and our little daughter's future.

A quarter of a century ago, when Bishu left my side, Indian culture prevented my parents from sanctioning their thirty-six-year-old daughter living on her own with a small child.

"I know you are very independent minded, Tia," my sister said, shortly after my husband died. "Sure, you could find a job. But wouldn't it be more reasonable for you to come and live in one of our flats and go to work from there? That way, Gina will have a father figure, and my daughter Shona and your daughter can grow up together."

Living in my sister's huge house, with three separate flats that could be rented out if need be, Gina would definitely have a father figure, but not a father. Gina lost her dad; no one could become her dad or dad figure. I politely refused my sister's offer.

It wasn't long before I began work as a tutor for children. Group after group, I taught between two-thirty and eight-thirty p.m. I could have taught more groups, as I received lots of calls from parents wanting me to help their kids. But as children must go to school during the day, and my late afternoon schedule already full, I turned most of them down.

One day, I received a call from a lady who insisted that I tutor her fifteen-year-old son. She offered such a high amount, I couldn't say no. Daily, this lady dropped off and then picked up her child. Slowly, we became friends, and she took me to a women's group where I met lots of very sophisticated, wealthy women. Almost every one of them was currently married to or divorced from a rich man. These ladies took me under their wings and offered to help me establish some kind of business. I declined their offer, explaining that I needed to feel I was good at whatever I did, and unfamiliar work made me uncomfortable. Accepting my explanation, they offered to build a tutorial home for me. I was shocked. *Why did they want to help me?*

During this same period, my restless mom would visit every month, then get worried about my dad and head back to Kolkata. Growing tired of what felt like continual interference by her, I started looking for a way to get Ma off my back without hurting her feelings. I needed a solution, one I knew already existed and I just had to find it. It was a lesson I learned from my dear Bishu, who shared these wise words: "Tia, when a problem comes, don't get upset; instead, try to think about the probable solution. Every problem has some solution, maybe not exactly what you want, but *there is always a solution.* You just need to think."

Wow! It was such a wise and powerful message. When he said it to me, I didn't realize that his *solution* lesson would become one of my lifelong problem solving tools. Bishu wasn't a talker. I was. Most times while I'd talk on-and-on, he'd just sit there listening, his divine smile so patient and caring. But once in a while, he would say something I would never forget for my whole life!

Looking for the solution that Bishu promised was available, I went to the library and began researching universities abroad. If I could study for my PhD somewhere far away, Ma would have no choice but to leave me alone. How many applications I wrote! We didn't even know the word 'online' back then, so I applied through the mail, writing so many applications that I lost track of the number I wrote. I do know that it was at least seventy, maybe over one hundred, and paper and stamps cost a lot of money. Aware that I was quickly using up our little savings, heart of hearts, I was getting scared. *What if my solution didn't work?*

My new lady friend was regularly taking me to the women's group. I felt kind of weird being there, but they were extremely helpful to a lot of people. One day, they asked me to meet with a gentleman, and I agreed to do so. The way he talked to me felt a little awkward. Wasn't I naïve! I didn't even consider what I might be getting into. The gentleman (What is the definition of a gentleman?) said that he had a luxury apartment, which was just around the corner. Perhaps, a beautiful young lady like me should move there and enjoy the place. "Why would I do that?" I asked, a little confused and very concerned. "I have a comfortable place to live. Why are you asking me to live at your place? Did I ask for that? And why would I use something which does not belong to me?" Seeming somewhat puzzled, he looked at me in a funny way.

I kept hunting for a university that would accept me. One day, I met another gentleman, who was supposed to know my late husband. While we were talking, I told him about my university hunt. He said that his older brother was a math professor in Canada, and promised me that he would talk to him. He suggested that I apply for admission where his brother worked at Simon Fraser University. He also said his brother was planning to visit India in a couple of months. *How nice!* I decided there were good people in this world!

Unable to rely on gaining admission to any university, I knew that I had to explore various opportunities. Before he became sick, Bishu had an established consulting business. I thought, "Why don't I try that?" But I did not have a clue about mechanical engineering. It was funny, without knowing anything, I decided to meet with a gentleman through whom Bishu had secured a big job, but couldn't finish. Maybe I could hire an engineer to complete the work.

I met this gentleman and we talked. I am certain that within a few minutes he was aware of my lack of knowledge, but he didn't say so to me. Following our meeting, he started coming to my house under the guise of wanting to talk business, and then hit on me! Puzzled by this man's actions at first, I slowly began to realize how much protection Bishu used to give me. From a very young age, I enjoyed attention from boys. But now, knowing I was somewhat helpless, what I felt was a lack of respect. I had no interest in being trapped in an extramarital affair. I tried to explain to this man that I could not do the job, but he kept on insisting he would help me, and that I shouldn't let go of such a big opportunity.

Growing tired of people's behavior, I again asked myself, "*Where is the solution?*" Though I'd been tutoring, I was barely making enough to survive, and applying to universities was still eating away at our little savings. Constantly, I wondered if I should look for a job. But even working and tutoring wouldn't provide the amount of income needed to give my daughter the best opportunities in life. I'd made a promise to Bishu and intended to keep it.

On the very last day of his life, holding my hand and looking at me with his divine, kind eyes, my husband pleaded, "Tia, do not die with me. Live your life fully." Smiling at my tears and the way I was shaking my head no, he finished with, "I have only one request, take good care of Gina…she is my soul."

In India, it is not easy to give every opportunity to your child, because everything costs a fortune. *How could I keep his last wish?!* A big chunk of our savings had been spent on my husband's medical treatments, and I wasn't earning enough to replace it. How many times I pleaded, "Oh, Bishu show me some direction. What is the solution?"

It was December when the gentleman I'd met called to say that the Canadian professor was in town. We made arrangements for me to meet him. "He's the nicest person in the world," I thought as he went through all my papers. Then he said, "I wish I could have you as my student, but your subject area is different than mine. However, I will talk to one of my colleagues and see if he is willing to take you as his student." I was so happy that day.

I met with the professor a few more times, and then invited him, along with his brother and his wife, for dinner at my place. Ma was there too, and didn't seem very pleased with my friends or my plans. A month later, I received a letter saying that I'd been accepted as a graduate student at Simon Fraser University in British Columbia, Canada. *Aha, I got it!* I started dancing with my daughter. Finally, I could fulfill all of Bishu's wishes.

I started wrapping up my affairs in India. There was so much to do, including lots of paperwork, which I hated doing. I bought our plane tickets, and then went to Kolkata to visit with Ma and my sister. No one seemed happy. Ma said, "I don't know what you are doing. You are gambling with your life, and you are gambling with Gina's life."

I was shaken. Sure, it was fine for me to take a chance to live my life fully. But did I have a right to take a chance with my child's life? I had no clue about Canada. *What if I got into bigger trouble?* Still, thinking of my promise to Bishu, I decided, "Oh, well, I guess I will find out!"

My sister conveyed what my brother had said to her: "Oh, that's Tia! She always has to give a stunt." Then she put in her own two cents. "Aren't you scared? You are a woman, Tia. You should think differently."

I was determined. In my Ma's language, I was *stubborn*. Whatever, I had made up my mind and wasn't going to change it.

My sister then offered, "How about leaving Gina with us? You go and see how it is in Canada."

I said, "No! My little girl has lost her father. She should not also lose her mother so soon. No matter what, we will be together. Thanks for the offer, though."

Gina and I left India with three suitcases and seven hundred and fifty dollars in our pockets! We boarded the plane scared. It was my first time travelling abroad. Although I could read and write English, I didn't speak it well. An Indian lady sat beside us. *Oh, wasn't she smart!* She could not read, write or speak English. She was a very friendly and confident person. She soon realized that I was a first-time traveler to Canada, and we made a deal. She would help us on the way to Vancouver, and I would help her with filling out forms and English translation. "English translation…me?! Okay, I suppose I can do that," I agreed, hoping that I could fulfill my promise to my new friend.

We had an overnight stopover in London, England. So there we were in a five star hotel in London! I could not even open the door or use the faucet without help. The next morning, Gina and I went for breakfast in the hotel. *Oh, my God! There are so many different kinds of food. Where should we start?* We started putting all those good looking foods on our plates. Suddenly, the Indian lady showed up and asked, "Do you think you can eat that stuff? They are all cold cut meats." We tried them. Yuck! They tasted horrible. Both Gina and I had to throw them away. Our new friend then helped us to choose the right food for us.

Later, we returned to Heathrow airport for our flight. Boarding our plane, I was excited. Here comes Vancouver, our final flight destination and probably our new home—new life!

The professor came to pick us up. It was my first ride in a Cadillac. *So smooth. So nice.* Mr. Professor said, "Let's go to my home first and I will find you a place in few days." He drove us to his nice apartment right on the ocean. We were tired and exhausted. But we were in Canada!

After a couple of days, he took me to the university, where I met my

PhD supervisor and a few other people. But something was not right. *What was it?* That night after Gina went to bed, Mr. Professor asked me to join him in the living room. Then he said, "I am divorced and you are a widow. How about we get together?"

What should I say? He was twenty-one years older than me. "Look, I am an Indian woman and grew up with Indian values. I can't even think about sleeping with someone out of wedlock."

"Okay," he said, "I am ready to marry you, if you are ready."

I had a sleepless night wondering what I should do. In a way, it would be nice to be married to the professor. Gina would get a perfect house. *What else could I ask for?* I accepted his proposal. Within a few days we moved into a bigger apartment. On the 31st of May, I married the professor. *Was I happy?* Under the circumstances, yes, I was happy.

We had a few good days, but I had a difficult time sleeping with him. I could not stop thinking about Bishu. Every single moment, my Bishu's divine smile and sweet face were on my mind and in my heart. *What did I do to myself? What next?*

Soon the reality of my life with the professor became clear. He just would not let me do my studies. Nor would he let me see my PhD supervisor. But he did help me get a job at the university as a teacher's assistant. Soon afterward, I was hired as a sessional instructor and given a course to teach.

Teaching in English was not easy for me and required many hours of preparation for each lesson. Although I had to quit my studies, my teacher's assistant job was not taken away. *But was I living my vision of a perfect family?*

The professor was a gambler and would often invite a few of his friends over to play cards. They would sometimes play for thirty-six hours at a stretch, sleeping on the couches for a few hours when they were tired, and then playing again. They would also drink alcohol. One thing was for sure, they did not look at me the way that some men ogle women. They were in their own world of gambling. Sometimes, the professor would disappear for a couple days. I never knew where he went. *Is that what I wanted? Was this my so called perfect house?* Finally, I'd had enough. I would do anything for Gina. She was Bishu's daughter and the most important person in my life. I could not let any bad things happen to her.

In the meantime, I met a nice lady, Lyla, from the Indian community. She suspected that I wasn't happy and going through some type of problem. One day she offered, "Tia, if you have anything you want to say, you can trust me. And you can come to my house anytime you want." It was good to know I had a friend I could trust and who wanted to help if need be.

One evening, the professor and I were having an argument when I said, "If I sensed before what the situation between us would be, I would have done things differently." He smiled before saying, "Do whatever you can do." I decided right then that it was time for me to do something about my partner problem!

I called Lyla, and Gina and I went to her home. She invited us to stay with her family for a few days, and offered to help us find a permanent place to live. It was wonderful staying in her brand new house. We felt welcomed and were comfortable staying in their downstairs guest suite.

The day after we arrived, Lyla and her husband were out and I was sitting at the kitchen table marking assignments. I was also looking after our children. Suddenly, Gina and Lyla's two kids came running to tell me that the basement was flooding. I hurried down the steps, shocked to find that the basement—and all my belongings—were under about three feet of muddy water. Stunned, at first, I wondered, *"What else could go wrong?"* Then I just stood there and laughed, because there was nothing else I could do. When Lyla returned, she said she was very sorry for me. Apparently the new drain was faulty. Well, one good thing happened as a result—we got a few thousand dollars from the insurance company!

After a week at Lyla's, we rented a basement suite, and Gina and I moved into it. My landlord had four girls. Gina was very happy in that tiny apartment, which was great because I had not seen her happy for a long time. So our mother and daughter life began! Now, we could live happily ever after. Was it time for *happily ever after*? Not quite. But that is another story of struggle that I will write about in the next *Heartmind Wisdom* book.

I sometimes ask myself, "Am I a proud lady now?" My answer is, "Yes!" Thanks to my late husband's wise advice that *"there is always a solution,"* I did fulfill Bishu's dying wish for Gina.

Losing Bishu, for a long while I also lost one valuable part of me.

What did I lose? I lost my attraction toward men. Having been married to the best man possible, I couldn't help but compare my professor partner, and all men, to Bishu. Not that my second marriage could have lasted. There was too much I didn't like, and I was worried about raising Gina in a home where there was drinking and gambling. A year ago, one of my neighbors asked if I was a lesbian. *Wouldn't my life have been easier if I were attracted to women!*

Last April, I had a bad flu and was so sick that I could hardly get out of my bed. After a few days, I woke up from my sick-induced coma, and wondered, "What am I doing? What is wrong with me? Why don't I start dating again and have the full life Bishu wished for me?"

So I started going out to dances, visiting with friends and having a social life. Am I a happy person? Yes, I am! I'm not materially rich, but I am very rich with experiences. Over my lifetime, there were some obstacles that seemed impossible to fix. Each time, I wondered, "Should I stop pursuing Bishu's wishes, or jump over, make a tunnel through, or pass around this barrier?" I did not stop, because as my sweet, sweet husband so wisely said, *"there is always a solution."*

Dying to Live

Susan Berger Thompson

Dedicated to Robin and Brandie—the loves of my
life. You are everything I dreamed of and more.

The day I died, October 26th, 1994, eased in with the minutia that
blurs most days: rise early, shower, eat breakfast, and drive to work.

As we had fought again the night before, I asked Liam to meet
me for lunch. I wanted to make up because I simply couldn't stand
being on the outs with him. I felt he was my soul mate, though our
coexistence defied any routine description of a heavenly match. We
fought constantly and passionately. That same passion defined the love
we shared—delight in each other's company, laughter, dancing, and
amazing love making. *Oh, how we loved.*

When we left the restaurant, Liam headed home. We had just
recently moved back to Prince George from Kelowna, so he was
currently unemployed and studying for his realtor's license exam. I
went to my optometrist appointment.

Excruciating headaches had been plaguing me for a couple of
weeks. I was told I would often sit holding my throbbing head in my
hands; however, I don't recall the many instances or intensity. I do
remember thinking perhaps I needed new glasses.

After checking in with the receptionist I took a seat in the waiting room.
Another headache began, but this time the pain escalated with such severity
that I knew something was very wrong. It felt as though my head was in a
steadily tightening vice. Then everything spiraled out of my control.

Like an uninvited party goer, punching holes in walls, leaving dirty
footprints on the carpet and drinking too much punch, death crashed
in to my life.

My next recollection was awaking in a strange place, holding letters
and concentrating intently as I tried to make sense of the words. Going

through the pages, I recognized the signatures: Robin, Brandie and Brenda. The rest of what was written just wouldn't sink in.

Noticing Liam out of the corner of my eye, I turned my head toward him and winced in pain.

"Hi!" he said, moving closer and kissing me. "You've been reading those letters over and over. Your kids and Brenda are worried about you."

"They are?" I questioned. "Why? Where am I?" His expression was tender, but his brown eyes held concern and relief.

"You're in the hospital, Sue." After squeezing my hand, he sat back in the chair, removed his glasses, and rubbed his eyes before pinching the top of his nose. His face was drawn and pale. I could see he was very tired.

"The hospital?" I rasped, lifting my head less than an inch, then immediately dropping it back on the pillow. *Why did my head feel as heavy as a twenty-pound bowling ball?*

"You had an aneurysm that burst a couple of weeks back. You've been in and out of consciousness since."

Two weeks? In and out of consciousness? Aneurysm? I tried to digest unfamiliar words coming from a familiar voice.

"You passed out in the optometrist's waiting room."

"The *optometrist's?*" I questioned, slowly remembering the exploding headache and thinking, "Oh, no, not now!" as the pain rapidly compounded until I screamed, "Something is wrong! Help me!"

"I thought I lost you," Liam confessed, his eyes tearing uncharacteristically.

I stared at the face I loved. His cautious smile brought light into a dreary room that reeked of human sweat and sickness.

"What day is it?" I asked, somewhat annoyed by the steady thrumming of what sounded like someone's megaphoned heartbeat.

"Friday."

"No, the actual date."

"November 11th, 1994." Liam indicated the letters I held. "Your kids were here for the first week, but had to return to Prince George because of school."

"Back to Prince George? Where am I?"

"You're in Vancouver General Hospital."

"How did I get here?"

"By air ambulance. Prince George Regional Hospital isn't equipped for neurosurgery."

I nodded, but stopped because it made my head hurt.

Immediately my thoughts jumped to my kids—*they must have been scared witless.* My heart in my throat, I blurted, "Where are Robin and Brandie? Are they alone? Who's looking after them?" At seventeen and sixteen, they were at ages when the desire to break free of parental control weighs heavily against the fear that you aren't quite able to stand alone. For them, a seesaw of hormone-fueled emotions ebbed and tided by the second. I wished I could hug them.

"Shh, relax, Brenda is staying with them."

I thought of my longtime friend who'd been at my side for many good times and bad. We had been best friends since each of our youngest kids started kindergarten and we began carpooling. Of course, she'd jumped to my rescue; it was her way. Relieved that my kids were safe, my eyes drifted back to the pages still in my hands.

"Dear Mom. How is everything in the aiding confines of Vancouver General Hospital? Sorry that I can't come and see you this weekend with Auntie Diane, Uncle Stanley, Wendy and whoever else is going with them. I have a lot of catching up to do in two of my three classes, seeing as I lost seven full days, whilst I was visiting you there. I love you dearly, the most of anything/anyone in the world (tied with dad of course), but there is a special bond between mother and her son(s), especially when they are this good-looking." *

I chuckled and cried as Robin's easy smile, mischievous hazel eyes and mop of long reddish-brown hair came to mind. Reading his witty letter was a treat for so many reasons; one being that my eldest didn't often express his feelings.

Suddenly exhausted, I nodded off with my daughter's letter clutched in my hand. Waking up some time later, I noticed Liam studying me, his smile tender, as if it were the first day we met playing slo-pitch. It brought back memories of the two of us flirting in the bright hot sun, totally exhilarated by our mutual attraction and the dusty thrill of the game. Ours was a relationship with as many innings as a tournament—hits and outs, tears and laughter, love and angst—we fit like a well-worn glove one day, and like an ill-fitted mitt the next. *Oh, how I loved him…will always love him.* Moving closer, he leaned over and kissed me gently. We looked at each other for a long moment. Then he sat back down, patiently waiting as I began to read.

> *"Dear Mom. Hi, how are you feeling? I really hope you are doing good. I'm sure you are, you're strong. I want you to know I'm so very proud of you for being strong and pulling through. Just the thought that you are going to be alright and that you miss me brings tears to my eyes. I miss you too mom. But I don't want you to try and rush anything. The very best you can do is rest and get all the strength you can for when the doctors say you can come back to Prince. I really wish I could be there with you always but I need to catch up at school."*

My beautiful daughter Brandie's letter was as warm and loving as she. As always, her words brought comfort into my often shadowed life. Crying, I asked Liam, "Was I awake when the kids were here? I don't remember them being here. Why can't I remember?"

"You've been in and out of the picture quite a bit. Sometimes you asked questions that didn't make sense; other times, you thought people were here, who weren't. You talked to Robin and Brandie when they were here, but you were groggy and not quite with it."

My time-line and memory out of whack, I felt confused, worried and disoriented. *What else had happened while I was comatose or incoherent? Why couldn't I remember? I needed to know!* My life had become a puzzle that I couldn't put together because there were too many pieces missing. It was so incredibly frustrating.

After a while, Liam handed me a pen and paper and began a barrage of questions to which I should know the answers. Where do we live? When is Brandie's birthday? When is Robin's birthday? Where do you bank? They seemed obvious and silly to me, but important to Liam. I wrote the answers down, watching his grin widen as I answered each correctly, only hesitating briefly as I tried to remember the street number of our house.

As I became increasingly aware, I noticed several other patients shared my room, including one hooked up to a heart monitor that was the cause of the thrumming noise. Looking out the window, in the distance I could see snow on the ground and knew that winter had arrived.

Later that day, my oldest sister Diane, along with two of her daughters, Wendy and Tracey, arrived from Prince George to visit. They surrounded my bed and I was able to chat and laugh a bit with them, though I tired quickly. Liam explained to them that my voice was harsh and weak because a feeding tube had been down my throat.

While combing a mass of tangles out of my long fine hair, Wendy casually asked if I remembered talking to some guy.

"Yes," I said cautiously, as a vague recollection came to mind. "I remember talking to a man I didn't know. I think I told him to tell Wendy I was going to be okay."

My niece smiled. "A few days after you were hospitalized, one of the guys at work asked me if I knew someone named Susan. I told him my Aunt Susan was in the hospital in Vancouver fighting for her life after suffering a burst aneurysm. He said that someone named Susan had visited his dream the night before and asked him to tell Wendy that she was going to be okay."

I gasped and tried to make sense of this extraordinary occurrence. *How was this possible? How had I contacted Wendy's coworker? Did an angel help me find a soul that was open to receiving a telepathic message? Did I have an out of body experience? If I did, how did I know whom to contact?* (I still don't remember any other details, and have never met her coworker and my messenger. I confess to still being curious, but remain grateful for the unexplainable communication that may have eased my family's worry.)

Two days later, after my sister and nieces left, I'm told I became extremely impatient and frustrated. Apparently, I carried on like a child, throwing tantrums and raging that I wanted to go home. I later learned that following a head trauma, people tend to be argumentative, angry and downright difficult. Obviously, I did nothing to dispel this notion. Having a shared history wrought with fervid and frequent arguments, I understood when poor Liam had a hard time not taking it personally. However, from what I remember he mostly managed to remain patient and kind, likely because he was relieved I was recovering.

Three weeks after the aneurysm burst, on November 17th, my thirty-ninth birthday, I was discharged from the hospital, feeling exhausted, but excited and anxious to get back to Prince George. After our long drive home, my kids and Brenda greeted me with hugs and kisses, then helped me up the stairs to the main level of our house. As everyone fussed about making sure I was comfortable, I felt both loved and relieved. *Home...finally.*

The normalcy of being home was bliss. After school, Robin and Brandie would sit on my bed, sometimes with a friend, and take turns telling me about their day. Throughout my recovery, they kept me buoyed with love, as did my many visitors who came by with warm wishes, gifts and flowers. Often too weak to socialize for long, I would go back to bed, leaving Liam and the kids to entertain our company. It was always nice to listen to their happy voices as I drifted off.

Incessantly fatigued, I slept through much of each day. With the exceptions of coffee, bread and tomato soup, meals were barely tolerable as most food literally tasted like mushrooms or dirt. Aside from possibly hurting Liam's feelings, it didn't really matter to me, however, because my appetite was nonexistent. I later learned my doctors had been concerned because food tasting like mushrooms and dirt is a warning sign of a pending stroke.

Standing in front of a mirror one day, I was disturbed by my image. I was bone skinny and my legs had atrophied. To facilitate surgery, much of my lovely long hair had been shaved off the back of my head. Thankfully, when my hair was down, you couldn't see the baldness. In the hospital, Liam had taken pictures of the tongue-shaped sutured flap on the back of my head. Viewing the photos didn't disturb me; however, they certainly bothered others, often eliciting exclamations of horror.

Perhaps because it was all he could do to help, while various medical professionals sought to save my life, Liam kept a journal. I can't remember how far along in my recovery it was that I propped myself up in bed on a snowy winter day, a coffee on the nightstand, and began to read. His diary was enlightening, because between passing out at the optometrist's office and November 11th, I remembered nothing.

Liam's Journal: Wednesday, October 26, 1994

"Things haven't been going very good for the both of us. Once again, we argued over something. Something because the reason we argue isn't the important thing to remember, but that we do argue."
Liam's opening words hurt my heart. He was facing the possibility of losing me, and the first thing he wrote was about our never-ending fighting. Since the reason we had met for lunch on that fateful day was to make up, I could understand why he would start with such a blatantly honest statement. But logic and facts aside, reading it made me incredibly sad. I wondered, "We love each other so much, why can't we get along?" Thrusting the troublesome thought away, I skipped over the bit about meeting for lunch and kept reading.

"At approximately 3:10 I received a phone call from Joan (an acquaintance and the receptionist at the optometrist's office) *advising that Sue was having severe headaches and was vomiting. She phoned 911 and an ambulance was there to take her to the hospital. Brandie arrived home shortly after the phone call and we went to the hospital emergency and they took me to see Sue."*
Pausing, my sorrowful ponderings became about my loved ones and what they'd been through. Waking up to learn that I'd nearly died was disconcerting, but it must have been terrifying for everyone else to live through the possibility of losing me—especially, Robin and Brandie.

"She was being assisted in her breathing with a manual ventilator. Talked to the doctor on duty who advised that Sue had a cardiac arrest while in the ambulance and had to be revived." (Later, I was told that I had actually arrested twice. The second time, moments before I was revived, they were ready to pronounce time of death.)
Reading that I'd nearly died but was revived made me realize how lucky I was to still be around. I set Liam's diary aside for a moment and concentrated on my blessings. There I was, snuggled up in a warm bed, out of the frostiness of the winter wind howling about our house, as the man I loved stayed close at hand in case I needed anything. In

a few hours, my kids would arrive, and after they shared their stories, we'd all have dinner. Closing my eyes, I silently thanked God.

"A cat-scan was done and they are sure that there is bleeding in the brain. Not sure it's an aneurysm, however, all indications and symptoms would appear that it was the probable cause of her headaches and vomiting. They have phoned Vancouver General to see if she can be flown down to their neurological ward, as the PG hospital is unable to treat an aneurysm attack, only to try and stabilize the patient. Received word that there is room at VGH and the air ambulance has been ordered and should be arriving around 7:00 p.m."

His journal further detailed how my family had been informed about my condition. It broke my heart to read about how my son's buddy had located Robin at his volleyball practice and taken him to the hospital. The more I realized the suffering of my loved ones, the more my emotions vacillated: sometimes, I was ecstatic to have survived; other times, I was sad to have put my family through so much.

"Plane had not arrived at 7 p.m. and staff was checking to see where it was. Winds were really strong that day and, therefore, I was worried that they couldn't fly. Sue by this time was heavily sedated to make sure she stayed still and to kill the pain. It's now a waiting game to see if the plane arrived and got her to Vancouver before anything else happened. Doctor warned that although the bleeding had apparently stopped, Sue was still in danger of bleeding again without warning. He was trying to give some comfort in saying that in 50% of the cases, the patient dies before reaching the hospital. They can see blood on the brain from the X-Rays however don't know where the bleeding is coming from."

Other than several times mentioning being worried, Liam's reporting of events didn't include any actual outpouring of emotions. Many times, imagining the fears and tears of others, I'd weep. When reading became too much to bear, I'd stop and listen to the comforting sounds of Liam puttering around the house, washing dishes, tidying up, or watching the news. Just as when he'd decided to keep a journal for me, he was doing whatever he could to help.

"Finally, the paramedics arrived at approximately 10:00 and they started to prepare Sue to be transported to Vancouver. It took about one-half an hour and they left the hospital around 10:30. I was worried about the turbulent weather (they said they were bucking 180 Km/hr winds around Williams Lake) and what the added air pressure would do to the aneurysm in Sue's brain. They said that they would be flying lower to keep the pressure down."

According to the journal, my brother Dale was working out of town when I fell ill. Kindly, his employer immediately flew him to Vancouver. He actually beat me to the hospital. Liam and my children's lengthy drive from Prince George to Vancouver began around 11:45 p.m. As cell phones weren't common in 1994, to check on my condition, they had to find a phone booth. Worried, they stopped in many little towns to call the hospital, each time learning that I was stable.

Liam's Journal: Thursday, October 27, 1994

"Arrived at Vancouver General Hospital at exactly 8:45 in the morning. Sue was in the Intensive Care Unit of Emergency Ward. Heavily sedated and lots of intravenous stuff. They were waiting to make sure she was "hooked up" properly before moving her to the Neurological ICU on the fifth floor. Met Dale and now it was a waiting game. Doctors were performing their examination to determine exactly what the problem(s) were. Later she was moved to the fifth floor and we were told by Dr. Turnbull that he was pretty sure it was an aneurysm and that an angiogram would be performed on Friday morning to determine where it was and if there were any more to be found. Visited with Sue the rest of the day and left after 10:00 p.m. for Jean's. (Liam's sister) *Hadn't slept for 39 hours."*

I shuddered, realizing how dangerous their drive down could have been. What had begun as a medical emergency for me could have resulted in a tragic accident involving Liam and my kids.

Liam's Journal: Friday, October 28 to Sunday, October 30, 1994

"Dr. Durity conferred with all of us that afternoon. He advised that the Aneurysm was located in the left rear of the brain and that the good news is that there is only one aneurysm and it isn't bleeding at present.

Its location was a surface artery located in the rear left part of the brain. Durity was scheduled to do the operation and that early Sunday morning had been reserved. If there is a simpler operation to perform a surface artery is but the location also causes problems."

Liam went on to explain the risks and potential complications of repairing a ruptured aneurysm. Ostensibly, though 'crude' by today's medical standards, the procedure's success rate was reasonable. However, the doctor was concerned about my lungs as I was a smoker.

According to Liam's diary, my sister Deborah and her husband Ed arrived from Alberta early Friday morning. They and the rest of my family visited throughout the weekend, mostly staying quiet so I could rest, and often holding my hands. Semi-coherent, I seemed to recognize everyone, but couldn't remember anything from the prior day.

My surgery was scheduled for early Sunday morning, but was postponed. Around noon, a nurse called Liam and asked him to return to the hospital as I was agitated and uncooperative. He was able to calm me down, and shortly afterward, I was transported to the operating room.

It was 9:30 Sunday evening when Dr. Durity gave Liam the news that the surgery was successful: my motor functions had returned and my eyes were responsive. However, my lungs were only working at forty-percent capacity.

Delirious for many days following my operation, I was unable to grasp being in Vancouver, not Prince George. I was also angry, because though they were often by my side, a short while after my family would leave, I couldn't remember anyone visiting.

Whenever Liam asked about my excruciating headaches, fever and extreme agitation, the nurses could only advise him to be patient... these things take time.

It's never easy to see someone you love lying in a hospital bed with tubes everywhere and no promise that everything will eventually be okay. Reading what he'd written, it was evident that Liam bore a heavy burden and endured much worry during my hospital stay.

Both of us thankful that I'd survived, and me incredibly grateful for Liam's attentive care in the hospital and at home, for a few weeks our relationship improved. It no longer seemed important who was right or wrong—we both understood that life was capricious, fleeting and precious.

In addition to reading and rereading Liam's diary, I struggled to accept that I'd almost died. Typical for head trauma survivors, my moods fluctuated unpredictably, extremely and frequently. One minute, I was content to sit quietly by myself in gratitude. The next, a wave of despair would whirl through my confused mind, and I'd bawl like a baby. My frustration with sporadic memory recall, being physically weak and totally dependent on others, elicited either more tears or spurts of grumbled complaints.

A week or so into my at-home recovery, when my eldest sister and her daughters arranged a party in my honor, I insisted on going. Fearing I was too weak and would likely make myself sicker, Liam argued that I wasn't yet well enough to leave the house. Of course, my wishes prevailed—and of course, he was right. A few days later I was sick.

Understandably, after a month of playing nursemaid, Liam's frustration surfaced, and once again, we resumed arguing about everything. For weeks he'd been faithfully keeping house, cooking and administering my suppository and oral medications. (Not exactly what he'd envisioned when we'd so blatantly flirted with one another on that hot summer day when we met.) Despite his great care, I couldn't keep food or fluids in my system and became dangerously dehydrated. In the midst of our series of daily verbal battles, I was admitted to the Prince George Hospital, where I remained for several days.

Incensed that he'd bothered fighting with me in my weakened state, Liam's visits with me at the hospital were mostly spent in uneasy silence. When I returned home, persistently exhausted, I slept the majority of each day. Liam, unable to endure much more, began accusing me of malingering on purpose, saying that I was lazy and didn't need to spend so much time sleeping.

When strong enough, I'd defend myself against his absurd accusations. When too weak to care, I simply ignored him. Hurt that he didn't understand, and too sick to truly consider how my lengthy recovery was affecting him, I often just buried my head under the covers and cried myself back to sleep.

By mid-December, I was finally able to stay awake for a few hours at a time. Deborah and Ed came for a visit from Alberta, and thanks to the use of a wheelchair and my mother's walker, I was able to go

Christmas shopping. Eternally grateful to be alive and well enough to celebrate the holidays with family and friends, each hug and burst of laughter was precious beyond measure. For one memorable (thank God) week, we were a normal, happy family.

Though it's never been quite as keen, my short-term memory gradually returned, as did the normal flavor of most food. Chocolate was the last taste to return, and was delightfully celebrated during the summer of 1996 when I devoured a Fudgsicle. (Now that I'm battling middle age weight gain, I sometimes wonder if it might not have been better if chocolate had continued to taste yucky.)

Further along in my recovery, through research, I discovered just how incredibly lucky I was to have survived a ruptured cerebral aneurysm without any notable residual side effects. I felt truly blessed. It was as if I'd won the lottery—a second chance to live the remainder of my life happily and with purpose. I knew it was time to edit my personal story.

There is a wonderfully profound quote by Rabbi H. Schachtel that I'd seen on a poster during a much earlier stay in the hospital when I'd suffered a stress-induced emotional breakdown: "Happiness is not having what you want, but wanting what you have." The quandary was—how should I apply this truism to my own life?

For the following few months, through journaling and talking with close friends and family, I searched for *my* truths, desires and needs. Being brutally honest about what needed scrapping, changing and nurturing in my life wasn't easy; especially, where Liam was concerned. *Were Liam and I capable of setting our relationship on a more positive and loving course?* I doubted it. *Had the continual stress of our fighting contributed to my getting sick?* Research said stress could be a factor. *Was it fair to me or my children to remain in a rocky relationship that robbed my joy and might well lead to another lengthy illness?* No, it wasn't fair to my children, me or Liam. *If the day my aneurysm burst had been my last, would how I felt on that particular day be something my soul would regret or treasure?* My answer was that I wanted to leave earth peacefully happy, not on the heels of a perpetual roller-coaster of highs and lows.

Gratitude was a major theme throughout my ponderings. I was grateful to God for letting me continue my journey so that I could enjoy my life and children. I was grateful for the constant and loving devotion shown by Liam while I was in the hospital. And grateful for my niece telling me about her coworker who I'd somehow contacted while in a coma. Apparently, I told Dale about a bright light at the end of a tunnel and feelings of tremendous love and peace. Though I don't recall that encounter, it must be registered deep within my subconscious for I've lost my fear of death.

Unable to allow Liam to continue shouldering our financial obligations, I returned to work; albeit, too soon health-wise. A few more months passed before I was strong enough to deal with both working and addressing the dreaded ending of life with Liam. The one thing I had wanted most from him, during our tumultuous relationship of breakup-after-breakup, was a commitment. It's sadly ironic that once he did commit, what I thought would bring abundant joy instead brought the exact opposite.

Mustering the courage to end our relationship took a while. One day, I'd cling to the great times and rationalize that he'd been such a prince during my initial recovery. The next, I'd fume about our latest argument. Some days, I'd just ignore him, hoping he'd somehow just disappear and the problem would be solved.

Of course, telling Liam I was finished with us, brought about another argument—putting the proverbial last nail in the coffin that had once seemed my life raft. Though a wrenching decision that shattered my heart and sickened my gut, through our flooding tears, I stood firm. To stay in the chaotic craziness we'd co-created would lead to a slow death. The idea of leaving him nearly killed me too; however, I clung to the hope that I'd eventually heal emotionally and be able to live peacefully happy.

It took almost a year to sell our house. As neither of us could afford to buy separate residences without first getting the equity from our mutually-owned home, we continued living together. Mostly we coexisted in cold silence. However, there were occasional fights and a few reconciliation attempts on Liam's part.

Confused, stressed and hurting, during that year I mourned the loss of my ex-husband. Having found joy with Liam soon after my divorce, I hadn't allowed myself time to grieve the loss of my marriage. With my sorrow came questions about whether I'd made the right decision in leaving my husband and musings of wanting him back. In the end, I realized that second-guessing my decision to divorce was part of the painful process of letting go.

Once our house sold, we started packing our belongings and looking for separate places. It was then that, like Liam, I started to wonder if maybe we should reconcile. One day, as we held each other, through sobs, I told him, "I don't *want* to never see you again!" It broke my heart to let go of the man I loved more than anything. But staying together broke my heart too. After many tears and sorrowful conversations, we each moved into new homes. We continued to see each other for a while, slowly releasing the love we felt but were unable to mesh into a happy union. In time, our eleven-year love affair came to an end.

My cute little house in Prince George became my haven. For the next several years, my children and first grandson filled our home with love. Determined to learn how to live in peaceful happiness, I devoured self-help books, meditated and practiced positive affirmations. Sometimes, I'd look in the mirror and say over and over, "You are beautiful. You are smart. I love you." Whenever I did or said something I regretted and automatically started chastising myself, I stopped, and instead would say, "I made a mistake that I want to correct. What do I need to do to right this misstep?"

Through my studies and reflections, I began to appreciate the little things I'd previously taken for granted. I hung onto such blessings as sliding into bed between freshly laundered sheets and the amazing fresh feeling of toweling off after a shower. When something annoying happened, I learned to laugh it off, instead of dwelling on it. Over time, I realized that what happens to us throughout life isn't as important as how we interpret events—the *power* we give to the good and the bad.

Positive interpretation of events, allowed me to stop mourning the loss of my relationship with Liam and to fondly remember and appreciate the time we did spend together. Living in appreciation of what was, instead of regretting what I'd lost, I became more content with myself and life without him.

Further realizing that we each have the power to decide how we feel, I *decided* to be happy and set about doing things that brought me joy. Toward the end of 1998, I began dating again. It was healing for me to be able to express my feelings to a man without sparking a fight.

It was freeing to encourage someone I was dating to express his feelings without taking anything negative he said as a personal affront. It was exciting to discover that I'd finally learned how to have a healthy, loving relationship.

When people learn of my ruptured brain aneurysm, they often comment that it must have been very difficult for me. My reply is always that I wasn't even aware that I nearly died; however, it was extremely difficult for my loved ones. People also say things such as *that must have been the worst thing that ever happened to you.* In response, I smile and say, "No, almost dying was one of the *best* things that ever happened to me. It gave me a much needed kick in the butt to change my life. It was as if God saw that I wasn't paying attention to what he was trying to show me, so He went Zap! You're dead!"

A corner in my heart will always belong to Liam. However, I've put aside memories of the fighting and hurt feelings, choosing to remember only the love, tenderness, happiness, and pure joy that we once shared. Doing so, allows me to treasure an elusive dream without feeling hurt, or as though my life is lacking. I suppose we could have avoided all the pain of our relationship and consequential breakup if we'd never gotten together, but that would have meant missing one of the best adventures of my life.

Perhaps the *true* 'love of my life' has still to come along. Regardless, I will continue to live happily—in gratitude for what I have, and for whatever gifts will unfold. I have amazing children, great children-in-law, and absolutely fantastic grandchildren. I'm healthy and my path is going forward in ever-increasing love and financial abundance. I am blessed. And, as my family sometimes reminds me, since my attitude and gratitude shifted, I'm now a laughing and happy person. I love my life.

Note: Throughout this chapter, letters from my children and diary entries from Liam are quoted exactly as written. Editing their spelling, grammar and punctuation choices would diminish the authenticity of my story.

Escape from the Green Room

Arnold Vingsnes

Images of my worthless butt hurtling like a broken twig along Vancouver's mean streets, I coiled beneath the prickly gray blankets of my much too short cot, listening to the winter storm claw and screech with undulating fury. Even the meager shelter of the windowless closet-sized Green Room would soon be outside my financial reach. *How in the world did I end up here? What happened to ME?*

I primarily blamed my miserable predicament on sporadic employment and ignorant financial decisions with me starring victim mid-center. In truth, it was infinitely more complicated. Although, during the initial moments I'm about to share, I found comfort in faulting outward, not inward.

It was either her sparkling wide eyes, the come hither allure hedging her girl-next-door smile, or the elation from being suddenly smitten, but whatever the reason, I blurted out, "I love sex!" mid polite introductory exchanges. Immediately regretting that my mouth had commandeered my brain and *manners*, and suddenly feeling as confident as a virgin teenager, I stifled a gasp. Had I actually said *that?*

What was surely the sweetness of romance victory dancing across her face, she coyly tilted her head as her brow lifted amusedly. Relieved that she hadn't slapped my face and run off, or denied enjoying my favorite sport—she suddenly owned my heart. A few months later we were common-law partners.

It wasn't her, but the employment events of 2008 onward, coupled with spats of depression that strangled and then killed our love; especially, when I found a second home at the casino.

"Where have you been?" she'd often ask, narrowing her brown-eyed gaze. "Have you been gambling again?"

"Of course not!" was always my incredulous reply. "How come you're always questioning me about where I've been? Don't you trust me?"

Silly, silly man!

In late 2009, we were both looking forward to a change in residence. As moving day approached, I snuck off to the casino to celebrate. That evening she confronted me, and as usual, I denied everything.

"But Arnold, I saw you there with my own eyes. How can you deny it?" she questioned, betrayal and hurt flashing first, then anger.

Glancing downward, I shook my shameful head, mentally preparing a defense of *How dare you spy on me!*

It was a weak and never voiced vindication, for without further discussion my love informed me, "Arnold, you are not welcome in our new home, and neither will you be allowed to stay there until you find somewhere else to live."

Well, that got my attention—real quick!

Begrudgingly, I accepted her decision, and relocated myself to the couch for the next couple of nights. Foolishly, I thought, "She'll change her mind because she knows I've no place to go." WRONG!

New Year's Eve 2009 was moving day. The weather mirrored my homeless horror: bone chilling, gusty southeast wind and stinging rain. Borrowing a truck from a friend that immediately broke down, some six hundred dollars later I helped my partner move into her new home. *Minus me, would she be happy or miserable?*

Exhausted, drenched and damn cold, I hauled my weary butt into the borrowed truck and drove away eyes forward. I didn't need to glimpse in the rearview mirror to know that my purpose for being was about to disappear.

Hours later, checked into a flea-bitten hotel on skid row in East Vancouver, staring out the grimy window at the long forgotten souls in the alley, terror struck. *How long before I was inextricably drawn within their miserable and hopeless midst?* Knocked down more times than an amateur boxer, I had my doubts that my view from above would last much longer. Certainly, none of those below had anticipated their lot; more likely, they were victims of direly consequential life-choices.

Unwilling to remain lodged one floor above permanent nowhere, between employment rejections I hunted for acceptable and cheap accommodation. Through luck and prayer, a mid-January ad search turned up an ideally located room for rent: on bus route, shops nearby, furnished, seven hundred per month, utilities included.

Off I went to check out this nugget; however, what I walked into wasn't even fool's gold: twelve-by-fourteen square feet, was once part of a garage, no window, drab prison-green walls, mattress on the floor, writing desk and chair, and closet with a TV perched atop. Oh, yes, it came with a shared kitchen and bathroom. I took it! And so it was that, for the next six months, the *Green Room* became my place of refuge and torment.

Distancing myself from family and friends, I set about righting my shipwrecked life. I needed an income, but employment opportunities were scarce. No one was looking for an ex-captain or ex-union leader. Nor were they interested in an aging fossil now in his late fifties, regardless of credentials or experience. It was the worst global recessionary period since the Great Depression, and despite dozens of interviews, I remained one of the crisis-fraught unemployed. Enduring endless job rejections, emotional darkness shrank the Green Room into a cavernous hell.

Where the bejesus had my life gone? Previously, I'd literally captained my own destiny! On more than one occasion, I'd saved my crew's butt. Once, on a delivery job to Guatemala, some ten miles off the coast of El Salvador, staring through binoculars at a Salvadoran warship readying their guns, it was my order to quickly raise the Canadian flag that averted a devastating fate. Our flag having been taken down so that it wasn't ripped to shreds in the gusting winds, the stern of our barge boldly emblazoned with its country of registry as Guatemala, we were suddenly the meat sandwiched between two neighboring countries' territorial dispute. That white-knuckle adventure, and a few others that followed, taxed my nerve and skill to the max; yet, each time I met the challenge. *I had brass and brains, so why couldn't I find a damn job?*

Oh, how I missed my love's quick smile and easy laughter. She'd been right to kick me out on my sorry butt, but realizing that bit of truthful debris didn't matter a blessed bit. Neither did endless hours of *if only I had or hadn't* contemplations. I was on a barren island of my own making. Regardless that there were many friends who'd gladly lend a helping hand, having run my life ashore, it was up to me to reset its course. Pride was the one shipmate I would not surrender.

Entombed in the hideous Green Room by night, and daily jeered by the miserable coastal winter, dwindling finances and joblessness—

suicide seemed my obvious savior. *But how best to kill myself? What if I survived maimed or in a vegetative state, trapped more than I was already?* Stalled by visions of a fate worse than the one currently endured, alter-coursed, hopeful thinking generally followed. *I'm tough, still alive and capable. I'll make it through this bleep-bleep mess. I have to!*

Perhaps spurned by the sweet sounds and smells of spring, like a shapeless fog enshrouding a distant ship, slowly, the true Arnold emerged through the mist. A long time ago, my idealistic purpose had become material centered. *I'd sold out to the man* as my back then hippy sisters and brothers would say. The recession was not at the root of my situation...chasing the elusive almighty buck was! The true me had vanished decades earlier when I'd exchanged my ideals for status.

Shored by the remembrance of a younger more idealistic self, and aware that I was still regarded by most as a trustworthy, influential and high-ranking trade union official, hope dawned. *Being jobless didn't equate with being worthless.* I was still a take charge, detail oriented, and get-things-done kinda guy. All that was missing was gainful employment.

Looking back, resigning my trade organization position (great pay, executive health plan, company vehicle, etc.) *hadn't* permanently skewed my life, it had furtively reset my compass homeward bound— albeit, only after a three-year-long stint in life's boxing ring.

Round One began in 2008 as a direct result of a questionable order from an executive officer to hire his young inexperienced offspring as a full-fledged union representative. Initially, I refused my superior's nepotistic demand. His rigid response, *"Arnold, you are going to hire my son, and that's all there is to it!"* Reluctantly, on that Friday, I brought the young lad in for a mock interview with myself and our office manager, and hired him.

When I arrived at work Monday morning, the executive officer stormed about my office cursing a blue streak and threatening me with physical harm. Although untrue, his son had apparently told his father that I'd treated him poorly during the interview and that he'd never work for me or the trade organization. Fists balled at the end of his stubby arms, bits of spit flying about, my superior bellowed, "You *#@*! I'll get even with you for this, mark my words!"

Mouth gaped wide, I watched as he marched from office-to-office repeating his threat. I hadn't mistreated his son, as the office manager who sat through the entire process could attest. Whatever had transpired between the two of them, I'd somehow become the young lad's scapegoat for not accepting the job offered—perhaps, he knew better than to accept work in the same office as his *rageaholic* father.

Having had enough of these kinds of theatrics, I tendered my notice of resignation with the generous concession that I'd stay until a suitable replacement was found.

Round Two: A few months later. Having advanced through the ranks, my unintentional nemesis stormed into my office and delivered his revenging swipe, "Arnold, I've commissioned a forensic audit of the books. I know there's been monkey business with the money, and for your sake, I hope you're clean!"

"What?" I stammered incredulously, unable to believe my ears. I'd been in charge of the books for years and prided myself on keeping them accurate and current. *Whatever was he talking about?*

"You heard me," he returned huffily.

"Listen, you *#@hole! I have nothing to hide. I welcome your audit. And by the way, I no longer care that you haven't found a suitable replacement for me. I quit!"

Several months and a rumored three hundred thousand dollars in audit costs later, the findings were that there *hadn't* been any fiddling with the funds. However, as quickly as this was determined, the documentation proving my innocence mysteriously vanished.

Although confident from the get-go that nothing was amiss, I confess that it was a troubling time. But at least it was over, or so I thought.

Round Three: Unemployed, I turned my attention toward kick-starting a Canadian Ship's Officer Recruitment Program for youth. Since meeting several years earlier, an international ship owner and I had been in ongoing discussions about such an initiative. With the ever-increasing retirement of baby boomers, the shipping community was suffering a manpower shortage, and in the summer of 2008 our conversations moved toward becoming a reality. Unaware of the calamity that would soon rear its ugly head, I flew to the Philippines for a weeklong set of meetings with ship owners and their representatives from South East Asia.

Delighted to be bumped to business class, I tucked into my personal cocoon for the journey across the Pacific. When I arrived at 5:30 a.m., my jetlag temporarily vanished as a driver holding a placard bearing my name greeted me and then whisked me off to my hotel in style. *Life in the fast lane, gotta love it.* Just as I settled in for a nap, the phone rang summoning me to an unscheduled meeting.

Eager, excited and confident, I stepped outside into the blaring heat, quickly realizing that my suit and tie attire was probably a bad choice, but it was too late to change. Arriving at the office bedraggled and sweaty, but thankful for the air-conditioned waiting area, I paced until ushered into a boardroom. A few minutes into our discussion, I learned that the shipping industry had taken a recessionary downward spiral. Owners were losing cargoes and fortunes by the hour. Consequently, the Ship's Officer Recruitment Program wasn't even discussed. My Manila business trip disappointedly collapsed amid the unfolding era of global uncertainty and market chaos.

Round Four: Begrudgingly accepting that retiring wasn't an option, I flew back to Canada, shoring my disappointment with waning hopeful thinking. *Everyone in the industry back home knows me, so surely there is something waiting for me. I'll just have to search it out.*

Managing to secure a ten-month contract, I was lulled into a renewed sense of security. But as quickly as salvation arrived, it disappeared. Suddenly and unexpectedly, the company president departed for greener pastures and my contract was immediately canceled. By then the global recession was in full swing and employment opportunities scarce.

Round Five: Since my departure, my former employer/nemesis and the newly hired Secretary Treasurer had orchestrated a Smear Arnold Campaign. Obviously, I'd become the scapegoat for the three hundred thousand dollars spent on the audit that had mysteriously disappeared. Rumor had it that I was still being accused of having mismanaged union funds, was solely responsible for an array of missing financial statements, and had stolen the office photocopiers under the cloak of darkness.

When told of the marks on my reputation and honor, stunned mute, I merely shook my head. *Are they bleeping kidding me? When I left the organization the books were in order. Stolen photocopiers, what the hell was that about?*

As time moved forward, their relentless Machiavellian campaign eventually became fairly effective, and some previous disbelievers of any wrongdoings on my part were swayed against me. It was as though I were a lone tree in the center of an advancing winter storm—what began as a swaying of a few branches, gradually became a crescendo of many accusers twisting in an uncontrolled frenzy, eerily moaning in unison, *That Arnold's a traitor; we'll get him!*

My patience waning along with my reputation, I composed a letter demanding specifics regarding all accusations. There was no response to my letter; instead, a Supreme Court action was filed ordering me to produce ten-year-old receipts that had long been properly discarded. *They were certainly creative in their quest to discredit me.* Fortunately, once my counsel relayed our intention to sue for character defamation and libelous accusations, as well as legal costs should their action fail, their court filing was immediately withdrawn.

Knockout Round: Angry and wanting my now blemished reputation restored, I decided to make good on my threat to sue. Unfortunately, four different lawyers offered the same legal opinion: "Sure, file an action. But first, we require a twenty-five-thousand-dollar retainer, and the best you can expect is an award of between twenty-five and thirty thousand dollars. And, of course, there's no guarantee of securing an apology when all the smoke clears." The answer to my question, "Cost-wise, what am I looking at realistically?" settled my deliberations. Should I proceed, my legal fees would likely amount to between fifty and one hundred thousand dollars! I forfeited the fight.

Deliverance in the Green Room

My reputation brutally battered into joblessness, coupled with my love's eviction, made the early days in the Green Room seem bleaker than death. I was damaged goods. My place within familiar circles that I'd once taken for granted was barred shut. Pondering my expelled fate, optimism plummeted one second and then rebounded the next, making my life an extreme rollercoaster of highs and lows.

Despite the Green Room's solitary bleakness, its confines slowly emerged as a quiet place, where alone with my thoughts and reflections, I could begin to weigh my options with circumstances. Toward the end of my stay there, the windowless room became a space shuttle, my place of reentry into life. But I didn't find liberation alone—deliverance came as a result of unexpected and unfamiliar territory, without which I firmly believe I would have remained lost.

In 2010, I sought professional counseling. Being an 'I can deal with my issues myself, thank you very much' kinda guy, helping others was much easier than accepting help. As a result, I resisted the counselor at every step. Breaking through my barriers a near impossible task until she one day asked, *"You're testing me, aren't you?"*

Well, that woke me up. Somewhat embarrassed, I confessed, "Yes, I have been."

Back in the Green Room, knowing it would require full disclosure and cooperation on my part, I pondered whether to continue with counseling. My conclusion was that I'd never before closed the door on something simply because it was new, and decided to go for it.

By becoming a participant, rather than an antagonistic observer, counseling brought release, wisdom and hope. It wasn't always easy, but with her skilled assistance and support, I worked through many interesting and often challenging issues. Although I'll never forget their actions, I succeeded in forgiving my ex-boss and those who'd rallied against me. Most importantly, I became reacquainted with my beliefs, skills and goals. Feeling confident and back in charge of my destiny, both the need for further counseling and my depression came to an end.

A renewed, wiser Arnold at the wheel, I contacted my love in hopes of rekindling our friendship. After some prodding, she agreed that although both of our hearts had been broken via my actions, there was much to be gained by staying connected. We began seeing each other occasionally, and though it saddened me to have lost a good woman, I was grateful to again have her friendship.

Next on my Move Forward List was somewhere decent to live. During a barbeque with friends, I learned our host had just bought an apartment that was now for rent. Intrigued, I checked it out: two bedrooms, a bathroom, kitchen with a dishwasher, dining room, living room, and, a balcony—all the comforts of a real home. Still unemployed, risking what remained of my retirement portfolio, I moved into the apartment more determined than ever to find work.

Summer bled into fall, then winter, and I was still unemployed. *Oh-oh, what now?* My finances were nearing nil, so I was more than a tad nervous. Counseling, however, had reawakened my lifelong sense of optimism, and although every door I knocked on went unanswered, I simply persevered with the belief something would materialize.

In February, tired of avoiding creditors, I considered giving notice to vacate my apartment and consulted a bankruptcy trustee. Short of winning the lottery, there was no way for me to meet my financial obligations. I left the trustee's office humbled, not broken. A scant year earlier, contemplating bankruptcy would likely have driven me over the edge.

The next day, I left a voicemail message for a potential employer I'd briefly met some years earlier, and suggested it might be mutually beneficial for us to have a chat. I didn't really expect to hear back from him, but lo and behold he returned my call! Our brief telephone exchange led to an informal chitchat, and then a ten month part-time consulting contract. As of January 2012 the consulting arrangement turned into an employment agreement.

At this moment, I don't have a mountain of savings. Perhaps, I don't even have that many more years to work, or live. But what I *do* have is abundant optimism and a peaceful coexistence with myself, my former common-law partner, friends, and family—all precious commodities that were almost lost.

Through counseling, I realized that although exploring my inner self honestly and openly was difficult, it was invaluable. I now know that even when absolutely everything seems sunken, lost or out of reach, it doesn't have to remain as such. The *mind* tends to be at the helm of many a plight; fortunately, with a few tweaks, it can greatly right a skewed course. When desperation or depression sets in, professional help is not only available, it's necessary. However, for counseling to be effective, an open mind is a definite prerequisite. Forever forward, when confronted with difficult decisions, challenges and even roadblocks, I'll view them as gifts that may very well hold the keys to a happier self.

The need for shelter, warmth and food necessitates that I continue to participate in a materially-centered world. However, with an unwavering mindset of hope, forgiveness and self-accountability, my path forward is much clearer. It would be easy to blame my Green Room circumstances on outward influences, but that would be a copout. The reality is that how we each *interpret* and *react* to events directly influence our individual choices and resulting circumstances. By exercising self-accountability, one maintains control of his or her unique destiny.

Some who read my story will conclude that the accumulation of numerous extraordinary and unpleasant events over a three year period—the breakup of my romantic relationship, instantly becoming homeless, losing my life's savings, dwelling in the Green Room, being accused of theft and fiddling with the union's books, employment slaughter by libel and slander, two Supreme Court actions, and filing for bankruptcy—would be too much for any man to handle. Well, it was a bit too much. As humans, though, it is sometimes necessary to persevere in spite of adversity, which is much easier when we remain true to ourselves. The alternative would be to give up, which I would never recommend.

As unpleasant as it was, without the Green Room experience, and all that befell me before and afterward, my life would have continued in a mindless direction much like the proverbial ship without a rudder, sailing aimlessly into troubled and uncertain waters. Although I almost succumbed to depression, I mustered the inner-determination to push on with my life and accept responsibility for the choices *I'd* made.

If you are at what you believe is *the end*, don't give up—it's merely a crossroad. Problems are simply issues in search of solutions—solutions that can be found by looking within, remembering who you are at your core, and pushing ahead with optimism as your personal guide. All things are possible so long as you remain true to your values, others and self. As with me, sometimes you may have to rediscover or redefine your truths until you realize that your fate was always and remains forever in your hands, no one else's.

Tears in my Ears

Monica Forster

"I can't be pregnant!"

"I know it's not what you were expecting to hear."

Three weeks earlier such blessed news would have had my husband Brad and me dancing a jig in the streets, screaming our joy to the world so loudly the neighbors would have called the police. Receiving it today, three weeks after the diagnosis of my cancer, seemed a cruel joke. *Did God and the angels just sit around trying to figure out a way to break our hearts?*

"Monica, are you still there?" asked the woman on the other end of the phone, whose voice I vaguely recognized as being Julie's, my family doctor's senior nurse. "Your *HCG* hormone levels are low, so it's possible you're not pregnant. And if you are, there's time to decide what you want to do."

"Decide what?" I asked, my innards flopping about like a hooked fish gasping for its last breath. But I knew what she meant—abortion was an option. *Oh my God, how could she even suggest that? Didn't she know that Brad and I had been trying to have a baby for three years? Three years!*

"The doctor wants you to come in tomorrow or the next day for another pregnancy test," she continued caringly. "Which day would be better for you?"

"I'll call you back," I mumbled, too distracted to know what was on my calendar, other than a string of appointments for my Non-Hodgkin's Lymphoma pre-treatment workup, and the possible collection of my death warrant. The latter was on my mental calendar in big red letters.

"What the heck's going on?" my sister Maria asked, puzzlement in her pretty blue eyes as she walked into my house a few seconds later. Standing just inside the door and holding hands with her new boyfriend, she added, "I can't tell if you're happy, sad or scared."

"I'm pregnant," I screeched, relieved to have her there to share in the good news, as well as help push the bad to the back of my mind. "I'm pregnant! I'm pregnant!" I hollered repeatedly, jumping up and down and clapping like a make-believe child princess as I bounced around the living room.

"That's great!" Maria said, catching me between leaps for a hug. "Have you told Brad?"

"He's golfing, do you think I should call him?" I asked, suddenly sad that my longtime dream of announcing our conceived child over a romantic dinner of shrimp served atop diaper placemats, followed by a rattle filled with chocolates, would never happen. Like red wine and fish, cancer and baby announcements shouldn't be served together.

"Call him!" my sister urged, the grin on her face matching the one making my cheeks ache.

With all that had happened in the past few weeks, I knew Brad would answer his cell phone even if he was in the process of putting for a birdie or swinging for a three-hundred-yard shot. *But how much emotion could one man handle?* Recalling the pain in his trusting blue eyes when I was first diagnosed with the disease threatening my life, and how we'd cried for hours, just holding each other and weeping, I hesitated. He was my rock, but even rocks could be crushed into thousands of pieces. *What if it turned out I wasn't pregnant?* But I also knew he'd want to know and would be disappointed if he didn't get to immediately share in the great news—even if it turned out to be *temporary* great news.

Brad answered on the third ring. "Hi, Monica. What's up?"

"I know you can't sit down, but put your club down…I'm pregnant!" I blurted into the phone, imagining his head jerking forward like it always did when he was shocked.

There was a few seconds of silence before he hesitantly asked, "You're kidding, right?"

"Nope, not kidding," I said, my aching smile still wide.

"What about your —?" he started to ask, but changed his mind. "I'll be home soon, sweetheart. That's great news."

"I love you," I said, hanging up the phone and worrying. Would our baby survive my disease? Would I?

It was February 26th 1997, a day forever etched in our minds as the most bizarre and happiest since we'd committed to being partners for life. Ironically, it was on the heels of January 29th, the day we learned about my cancer, which was the most fearful day of our then four year marriage. What had for a month been a stupid joke intended to ease our worry—about how instead of having the baby we'd been desperately hoping for, we were having a bouncing baby lymphoma—came to a welcomed end. I didn't need a second pregnancy test to know I was carrying Brad's baby; just as, a few days earlier, I'd somehow known to cancel my scheduled chemotherapy.

I worked for the British Columbia Cancer Agency, and had often held a patient's hand, hoping he or she would beat the odds and survive the same insidious disease now plaguing my own body. I was aware that, with early treatment, across all types of Non-Hodgkin's Lymphoma, the survival rate was favorable. Unfortunately, at the time, my form of Non-Hodgkin's was diagnosed as incurable. Fortunately, the disease doesn't tend to run in families, so my diagnosis wasn't a pending threat to my five siblings or my unborn child.

My patient and friend Terry, who also had Non-Hodgkin's, died because he needed a bone marrow transplant and none of his relatives was a match. After six years, his body gave up the fight. When he passed, I cried buckets of tears. When cancer strikes, there's nowhere to run and nowhere to hide. The life you've taken for granted and imagined will expand into decades of laughter and memories, simply shortens and shrivels—the only thing making it seem long is the time you spend in worry and wonder.

When diagnosed, feeling fit and fine, grasping that I was sick didn't completely register. Neither did finding out that I was pregnant too. Both news bulletins had trouble finding a nest in my brain and in my heart. Through tests and biopsies, Brad held my hand, each of us sometimes reaching for humor to lighten our fear.

It was a month prior to finding out that we were pregnant, while waiting for a CT scan that the bouncing baby lymphoma joke popped out of my mouth; thankfully, causing my husband to laugh. It was a rare treat among weeks of crying.

"Monica Forster."

Jerking my head toward the technician, my heart thudded. After handing my purse to Brad and exchanging weak smiles, I headed into the CT scan room dreading the test I was about to undergo. *How many times had I reassured patients that there was nothing to this test?* It didn't hurt, and was the only way to be certain what was happening inside one's body. Though my blue hospital gown was flimsy, the room was warm, so why was I suddenly shaking like a thief facing down a guard dog?

"The test will take about half an hour," the technician explained, as I stared at the skinny motorized table that would slowly move me into the donut-shaped hole effacing the machine that would detect how far my disease had progressed. It was the only way to be certain if the cancer had metastasized throughout my body, or had been caught early enough for treatment to be effective.

Leading me toward the table, she further explained how important it was that I stay perfectly still. I don't know what else she might have said, because past that, I wasn't really listening. Dominating my thoughts was how much, since being diagnosed, I now dreaded being alone—and how dreadfully long a half hour was going to seem.

Sliding headfirst into what was surely to be a half hour of mental torture, thinking about my husband waiting for me just outside the room and our silly bouncing baby lymphoma joke, I started to cry. Big crocodile tears flooded and filled my ears as the machine whirled and whirred around me. *Would we still be able to have kids? If we did conceive, would I live long enough to watch them grow up? How would Brad manage having kids and a sick wife? Or worse yet, how would he survive with no wife at all should my disease kill me?*

Willing my tears to stop, just increased them in number and size. As each pair streamed down my temples, tickling as they meandered into one ear and then the other, unable to shudder, tilt my head sideways or wipe them away, I cried harder. Neither my unspoken repeated commands of *Stop crying, Monica* nor my begging *Oh, please stop crying,* ceased the flood. The tears in my ears pooled until they overflowed down my neck, announcing their exit with more tickling. *Oh, how long a half hour can seem.*

On February 14th, two weeks after being diagnosed with Lymphoma, Brad and I went on a trip to Harrison Hot Springs, which was about a two hour drive from where we lived in Greater Vancouver. It was my parents' fortieth wedding anniversary, and for four months prior we'd been busy creating a beautiful cardboard heart donning at least a hundred family pictures. Successfully sneaking Mom's photos out of her home was quite a feat. The heart was four feet wide and three feet tall. In the center was a photograph of Mom and Dad looking insanely happy on their wedding day. Surrounding them, in a circle, were baby pictures of their seven children spanning into photos of us at various ages. On the outer rim of the heart there were photos of their grandchildren, in-laws and outlaws. Every milestone and triumph was proudly displayed in grand celebration of their lasting love.

It was difficult to stay focused on a celebratory milestone that my husband and I were never likely to reach. Still, I hung in there, concentrating and helping when I could, resting and crying when I couldn't.

Brad, Maria and I checked into our shared hotel suite on Friday. After some typical sister bantering, she took the double bed in the attached bedroom and we flopped down on the king-sized bed in the living area.

Saturday February 15th, the anniversary of my parents' 1957 wedding, we celebrated with dozens of relatives and friends in the hotel's lovely Copper Room, famous for its great food and charming atmosphere. It was so nice seeing everyone dressed to the nines and happy. When we presented the heart to our parents after dinner, they both cried.

Later, having danced and laughed the night away along with our worries, Brad and I made love for the first time since I was diagnosed with Non-Hodgkin's Lymphoma.

I was booked for my first chemo treatment the following Friday morning, but couldn't bring myself to even get dressed. Having worked for the B.C. Cancer Agency for over two decades, and currently a secretary in the oncology department, I knew if I canceled it was too late to schedule someone else. Sitting at my kitchen table in my pink housecoat and slippers, calling friend after friend for advice they weren't qualified to supply, I tried to decipher the knot in my gut that had me immobilized. *Was I embarrassed being a patient under the care of doctors and nurses I knew personally, some of who had become friends? Was I afraid of the treatment?* Maybe, it was a bit of both; regardless, each time my head convinced me to go, my heart screamed NO DON'T! My heart won. Riddled with guilt and crying, I canceled my appointment.

Even in the most desperate of times, when all seems lost to a cruel twist of fate, the angels intervene. An oncologist at the cancer agency had prescribed birth control to ensure I wouldn't get pregnant during my chemotherapy treatments. Before taking it, I decided to check with my family doctor to ensure that the pill prescribed wasn't one that had caused complications for me in the past. My period was five days late, which wouldn't be abnormal considering the stress I'd been under, but to be absolutely certain, she ordered a pregnancy test. It was the very next day that her nurse called with the elating news.

As the news of my pregnancy spread around work, nearly every doctor at the agency made a point of visiting and chatting with me about my options, each of them delivering similar sentiments and information. It was understandable if I chose to have an abortion. It was possible that my pregnancy might put my cancer in remission. It was also possible that being pregnant would speed the disease. Basically, it was impossible to know how my body would react to the hormonal changes.

Workmates reacted in various ways: some with laughter, congratulations and hugs; others with sober faces that should be reserved for funerals. I received cheerful cards, bouquets of bright colorful flowers and sweet gifts. One of the nurses gave me a card with fawns on it that expressed the sentiment that God would bless my socks off for making the decision to keep the baby. *Decision! What decision?* My baby was a heaven sent gift—a miracle from above. *Why would I reject such a wonderful gift?*

Over the next few days, I made a decision—cancer was going to have to fade into the background while I focused on becoming a mom. Being pregnant was all that mattered. What would happen would unfold without me feeding it with fear or buying into anyone else's qualms or predictions. Brad and I wanted a child and we were going to have one.

A few times at the office, in their awkwardness and need to soothe, some coworkers said the strangest things, making me initially wish they'd just forget about me having cancer and being pregnant. But after thinking about it, I changed my mind. Even if their words were often strained and sometimes hurtful, the fact that they cared enough about me to want to express their feelings and thoughts was what was important, not what they said or didn't say. From that day forward, I welcomed their concerns and sometimes awkward congratulations. When the skies are gray, even a weak ray of sun provides warmth.

Though I loved my job and the staff, working where I was daily confronted by people suffering with the same disease, took a toll on my psyche, sometimes dismantling my house of hope into scattered bits that Brad had to reconstruct at home. To save my sanity and concentrate on delivering a healthy baby, I applied for a job away from direct patient care. Changing jobs helped, but my mind still jumbled between all I'd read about cancer treatments, survival rates and what to expect during pregnancy. Whatever fear or doubt came to the forefront, I pushed it back by steadily repeating, "I'm pregnant and that's all my *brain* has room for. I'm pregnant and that's all my *body* has room for."

Brad and I made a concerted effort to live as normally and healthily as possible. I continued to play volleyball once a week, and though relegated to the bleachers during softball, I didn't miss a game. Instead, I cheered on my husband and his team, often hollering, "You're out!" as loud as the umpire. Used to playing the sport four or five times per week, being sidelined seemed a cruel penance; however, my yearnings weren't worth the risk of hurting the baby, or scarring another player's heart should he or she knock me down. Volleyball was a little less risky, although I had to hold myself back there too. No longer could I dive for the ball or aggressively jump for a winning spike. Just the same, participating in sports together continued to bring us both great joy.

Brad continued playing baseball throughout the season. During the second to last game, he broke his thumb. In the early spring we regularly rollerbladed between Science World and Stanley Park in downtown, Vancouver. Regrettably, as my center of gravity changed, that bit of shared fun stopped. In June, our core team of four close buddies, including my sister Maria, won a beach volleyball tournament. Though playing was exhausting, collecting my T-shirt prize and telling the young lady handing them out that I was four months pregnant gave me double bragging rights.

Unable to completely ignore my disease medically, I continued having regular ultrasounds; some were to monitor the baby's growth and others to monitor the tumorous cancer. One happy finding was that as the baby grew, my cancer shrunk. Another was finding out on July 28th that our unborn baby was a boy. We promptly decided to name him Alexander Matthew Harrison: *Alexander* was the name of the mountain on which Brad and I were married; Matthew had no particular significance other than it was a name that Brad liked; *Harrison* was chosen by me because our son was conceived following my parents' fortieth wedding anniversary celebration at Harrison Hot Springs. How fitting, we thought, that our own family began on such a special night.

Knowing the baby's sex made becoming a mother seem more real and my cancer surreal. Nearing six months into the pregnancy, life was again blooming along with my ballooning belly. I was finally able to relax into pending motherhood. Relaxing, however, was short-lived. A friend invited us to watch Vancouver's Celebration of Lights International Fireworks from his boat. I was just climbing into the cabin, when a speedboat crashed into us, mounting our craft from the back and slicing through to the door I'd just closed! Within minutes, the coastguard hovercraft was on scene, as fire trucks and police vehicles lined the nearby shore. My legs were bruised as a result of another woman diving into the cabin on top of me in order to escape harm's way. Shaken, more than physically injured, I refused a hovercraft ride followed by an ambulance drive to the hospital. I'd simply had my fill of doctors and nurses. Brad and our friend had jumped out of the way just in time. Neither of them was injured. The speedboat driver's face was covered in blood, but he stayed with his sinking craft until he made shore, where he took off running. Apparently, he was drunk and had passed out just before crashing into us.

Once again reminded of how quickly one's life can spiral off course, I was immediately back on high alert, worrying incessantly, and being extra cautious. After all, I was carrying precious cargo and responsible for two lives, not just one.

To make ends meet, my husband and I started a weekend business cleaning the common areas, washrooms, elevators, and pools of an apartment building. It was tiring work, but we were house-poor and needed the money; especially, since I'd soon be on maternity leave. We must have been quite the sight for residents, me six months pregnant and Brad with his thumb in a cast that extended halfway up his arm. "You do what you have to do," became our shared mantra. "I'm stronger than I think," was what I uttered under my breath whenever I'd become discouraged or too tired to take another step. Brad had enough on his plate; he didn't need to listen to me whining and complaining.

Constantly tired, used to aches and pains, and a bit numb from all that had happened, in late August, when my back began aching continually and the pressure to urinate had me trotting off to the washroom every five minutes, I chalked it up to my advancing pregnancy. Daphne McIntyre, one of the nurses in the Acute Care Unit where I'd transferred to avoid patients with Non-Hodgkin's, noticed me wincing and holding my back. After a brief caring interrogation, she suggested that I immediately go to my doctor's office. Being the heroine that I am, I didn't do as she recommended, knowing I had an appointment the next day. By midafternoon, I could no longer argue with her advice—the pain was unbearable.

As with most calamities of late, just when I needed it most our car was stolen. I'd taken the bus to work, and now had to bus it to my high-risk-pregnancy physician's office. It was a long, bumpy ride, spent with me sitting on my hands to cushion myself.

When Dr. Petra Selke called me into her exam room, and I could barely get off the couch, concern flattened her usual friendly demeanor. "Monica, how long have you been feeling this way?"

"For a couple of days, I guess," I replied, wincing as she took my arm and I limped toward the exam room.

"Besides being tired, what else are you experiencing?"

"Mostly pressure on my bladder and a backache that would bring a man to his knees," I joked, thinking of how many times I'd teased Brad that he should take a turn carrying our son.

Smiling her understanding, Doctor Selke helped me onto the exam table. Undoubtedly, she'd heard many a similar quip.

"Is something wrong?" I asked as she felt my belly, her expression again concerned.

"That's what I'm trying to find out," she returned in a pleasant bedside tone. "Just to be certain all is as well as we're hoping, I'll be back in a moment with the fetal heart monitor."

"Fetal heart monitor," I repeated, as she exited and I was alone to worry. *Was something wrong with my son?* Kicking my feet to calm myself, I waited. Brad and I'd been through enough. We were tired and scared most of the time. There were just too many unanswered questions. *Would I carry to full term? Would our baby be born healthy? Afterward, would my cancer return with a vengeance?*

"Okay, let's get you hooked up and listen to that little guy of yours," the doctor said as she returned, monitor in hand.

Closing my eyes as she spread warm jelly on my belly, I repeatedly uttered, "The baby's healthy, I'm pregnant and that's all my *brain* has room for. Alexander Matthew Harrison is healthy, I'm pregnant and that's all my *body* has room for." A few dozen missed breaths and beats of my own heart later, I heard my son's soft whump, whump, whump. Goosebumps and butterflies delighted, I listened in awe. Too enthralled to cry, I just listened.

After further examination, Dr. Selke announced, "You're fully effaced and have likely been in labor for about three days."

"In labor!" I shrieked, lifting my shoulders off the table and staring at her.

"Monica, it's much too early. We have to stop your labor. You need to stay calm and get yourself to Grace Maternity Hospital. You should call Brad and get him to drive you."

"Brad can't drive me," I said, tears springing from my eyes. "Our car was stolen this morning. I came here by bus."

"By bus!" It was the doctor's turn to shriek. "You're too brave for your own good, Monica Forster. You shouldn't be alone, and taking the bus to Grace is out of the question. I'll drive you there myself."

"You don't have to do that," I argued, thinking of who else I might call. Maybe I could reach Maria or one of my brothers.

"Trying to find you a ride will take too much time," Dr. Selke said before exiting the room. She came back a few minutes later, keys in hand and donning a smile. "Let's go!"

Dr. Selke not only drove me to the hospital, she stayed with me until I was safely admitted to the Intensive Care Unit and had contacted poor Brad. Of course, he came immediately, and was there in time to hold my hand as I was transferred onto the general ward.

Because he had to get up early for work, Brad left about midnight, leaving me alone with my fears. I cried most of the night, wishing I was home instead of hooked up to machines, once again, waiting and waiting. *Waiting to see* was beginning to fray my nerves. But what choice did I have? If Alexander was born prematurely, he'd begin his life in an incubator, not in my arms. For now he was safe in my belly, and I would do my best to keep him there.

The next morning, red-eyed, exhausted and feeling guilty for keeping them awake, I intended to apologize to the other two women in my room. But before I did, one of my roommates said, "I heard you crying last night. I know it's hard right now, but it *will* get better."

"I'm sorry for keeping you awake," I said, while wondering how anyone could possibly know if my life would *ever* get better.

"Losing sleep is a gift," she replied, smiling in a Gandhi sort of way.

"The more hours one is consciously aware of life's gifts, the brighter one's life will be."

Had they roomed me with Mother Teresa? I apologized again, listening the best I could as she shared her story about how hard she'd prayed to conceive, and how when she did, her pregnancy had been wrought with troubles. This wasn't her first baby, and she assured me that the key to a healthy delivery, or anything else one desired, was to lock onto your dreams with a willful determination so ferocious that it defied matters to proceed in any other direction than intended. She also advised that I pray as though my prayers were already answered. She completed her words of encouragement by saying, "There is no room for doubt in miracles."

I never did catch the lovely, wise woman's name. What I did catch was renewed hope.

After three long, fretful, precarious days, my labor finally stopped. A week after that, following an ultrasound, my oncologist personally delivered the fantastic news that there was no longer any evidence of my lymphoma. Wow! What a week—still pregnant *and* cancer free! Though she'd been released, the words of my wise hospital roommate came to mind: with determination, belief and prayer, miracles do happen.

Ten days later, the doctor said I could go home *if* I remained on total bed rest. Knowing me well, my family gathered in my hospital room for a discussion. The general consensus was that there wasn't a hope in heaven I'd follow the doctor's orders, unless they physically tied me to the bedposts and stole all of my clothes. Though I cried buckets and flailed my arms in protest, I knew they were right. It wasn't my nature to sit still, and if I went home, I'd surely find a zillion excuses why it would be okay for me to get up to do this and that. I conceded to staying in the hospital—jailed!

By day, to drive off resentment, I thought of Alexander and how I was staying put for him. At night, I dreamed of literally being in prison and trying to escape. The time passed agonizingly slow. Though everyone came to visit and brought magazines, flowers and food, I actually kept track of how many hours and minutes needed to pass before I was released. *Would my life forever be on wait and see?*

While in the hospital, Princess Diana died. I was devastated, not only by the news of the death of someone I admired and shared a distant kinship, but also because I couldn't even attend a gathering of mourners to pay my respect. My brother Georg went to a gathering and signed a gigantic condolence card on my behalf. Later, he visited me, sharing how amazed he was by the beautiful flower memorials and people wailing in the streets. He also brought me a CD of Elton John's "A Candle in the Wind," vicariously and gratefully connecting me with others grieving the loss of the princess who'd extended the world such kindness.

Four weeks into my hospital sentence, with the baby and I both doing great, I was released as promised. Having sat on my butt for a month, I was as big as a house and low on energy. Mom and Dad helped out while Brad was at work, taking me grocery shopping and to doctors' appointments. For the next few weeks, I was happy baking, cooking and nesting.

At four in the morning on October 15th, my water broke, but I wasn't having contractions. On my doctor's advice I stayed home and tried to go back to sleep. Just before noon, we went to the hospital only to be told to go back home. Excited, hungry and wanting to celebrate early, Brad and I headed for the De Dutch Pannekoek House for lunch. Peering at my large belly, the waitress asked, "When are you due?"

"Well," I declared, enjoying the theatrics, "my water broke about four this morning."

"What?" she exclaimed, the cup she was filling with coffee suddenly a tsunami of waves.

I laughed while Brad explained that we'd just come from the hospital and all was fine.

At ten that evening, after two earlier trips between the hospital and home, my labor intensified and I was finally admitted. Not yet fully dilated, I began begging for the epidural I swore I wouldn't have. It was two hours later when the nurse actually administered the magic needle that eased my pain. Brad and I both managed to get some rest, until the baby's heartbeat slowed.

"Gown up and prepare for surgery," yelled one nurse as the room became a scurry of activity. I frantically searched the room for Brad. He was missing. *Where was he?*

"Do you know where my husband is?" I asked as they maneuvered me onto my left side, and turned the baby's heart monitor down so I wouldn't be able to hear it. But I could still hear the faint whumping of my son's heart. "Alexander, don't do this to me. Mommy's scared and she wants to have a natural childbirth. And so do you. Be strong baby boy. Be strong, mommy loves you."

"What the heck is going on, Monica?" my white-faced husband demanded to know as he suddenly appeared over top of me.

"The baby's heart slowed," I explained through panicked tears. "Talk to him with me. Please make him come out on his own, Brad. I'm scared."

His hand on my belly, Brad gave our son the first of many loving lectures that were sure to follow. "Son," he said, sounding so fatherly I almost giggled. "Be a good kid and give your mom and me a break. Forsters are fighters. We don't give up easily and we are in this together."

After about five minutes, we looked into each other's eyes and smiled. The baby's heartbeat was back to normal. Two hours later on October 16th, 1997, Alexander Matthew Harrison Forster was delivered naturally, weighing in at six pounds, eleven ounces. His arrival was nineteen days early, on his great grandfather's eighty-eighth birthday.

As I sit here writing this story, my now fourteen-year-old son is in the other room watching a movie with his dad. I now celebrate two birthdays per year—one for the day I was born, and one for the number of years I've been cancer free. After the birth of our son, my cancer did return. Thanks to my brother Georg who donated his bone marrow for my transplant, a team of medical specialists, and the tremendous support of family, friends, community, and health retreat workers, I am alive and well.

As paradoxical as it may seem, once the business of preparing to die was behind me—letting my family know how much I loved them, getting my financial affairs in order, and recording a goodbye video for my son—I was able to concentrate on the fight for my life. A fight, I continue to win as life unfolds its magic for Brad, Alexander and me.

The threat of death;
the joy of life.
We are strong.
We are brave.
We are the neighborhood heroes
in each other's lives.
— Monica Forster

Self-Actualization

www.kindnessiskey.com

From Emptiness to Living, Loving and Laughing
The Miracle of Connection

Georgina Grace

It wasn't that I wanted to die—I just wanted to escape the monotony of never-ending stress. The night my outlook shifted was no different than any other. I went to bed with the TV on for background noise, floating in and out of consciousness in that delicious moment before sleep, when suddenly what had been mumble jumble became crystal clear.

"God dwells within, not above."

What did he just say? Barely awake, I half listened.

"Life is everlasting and the spirit goes forward eternally."

Now you're talking! I snatched up my glasses, scurried to the end of the bed and hazily peered at the screen in time to see the credits at the end of the show. The guy was from a local church that was a mere thirty minutes from my place. A place where people thought like me! People who knew that although a loved one passes over, they never really leave your side.

Sitting at the foot of the bed, frozen in disbelief at my good fortune, I wondered if I'd heard correctly. *Were there others close by who thought like me? Was this church the answer I'd been searching for?* Limbs vibrating, ears ringing, I tried to absorb and digest thoughts exploding in my head like fireworks. Long dormant butterflies flittered and floated in my stomach that churned with excitement. It had been years since something—anything—truly felt right. From head to toe and heart to soul, the idea of exploring this church felt right. Suddenly, I knew that everything was about to change—for the better!

If I'd understood correctly, the people at this church could communicate with people who'd passed over. I'd been talking to my Uncle Alvin since he died when I was five years old. The only alive adult who encouraged his visits was Grandma, and thanks to a hated move from Ontario to British Columbia when I was thirteen, she lived a zillion miles away. We wrote back and forth, but there was no one nearby who cared about my conversations with Uncle Alvin. Away from Grandma and our oft teatime chats, I began to lose contact with my uncle. Confused and dreadfully missing them both, late in my teen years, suicidal ponderings trickled into my conscience, fingering their way into every disenchantment, yearning and void.

By my twenties I had a preferred exit strategy involving a Friday night. Why Friday? I liked Friday. It was the beginning of the weekend and somehow reinforced my belief that I didn't matter. No one would notice I was gone until Monday when I didn't report for work. Earth minus me was really not a big deal.

It wasn't until that fateful evening, when someone or something pulled me back from sleep and toward life, that I realized I wasn't alone. A few miles away, others knew what I knew. My chest filled with a warm, fuzzy peace; where I'd once felt nothing, I suddenly felt hope. A mind that predominantly doubted, raced and screamed—became quiet, assured and calm.

The next day, more jazzed than a hyena on laughing gas, talking with a coworker, I shared what I'd learned about the church.

"Ya, I've been there. I know where it is," she returned with a shrug.

"You have to take me there!" I eagerly implored. I couldn't believe my good fortune. Since moving away from Grandma in my early teens, life had been either empty or a bitch, one challenge shoring up the next. Finding a church full of like-minded people—who openly celebrated communicating with the dead, who knew life was eternal, and who had dismissed the devil as fear mongering—unlocked parts of me that had been frozen in secrecy.

"When do you want to go?" my coworker asked, as if it were possible that any other Sunday than the very next would do.

"This Sunday!" I chirped, already planning what I'd wear.

"If you want," she responded, rolling her shoulders in a no-big-deal fashion.

She was obviously unaware of the emptiness that filled my soul. But then, no one knew that my smiles and happy words were mere counterbalances for my dark, weighty thoughts.

Like many who suffer from depression, mine had a set of triggers: Dad and Mom's divorce, Grandpa's death, and our move from a small village of four hundred to a metropolis of over one million. Leaving behind my dad, Grandma, relatives, and friends, triggered my spiral into a deep black hole.

Arriving in Vancouver—our family decimated to just Mom, our cat Duchess and me—emptiness became a new way of life. Gone were all the familiar faces and the laughter of cousins and friends. For me, there were no more bike rides, games of hide-and-seek or pal time. Everything and everyone seemed strange. Angry at being transported to the planet Zircon, and overwhelmed by the thousand-plus students in my new high school, my chatterbox self, coiled inward, clamped closed and became mute. Mom did her loving best to care for me while struggling to rebuild her own life; however, within weeks of our move, I became a self-imposed shut-in. Anchorless, and bumbling about the noisy, confusing city, my gloom glommed on and devoured me one day at a time. A couple of cousins, whom I seldom saw until I moved to B.C., tried to coax me into socializing with them; however, paralyzed by emotions I didn't understand, I remained housebound.

In the 1970's, no one spoke of depression, and you certainly didn't seek counseling. I didn't trust anyone enough to talk about my fears or bleakness, so I hid out in our basement suite baking Grandma's chocolate-chip cookies, cakes and biscuit recipes. Eating the treats we'd once baked together helped to soothe the three-thousand-mile gap between us. It was also the beginning of my yo-yoing weight.

Television was my only teenage companion—more accurately, *best friend;* especially, when run-amuck insomnia droned into a nightmarish marathon of bleak endless hours. Most stations went off the air before exhaustion rendered me unconscious. I could rely on only two surefire sleeping tonics: the theme music from late-night reruns of Hawaii 5-0 or sunrise.

Dad died when I was eighteen. Even though my parents were divorced and I hadn't lived in the same province as my father for over five years, the finality of our separation numbed me into shock. When I learned of his passing, I sat on the edge of my bed, saddened that I no longer had the option of calling him, sending a birthday card, or flying his way for a visit.

I'm not sure why Dad's passing was so much different from when Uncle Alvin died. I'd handled death much better when I was five years old. My father was an alcoholic, and although I wished he could have given up the bottle, I never judged him. His destiny was skewed from the moment he was born as the fifth child of a struggling Depression Era family. His father died when Dad was just three months old. In grade three, my father quit school to help his mother financially. As the saying goes, he did the best he could with what he knew. We each do the best we can with what we know. It was twenty years before Dad's spirit reconnected with me. His never-too-late threefold message: *I love you. I'm proud of you. And I'm sorry I let you down on earth.*

Dad's dying, coupled with the fact that I'd just graduated from high school and couldn't find a job, became the catalyst for my new friendship with alcohol. Gone was my status as *Daddy's little girl*; in its place came frustrated joblessness. Weary from endless despondency, I easily adopted the let's-make-things-go-away approach to misery. Following his death, I didn't fall apart—I flew apart, gleefully imbibing in fountains of booze to medicate loss, boredom and isolation. During my two-year alcohol binge, I totally missed that I was suffering from anxiety-riddled panic attacks and acute depression. *Well, who knew? Clearly not drunken me!* (Now realizing that I have an addictive personality—numbing my troubles away, was obviously not the best option.)

Without questioning the cause or seeking a cure, throughout my twenties, I stoically endured my racing heart, sweating hands, ringing ears, and excruciating migraines that made me want to pop my head like a zit. My mind sped faster than Giorgio Andretti on the homeward stretch, without any consideration that this might not be normal and even might be curable. Funnily enough, some people nicknamed me Georg*ieo*, but in comparison to my driving, not my runaway mind.

When I was twenty-five, my cat Duchess died. She'd been my best friend and only confidant since I was a wee tot learning to tell time. Duchess's death was one more blow to an already fragile existence. Smack-up-the-side-of-the-head realization: I had more memories of being with my cat than I did of being with my deceased father! Losing my furry shadow ached in every crevice of my heart, mind and body—even my soul. I was more lost, confused and desperate than before. Emptiness grew in me like a tumor.

For the next several years, my friends urged me to get another cat. *Seriously?* Most days I didn't have enough oars in the water to care for myself. Plus, it seemed a betrayal to simply replace Duchess. However, when I was around thirty-two, my friend's cat had kittens. I went over

:m. Of course, I walked out with *two*—Teala, a long-haired
hite feline, and Bailey. I swear Bailey was part dog because
etch, came when I called her, and growled to warn me when
as coming near the door. (Word to the wise: Unless you're
rket to increase you family, never make eye contact with
purring that can fit in the palm of your hand.)
help heal humans in unexpected and wonderful ways. As
ney make you feel loved, needed and somewhat essential.
er I was upset or migraine comatose, Bailey would always
comfort me. When it became apparent that she was allergic to
cigarette smoke, I quit the tar and nicotine. Ironically, and sadly, Bailey
died of cancer when she was only thirteen.

Though I no longer contemplated suicide, for many more years depression
remained my nemesis; particularly, in September—the anniversary month
of loss after loss. Dad, his mom and Duchess all died in September, which
coincided with the height of the Seasonally Affected Disorder (SAD) that
enshrouded and heightened my glumness six months per year. I couldn't
focus on anything. Work was a haze of busy confusion that left me fretting
about going back the second I left. Days on end, paralyzed by whatever
fear beckoned, I stayed hidden in my apartment watching stockpiled
movies. Forever the proverbial mouse on an endless wheel going nowhere, I
continually wondered, "Is this all life has to offer?"

Depressed people often go from one extreme to the next; hence, my
let's party interludes of drunken madness and shopping sprees. Skewed
thinking also plagues the despondent. I was no exception. *Happiness
is a fraud. Is normal an illusion? What is normal? Maybe this is normal?
Perhaps this is as good as it gets. It's only a matter of time until I feel better.
I'm not going to take antidepressants; I'm coping just fine without them.
Everything is fine.*

Perhaps you're familiar with drunken bed-spins; that horrendous
sensation where you can't focus because the room is whipping about
you at sonic speed. Well, that was my mind twenty-four-seven. It was
six years before I had my lovely bouquet of afflictions diagnosed—a
daunting six years with lunar-length days. (FYI: The moon's axis
rotation is kind of slow, so days span a quarter-century.)

Persuaded by a friend who also suffered from depression, I booked

an appointment with my family physician. Plastic smile in place, knees knocking and a bag full of vitamins sure to cure my soon-to-be-diagnosed A, B and C deficiencies, I sat in the doctor's office, waiting for her and anticipating how our visit would progress. I was fairly certain her opening question would be, "What can I do for you today?" What I would answer wasn't completely clear; however, my imaginings of her response to whatever I finally mumbled, zinged about my speedy mind Georg*ieo* style. *You're just silly! You're not depressed. You can smile. You can laugh. You don't suffer from depression. Chin-up, gal; nothing's wrong with you at all. Why ever did you bother booking an appointment? You should leave.*

Ears ringing, frenzied mind, fluttering mid-region, heart thumping ribcage-painful, escape route mentally secured, I neatly lined the vitamin bottles on the doctor's desk, ignoring that my shaking hands were leaving tiny little sweat pools behind. Certain that an excruciating migraine would soon rotate my eyeballs backward, animatedly validating the severity of my neurotic existence, I waited.

My doctor arrived, surveyed my vitamin collection and nodded. I haven't a clue as to what she then said, but remain certain that it was a caring, probing question. However, what I heard was, "Charlie Brown's teacher," followed by a series of nasally quacking sounds. Then the doctor smiled.

I tried to smile. Couldn't! Darn lips froze—but not my legs; they jerked my trembling frame upward so fast that the room spun in unison with my whirling fears. Stammering something such as, "I can't do this," rubbery-legged me bolted for the door. *My problem, not hers! Fix it yourself, or live broken.*

Obviously an Olympian sprinter, the doctor beat me to the door, blocking my exit in patient-stealing-triplicate-prescription-pad fashion.

Stunned silly, I just stood there. *Now what? Should I wrestle her down?* She was kind of puny, so I knew I could take her. Imagining sounds of *ha-ha hee-hee* and men in white coats coming to take me away to the funny farm soon thwarted that pondering.

After some coaxing, much talking and many tears, I left the doctor's office armed with knowledge, a few prescriptions that would right my chemical imbalance, and a sense that I'd be okay.

You'd think from there forward that life would have become perfect, right? Wrong!!!

I couldn't decipher a cause, but the *void* persisted and my mind still raced around nothingness in search of somethingness. *I was taking my meds, why wasn't I better?* Perhaps, I needed a stronger dose of Ativan. More likely,

I often concluded, was that my fate included an unyielding tug-of-war with depression and/or emptiness, with me always landing face-mud-forward.

Still, somewhere deep inside I realized something was missing or amiss, but what?

Unable to find a solution, I returned to self-medicating via: drinking, busyness, food binging, and retail therapy. My mood didn't elevate; however, my weight and credit-card bills certainly did! Somewhat failed by medication, and absolutely failed by self-destructive remedies, I felt myself being pulled toward religion. Perhaps, Jesus or God would calm my hurricane existence by slowing the whirling and filling the void with something other than fear and hopelessness. A few varying religions and church services later, I was still lost. For me, attending church wasn't the answer. *Maybe there was no cure for depression or emptiness.*

Advised as a youngster to give myself to Jesus, I rebelled on the principle of self-reliance instilled in me by parents who adhered to the Protestant work ethic as though it were the key to Heaven. *If you can't afford to pay your own way, stay home. Need money, work endless hours like Dad, who daily clocked upwards of ten hours. Not feeling well, too bad. Be like your Mom and go to work regardless of how you feel. Afterward, make dinner, clean the house, and prepare lunches for the next day. Once all that's done and you are totally exhausted, go ahead and drop your fatigued head on a pillow. It'll be bedtime, anyway.*

Asking for help, even from our Creator, I viewed as too weak, too lazy, and too scary. Plus, it required forfeiting control in favor of trusting—was never going to happen. I had a backpack of proof that everyone alive would find some way to let me down. Though, always having prided myself on being a good friend, I'd drop everything to help another.

Truth is an equally vital family virtue, and haunted me each time I claimed to be *fine*, when clearly I wasn't. To this day I have zero tolerance for lying, so as you can imagine, feeling like a fake did daily damage.

The Miracle of Connection

On Sunday morning, my less-than-enthusiastic workmate and I parked in front of the quaint, wood-sided two-story house that had been converted into a spiritualist church. My head was spinning tornado fast; however, on that rare occasion the spinning was fueled by excitement, not fear. The luscious green grounds were warm and inviting. Surveying the outside premises, I noticed that the backyard sported an expansive spiraling labyrinth—one-way-in and one-way-out. It was obviously purposeful, but past its mesmerizing magic, it eluded me as to what that purpose might be.

Each step up the stairs to the church doorway intensified my awareness that I needed to be at this place. I could feel it. Seated at the back of the church, marveling at the wood craftsmanship, stained-glass windows and assorted crystals on the podium, my mind started to calm. As various speakers spoke of love over fear and acceptance over judgment, the ringing in my ears quieted. When the congregation sang of brotherhood and community, my heart swelled in awe.

Toward the end of the service, when mediums took turns delivering loving messages from those who'd passed, I dared to think I'd found where I belonged. Embracing this brave spiritual fellowship, who openly and fearlessly shared their mediumship gifts, I silently prayed that they'd welcome me as their friend. Yet, I still questioned, "Do I really fit in here? Is this place truly what I've been searching for?" *Oh, how I wanted it to be.*

I returned to the church the very next week, anxiety jiggling throughout. But as the service began, for the first time since baking cookies with Grandma, I peacefully enjoyed myself. From that day forward, the welcomed sense of peace I found at the Sunday services slowly seeped into my everyday life. In response, I dared to poke my head from my shell and trust.

For two years, I attended the quaint little church *living, loving and laughing.* It was there that I met, Barbara Leonard, the founder and minister of the Inner Garden Balance Point Chapel. Immediately drawn to her motherly wisdom and love—so much like Grandma's—I started attending Reverend Barbara's Sunday services. With her steadfast support, encouragement and mentoring I blossomed.

Smile countrywide, during one Sunday service her kindly blue eyes peered at me from the podium, as she said, "If I were to tell Georgina that she'll be up here speaking one day, it would scare the bejabbers out of her."

Darn certain there wasn't a hope in heaven I'd ever speak publicly, I guffawed. It wasn't until later that night that I thought—"Yikes! Barbara's a psychic and a good one. Oh, no!!!"

Fast forward a year to when the Inner Garden Chapel offered a public speaking course taught by a Toastmaster leader and fellow churchgoer, Ray Helm. "Do you think I need to take Ray's Relational Presence class?"

I asked a trusted friend who was well-aware that I clammed up whenever there were four or more people in a group. However, as much as I didn't want to get up in front of people and speak, deep inside I knew it was a step I needed to take. My friend confirmed my inner knowing with a smile backed, "Yes, you'll be an excellent speaker. Take the course!"

I soon found out that keeping quiet can be even more difficult than speaking in front of others. First class, me front stage, Ray instructed, "Don't talk for one minute while making eye contact with your audience, one person at a time." *Are you kidding? He wants me to endure ten people staring at me for a solid minute while I keep my mouth shut! I'm the gal whose Dad couldn't even cash-bribe her to keep quiet. I need my words to joke and make people laugh. I don't do awkward—I run!*

Heart and mind speeding George*ieo* fashion, I did as instructed and, surprisingly, learned that I could survive scrutiny without my veil of humorous quips. *Who would have known?*

Watching as my word-naked classmates took turns on stage, I inwardly smiled. Not one seemed any more comfortable than I had been. *Perhaps, I was normal.*

Next exercise, Ray instructed, "While maintaining eye contact with your audience, speak from your heart for one minute."

Crap! I slumped to the stage, aware that there were three times more pairs of eyes on me than at any other time in my life! *Talk from the heart. Okay, here goes.* "I used to suffer from depression. But I don't anymore. It all started when I was uprooted from a small town and dropped on my neurotic head in the metropolis of a zillion strangers. For many years, I handled my spinning head, ringing ears, anxiety, and blinding migraines with a variety of self-prescribed psychotherapy: retail therapy, which was very effective until my cards maxed-out; alcohol therapy, which pretty much numbed everything for a few hours, but apparently isn't a great nine-to-five solution; seclusion therapy, which involved stockpiling movies and books, then locking myself in my apartment and not answering the phone that seldom rang, anyway; and, pet therapy. Pet therapy was my only non-destructive remedy, and it helped a lot. I'm a cat lover. Always have been, always will be."

"Time's up," a smiling Ray announced just as I was about to issue my warning about not making eye contact with anything purring that you can hold in the palm of your hand. Surprisingly, I didn't scat off the stage faster than a kitten caught on the kitchen table. I actually had more I wanted to say. I wasn't frightened that others were listening; I was gleefully flabbergasted. Wow! What went on in my zigzag, zip-here-and-there George*ieo* runaway-mind actually interested others, maybe even helped some.

It was my turn to listen without responding as each of my classmates spoke about what she or he held dear, feared and/or treasured. I was amazed. Everyone opened up, revealing more and more during each class. By the end of the six week course, I had ten close friendships, a new appreciation for listening, and the confidence that I could help others learn from my triumphs and tribulations.

At Barbara's urging, in return for all I've gained through my friendship with her and the people at the Inner Garden Chapel, I now regularly lead classes in everything from vision board creation to mediumship. Leading, for me, is pure joy manifested via a two-way exchange of life-gained wisdom, love and laughter.

Before regularly attending Barbara's spiritual church, I wasn't engaged as a life participant, but was more of a robotic imposter in a society I'd alienated under the pretense that its citizens had alienated me. Today, I'm mostly happy, and when I feel down, I don't fake being happy. My nine-to-five world occasionally presents challenges that overwhelm my sense of well-being, but all-in-all, I'm grateful for every aspect of my life. When my OCD or ADHD kick into overdrive, I don't recoil in fear or confusion, I own and share what's unique about me. Funnily enough, by simply explaining my George*ieo* mind, people not only understand, they accept me for who I am. Laughing with me, sometimes even confessing to a similar fate as I explain, "Oh, by the way, I'm an OCD graduate, so if my Obsessive Compulsive Disorder makes me seem a little out-there, or over the top, please understand. Of course, I don't expect you to differentiate between that affliction and my Attention Deficit Hyperactivity Disorder, which could very well be at the helm today. So if I seem inattentive, fidgety or frenzied, please feel free to call me on it."

There's a lot of freedom in embracing, rather than shrinking from or denying my uniqueness. Perhaps I'll one day add my blend of afflictions to my business card—GEORGINA GRACE: Psychic Medium, Writer, Inspirational Speaker, and Chemically-Challenged Comedian with ADHD and OCD.

As you may have noticed I remain a little quirky, but with good reason, wouldn't you say?

What transformed my once desperate bleak existence is that I've *found* and *allowed* the abundant love, support, and encouragement of friends and Spirit. We all encounter challenges that bring life lessons, some of which are more difficult than others. What matters most is that we each accept and face what troubles our unique beings, thereby prospering from wisdoms gained.

I no longer entertain the notion that the universe might be picking on me. I now welcome and explore each encountered hardship or misfortune, changing what I can and 'allowing' that which can't be altered. I must say, though, that I wholeheartedly agree with a friend of mine, who when confronted with an overwhelming situation, addresses her divine inspirer as follows: "Thanks for that lesson; but next time, please don't make it so difficult."

Much of my healing closely aligns with my companionship choices and recently gained ability to accept the continued metamorphoses of all friendships. Born an only child, a younger Georgina sometimes clung to many less-than-trustworthy pseudo-friends. When I left Ontario minus my friends and cousins from that area of Canada, I longed for their familiar faces. I fearfully refused all new wannabe chums as though they were somehow responsible for my great loss. In my later teens, afraid to let go, I cringed whenever a close buddy grew in directions that didn't include us both. How liberating it was to realize that it's okay to let people go, to never hear from or see them again, and to move forward without clinging to the status quo.

There is magic in challenge, in change and in friendships. I could devote an entire book to the wonderful people I've met in the past few years. I now realize that no matter how brief or lengthy our exchange, various people come into our lives to help us grow and become better people. It's life's circle of ever-expanding love connections—human and animal—that shore our foundation, learning and growth. In open, honest relationship with others we become better people. *How great is that?*

As suggested earlier, be easy on yourself and others—if we each *knew* better, we'd each *do* better.

Live Heartily! Love Fully! Laugh Often!

From Neediness to Wholeness

Erika Taylor

The voice at the other end of the line was solemn. "I'm afraid I have some sad news for you. Ben has died. It was his wish that you receive this message. He lived with the regret of having lost you, and never found anyone with whom he had the same depth of connection."

I sat wordlessly on my sofa, remembering that romantic love relationship of forty years ago and its devastating end. The caller's words brought back to mind the sharp sting of rejection, as I recalled how many a night my anguished sobs sought release in the dark solitude of my room. *How was I to integrate the caller's message with these painful memories?*

My thoughts turned to that hot summer night in Saskatoon when love first beckoned and I innocently followed. How my heart raced when a tall attractive young man invitingly extended his hand to me, drawing me onto the dance floor. A moment later we were moving in sync to the sultry sounds of the R 'n' B band, enjoying the palpable energy and vibrancy between us. Conversation flowed as though we were kindred spirits, and with youthful exuberance, we shared significant parts of our past and visions of our future. We laughed with a lightness of being, and delighted in the compatibility and harmony seemingly bestowed on us by grace.

I believed I had met HIM, as our interactions that first night held the promise of a blossoming love. Long after the singer's soulful sounds fell silent, we maintained this 'love-at-first-sight' connection. After saying a reluctant good night, we eagerly awaited our next day reunion.

When Ben picked me up in his flashy yellow convertible open to the sky, I felt I'd entered a higher realm in the ethereal world. It was a giddy and exciting time, with weekends spent sunbathing on sandy beaches and splashing in cool lake waters with childlike abandonment.

We savored the pleasant sensations of that young love, and soon he introduced me to his family members as their future daughter/sister-in-law. I felt beautiful, lovable and desirable.

Alas, by late fall of that same year, my 'beloved' Ben began to backpedal, finding fault with my clothes, my hair, my name. He became critical of my career choices, friends and hobbies. I felt panic welling up in me. Needing his love and approval, I slipped into pleasing mode, taking on the nickname he gave me, and making changes that were more in keeping with his taste. It was all to no avail. He seemed to have lost that loving feeling, and by New Year's Eve our relationship ended. My psychological underpinnings collapsed like a house of cards.

Distress propelled me to seek help, and I took the first step on a healing journey of a thousand miles. I found some solace in the wonderful book *Psycho-Cybernetics* by Maxwell Maltz in which he teaches the reader to call forth 'that winning feeling' to overlay currently active painful emotions. I began to explore other self-help tools such as metaphysical tapes and introduced myself to the world of counseling. I also started attending growth workshops to help me lift upward in my understanding of love.

I treasured Kahlil Gibran's writings on love in his book *The Prophet*. He suggested that if you must have desires, let these be your desires: "...to sleep with a prayer for the beloved in your heart and a song of praise upon your lips." Oh, how my life had to thresh, sift, grind and knead, before my heart was capable of holding such love for another. I recognized that in my early twenties it was my heart's desire to hear love and praise coming *from* my beloved *to me*. In fact, it was an urgent need, an intense longing. Small wonder, when the theme of the romantic novels, magazines and movies I had hungrily been consuming, reinforced the false conception that love was something we sought 'out there' and 'fell into' if we were lucky enough to find that individual who would make us feel lovable and whole. My understanding of love in those early years emphasized finding the 'love object' rather than learning how to expand my own capacity to love.

When the pain of my relationship with Ben subsided, I could see that he had unknowingly played an important role in awakening me to those parts of myself that were calling out for healing. At some point in our relationship, he must have sensed my neediness and wanted to run. No doubt, there was *fear* underlying his criticism of me. Perhaps, he was no more capable of loving than I was at that time. Regardless, I had to accept that *I had given HIM the power to define ME*—if he loved me, I felt happy and worthwhile; if he withdrew his love, I experienced myself as being 'less than' and felt despondent. I resolved to transform this fragile part of myself.

With the exception of a letter asking for my forgiveness, which I received ten years after our relationship ended, Ben and I had no further contact. Committed to another at the time, I did not wish to reconnect with him. However, I unhesitatingly extended forgiveness to both him and myself, for forgiveness is the path to freedom.

The unexpected phone call from his brother forty years later helped me to further embrace the Learning-Through-Relationship 101 course Ben and I'd once shared, with greater tenderness toward us both.

"I'd like to spend a lot more time with you," Matt whispered tenderly, pulling me close and wrapping his long woolen scarf in a figure-eight around our necks as we stood in the chilly winter air. Such warm words were welcomed—synonymous with a marriage proposal to my hungry ears. Recalling the agonizing breakup with Ben, after a six-month venture into the uncharted waters of love, I married Matt—and stayed for seventeen years. *After all, what could be more validating than marriage? Was that not the ultimate proof of my lovability?* I was reluctant to acknowledge that the urgent need and intense longing to be loved was still very much a part of my psyche.

The summer sun streaming down on our sailboat as we bobbed about in a coastal bay, it was as if our wedding day had nature's blessing. With a few sailing friends on board our handcrafted wooden vessel, the sailor-minister ceremoniously joined us in what we hoped would be holy matrimony. Pink champagne and cake sealed our pledge "to love, share and grow together; to discover a deeper, fuller life." Even with the level of anxiety and need that I carried in regard to relationship success, I noticed that my 'feistiness quotient' must have expanded since my days with Ben, for I felt bold enough to insist that the traditional vow to 'obey' not be included in our wedding service. The acorn holding the mighty oak inside of me could not be encumbered by such a nebulous promise!

Reveling in the emotional security of 'having someone' in my life, I turned my attention to domestic matters, determined to become a good wife and partner. To create a welcoming home environment, a sanctuary to return to after our day's work, I enthusiastically signed up for classes in cooking and interior decorating. I believed that the onus was on me to make this relationship work, and with joyful willingness I pleased and compromised 'on an as-needed basis.'

This prescription carried me through the first number of years of our marriage, and it was some time before significant differences in our core values became apparent in our daily interactions. The differences loomed ever larger over time, shaping our lives into patterns of separate interests and activities, with no common friends, few family connections, and a lack of unifying dreams and goals. The pilot light of our love was barely flickering and, to be sure, there was nothing cooking. 'Roommates' would have been a more accurate description of our relationship—living under the same roof but sharing only household expenses.

Addressing this painful issue with Matt proved to be fruitless, and from his point of view, counseling was out of the question. The disappointment of our savorless existence weighed heavily on me— going to Mrs. from Miss had not brought me wedded bliss.

"I CAN'T STAY IN THIS RELATIONSHIP!" The thought surfaced sharply. I pushed it down determinedly. It was year ten before such an anxiety-producing energy first dared to seek expression. This was an unwelcome visitor; one I was not about to entertain. However, in its persistence it would find an opening the moment I inattentively left my post as the gatekeeper of my thoughts. It would reap havoc with me then, stirring up angst in my being and leaving me deeply conflicted.

Seeking guidance from higher sources, I directed more of my energy into the practice of meditation. I frequented spiritual centers and ashrams to integrate western teachings with those of the east. I felt myself drawn to the light of the angels and ascended masters, and enveloped myself in their loving energies. It was my longing to heal the wounds that kept me in bondage and to expand my understanding of love.

In response to my query regarding separation, a wise being of light offered me the following nugget: "It does not matter which roof you live under. The important thing is what you carry in your consciousness— what thoughts, feelings, attitudes, and beliefs you harbor. When there is mutual respect between the two of you, and you have released judgment, fear and guilt, *then* you can choose whether to stay or go."

I spent the last five years of my relationship with Matt reaching toward this higher state of being. It became ever clearer to me that I did *want* to leave, but before I could do so harmoniously, I had to continue strengthening my inner resources. My desire was to leave with a feeling of compassion for both of us, knowing that we had loved to the best of our capacity.

Matt reluctantly accepted my decision, but was dubious about my ability to act on it. A few 'go and stop' trials were necessary before I could follow through with my intention. On two separate occasions, I located a suitable apartment and secured it with the first month's rent. Both times, an intense bout of anxiety paralyzed me and halted the entire process, leaving me convinced I couldn't 'make it on my own.' The third trial, however, allowed me to claim victory.

Forever etched in my memory is a moving day vision of two stocky men maneuvering pieces of furniture with relative ease, skillfully stacking them in the miniature truck parked in front of our home. To them it was a small job; there were few, if any, indicators to reveal the enormous undertaking it was for me. I kept my energies calm, and stayed steady in my resolve by holding a continuous prayer of blessing in my heart for both Matt and myself as we moved through the tasks that lay before us. In a spirit of cooperation, we divided our furnishings and attended to the necessary details of setting up two separate households. There were no angry words between us, no legal counsel to guide us. We simply thanked each other for the part of the journey we had walked together, and wished one another well. I said goodbye to that chapter of my life.

Although we were now living under separate roofs, our concern for each other's continued wellbeing was of uppermost importance to us both. The harmony between us eased that time of transition, paving the way for us to maintain friendly intermittent contact throughout the ensuing years. If one must separate, this was surely the way to go!

Being in a relationship with Matt, as well as having courageously made it through our separation, helped to move me along the path toward wholeness. The increased strength and confidence that I was able to unearth within myself were clear indicators of my progress. The treasures I carried with me as I stepped into the next chapter of my life were—a little *more* capacity for self-love and a little *less* need for love from 'that special someone.'

Waves of blissful freedom flowed through me as the natural child within playfully cartwheeled, somersaulted, leap-frogged and clicked-her-heels with gleeful abandon. *Oh, what a feeling!* The relentless anxiety that had so tightly held me in its grip, had compassionately released me into the hands of freedom. This was the state of being for which I'd been reaching as the Learning-Through-Relationship course continued to unfold in my life.

Before I could claim this gift of freedom, however, it seemed that, yet again, I had to step into the relationship arena to complete the weaving of that part of the giant tapestry of my life. It was an eleven-year step.

My new prize package came attractively wrapped in qualities I found irresistible. Ron was a well-educated man with a successful career. As well, he was interested in personal growth and spiritual awakening. His beautiful home shelved hundreds of books on philosophy, religion, psychology, and literature, revealing an intellectual curiosity about subjects that intrigued me also. His demeanor was that of someone holding a quiet wisdom. I was magnetically drawn to him.

Given all the experiences that life had brought to me in the past few decades, I believed my tastes had matured, and I was now capable of making wiser men choices. I acknowledged the inner work I'd done to release past limitations, and confidently embarked on the new venture before me.

Ron brought a loyal, steadfast energy to our relationship. At first, I appreciated his interest in my life and his desire to participate in my world. In the fullness of time, however, it became apparent that there was a confining quality to our togetherness, a lack of ease and freedom I found stifling.

In contrast to my later years with Matt when we had shared *only* household expenses, Ron seemed to cling to my hip like a static-filled slip. At his insistence, he would accompany me on all my outings—yoga, walks, non-impact-aerobics—and expected the same from me in return. Our tethered togetherness thwarted any expression of *me* in the coupledom of *we*. However, the needy part of me that was still looking for external validation, rationalized this togetherness as proof of my *lovability*. This man clearly wanted to be with me.

For several years of our relationship, Sunday mornings would find us primly perched on our pew, participating—albeit, reluctantly on my part—in the rituals and observances of a traditional worship service. During the scriptural readings and theological interpretations, I would give my mind free reign, allowing my gaze to be fixed on the magnificent colors and symbolic images depicted on the stained-glass windows, as my auditory attention absorbed the sounds of the pipe organ soaring dramatically to the apex of the ceiling.

Even though I could appreciate the beauty of the church's stonework, the luster of the Douglas-fir flooring, and the craftsmanship of the cedar-planked ceiling, these artifacts did not feed my spiritual hunger. One pivotal Sunday morning while sitting dutifully by Ron's side, I allowed myself to recall how the limited experimenting we'd done with churches of my choosing, had rendered him uncommunicative, withdrawn and expressionless. Alongside, came an acknowledgement of the *pleaser* in me that willingly and habitually rushed to accommodate him whenever he seemed unhappy. It was then that a powerful surge of anger gripped my being, catapulting me into the realization that I could no longer accept having abandoned my spiritual needs in favor of his. The gift of this unsettling and strong emotional response—it was time to honor my soul's promptings.

The constriction and constraint that I experienced over the years, coupled with the discordant energies that seemingly had no solution, resulted in that old familiar pattern asserting itself again. I felt deep inner stirrings of wanting my freedom, but at the same time, I felt conflicted by the accompanying anxiety.

In spite of the ensuing tension between us, I became more assertive about claiming time for myself. Having this *personal space* allowed me to delve more deeply into my own spiritual practices. Once again, I focused on strengthening my inner core. I was particularly drawn to a heart-opening exercise that helped me ignite and activate the *divine love* deep within my own being. This exercise, combined with the cumulative effect of all the inner work I'd done previously, brought about my desired result. I began to experience a vaster, more expanded version of myself—one that felt nurtured from within. As I increased my capacity to love both myself and others in a more *all-encompassing* way, I was able to release the need for love from a specific person.

I have felt a wonderful, uplifting freedom since my separation from

Ron. Ironically, it was my relationship with him and prior partners that helped free me from my *need* to be coupled in order to feel whole.

Divine Love Light Affirmation

I invite you to use a transformational affirmation I learned at a spiritual healing center in Vancouver, B.C. in the mid-eighties. This healing tool continues to assist me in the ongoing process of activating the love within myself. With full attention and feeling, affirm daily: *"My heart center is aglow with Divine Love Light, ever reaching outward, ever expanding, touching all that I meet."* With every in-breath, visualize a soft pink light at the center of your heart. See it grow and expand until it completely fills you. With every out-breath, visualize this light forming a far-reaching circle all around you, creating an aura of shimmering, shining luminescence.

"To be able to look back upon one's life
in satisfaction is to live twice."
—Kahlil Gibran

Heart Connections: A Matrix

E. Patricia Connor

There's a moment from a few years ago that beckons like a lighthouse in my heart. After shopping for groceries, I paused a few minutes to breathe in the fresh cool air and welcome my old friend sunshine. It was early morning in late January and it had been a long time since we had seen each other. The golden adorned white temple dome across the street looked striking against the crystal blue sky. I anticipated with great joy the springtime, which was surely around the corner. Sunshine and I would spend more time together soon, I was certain. I could almost hear the song of the birds announcing the good weather. But it was silent. Too early in the year for my little companions, I reflected, sighing deeply.

It was then that I heard happy whistling coming from someone behind me. So welcoming was the tune that I quickly turned around. To my amazement, I spotted a man rummaging through the garbage can outside the store. He was in his fifties, dressed in tattered clothing, and was closely guarding his shopping cart with one hand as he sifted through the garbage can with the other.

"Find anything interesting?" I asked him. *Why did I ask that?*

"Always," was his answer. "How can I not find anything interesting in a container like this one? There is so much to choose from. You just need to know where to look."

Not an expected answer from a homeless person, but a curious one. He had my attention. I took a closer look at my conversation partner. He was a nice looking man with sandy colored hair and blue eyes. It wasn't so much his physical characteristics that I noticed, but his aura. He exuded lightness and happiness. For me, our friendly exchange was both disconcerting and comforting. We were connecting—a total stranger whose money troubles were obvious, but whose heart beat with the same love as mine did.

As he stood straighter and faced me more directly, an energetic circle encompassed us. I was very much aware that the customers coming in and out of the store were staring our way as they walked around him and me, not in between. Perhaps, they didn't want to disturb us.

Dragging his cart behind him, he closed the distance between us just a little. As he did so, I noticed the two colorful windmill flowers on sticks, which he'd firmly secured at the front of his cart. "Would you like a flower?" he offered.

I declined, but complemented him on his decorations.

"I can't have real ones, you know. Not where I live now. I used to have a garden in Alberta. It was a nice backyard. My wife and I gardened together when the weather warmed up. The kids and I played touch football there. They don't speak to me anymore."

His words faltered as sadness swept across his face like a cloud blocking the sun. But before I could comment, he piped right back up again, "Maybe one day I'll talk to them again."

"Maybe sooner than you think," I offered, smiling against the ache in my chest.

With a slight nod of his head, his lips curled slightly as he bid his farewell. It seemed that he wanted to be alone with the treasured memories he pulled along as he did his shopping cart full of reclaimed gems.

Taking ten dollars from my wallet, I handed it to him. "Go get yourself a good breakfast."

After thanking me, he walked away, whistling his happy tune.

I stood frozen in place contemplating what had just happened. The encounter left me with warmth in my heart and a smile on my face. I'd truly connected with this homeless stranger; perhaps, even brightened his day, as he had mine.

Driving home, I recalled long periods in my life when I didn't connect with anyone. The years when it was difficult to connect with myself, let alone with another human being. That is not to say that I wasn't in the company of others. I was. However, a terrifying fear that people might discover how horribly I felt inside my own skin, prevented me from openly embracing any relationship—outward or inward. People viewed me as a competent business woman: nicely groomed, university educated and well-spoken. Certainly, I couldn't disappoint them, or myself, by revealing my struggles through the ever elusive internal light. So, for years, I led a dual life—happy on the outside, lost on the inside. Until, little by little, my world became lightless. For a time, I lived in darkness.

"Please stand in a circle in the middle of the room."

Twenty-one of us rose from our desks and heeded our herbology teacher's instructions.

Handing out our diplomas, one by one he congratulated my classmates, as I pursed my lips in a vain attempt to cease the flow of my tears of joy and gratitude.

"Patricia Connor," he called out.

My heart skipping beats, I stepped forward to accept my diploma. *I'd passed the course!* For reasons I didn't immediately understand, receiving my herbology course diploma meant more to me than the one I received for my Bachelor of Arts degree.

"You, my friend, earned the second-highest mark in our group—ninety-eight percent. Well done!"

A barely audible "thank you" slipped past my lips as I shyly bowed to the group's applause.

What our instructor didn't share, was that halfway through the nine month course, I'd almost quit. A course I'd enrolled in to help disperse the clouds that still shadowed my search for light. However, our wise and kind instructor refused to buy into my reasons for wanting to quit: "My thoughts are too scattered. I can't concentrate because my hip hurts all the time and there is so much material to learn. I can't go on the field trips to the forest and beach with everyone else, because I can't walk very far."

"Patricia, you can do this," he had encouraged after hearing my plight. "You are a smart and capable person. You will pass this course in celebration of the challenges you face in your life and mind. You will succeed because of them, not in spite of them."

I knew he was right. *Quitting* would set me back. *Continuing* might help free the depression that had latched onto my self-doubt and threatened to pull me further under the darkness. I decided to persevere; albeit, it was a decision based more in his faith than mine.

My life had crumbled three years earlier when I quit a high-powered corporate job. Amid *where to from here* quandaries, I worried about my aged-father, whose illnesses were multiplying and progressing. At the time, I was also suffering from debilitating pain in the upper portion of my right thigh and anxiously awaiting a total hip replacement. The relentless leg pain and constant worry were a bit too much to handle, so I went to counseling and took prescribed antidepressants. My only interaction was with my husband and others closest to me, as I struggled through a near-catatonic state in a bid to survive. At first, I disconnected from myself to avoid the physical and emotional pain, and then from others, because I simply couldn't endure any stimulation— even positive stimulation. Totally disconnected from myself and people, my world turned bleak and black.

My most trusted confidant and companion was Batza, my guardian Polish sheepdog, who spent endless hours watching me staring into space or sleeping. I felt safe with him. He didn't give me suggestions on what I should do to get well again. It wasn't that my family and friends weren't supportive. They simply weren't aware of what was happening for me, because I didn't tell them. Answering questions about my health or state of mind was more than I could bear. I couldn't decipher the confused thoughts tumbling about my head like a tornado, continually sucking up more bits of debris for me to sort through and order—how could I answer any questions or concerns that my loved ones might have? It was better to stay quiet and keep things to myself. My dog and I would figure things out.

Allying with outward silence to shelter myself was easy. My inner voice was deafening and relentless. *How could this happen to you? I thought you were a strong person. What are people going to think? You'll never get another job! What if your husband leaves you? What a failure! You have nothing to offer. You let everyone down. You thought you were superior. Ha! Look at you now!*

I'd become silent and turned inward in search of peace of mind. Unfortunately, the more I sought to quiet my chaotic and belittling thinking, the more entrenched my derogatory self-talk. How was I to achieve tranquility, when the traitor making it an impossible feat was my own mind? There had to be a way, and with the angels' help, I'd find it.

After threading my needle, my very first cross-stitch resulted in a knot. The instructions the sales lady had given me forgotten, I consulted the how-to booklet before starting all over again. I didn't miss that this was a perfect metaphor for my personal journey.

Cross-stitching became my solace. Concentrating on creating a beautiful image on a material canvas quieted my inner world. I was still very much aware of the aggrieved voice that jeered and jabbed, but it was slowly fading. Each stitch sutured a puncture in the wounds of my heart and mind. Like sunlight slowly cresting to cast a glow across a meadow, as each beautiful design began to take form on the canvas, light seeped into my darkness. Stitch by stitch, day by day, the possibility of escaping the endless self-berating chatter seemed more attainable. Perhaps, I'd soon be able to connect with myself in love.

The imagined joy in gifting my finished creations to family and friends nudged at feelings long dormant. It was more rewarding, perhaps safer, to connect with others via a lovingly crafted piece of art, than to reveal the turmoil that brewed within. At Christmas, my presents to family and friends were cross-stitched angels encased in picture frames of gold or silver. Throughout the spring, colorful birds and dainty flowers slowly appeared on canvas after canvas. Upon viewing one of my five-by-five creations, many people would fondly comment on how they'd once cross-stitched, some adding that their designs were much larger. My response to the latter was always to smile. My pictures were just the right size—each creation a stepping stone in my recovery.

Getting in touch with my feelings was painful. At the beginning of this process, my primary emotions were anger, sadness and fear. When asked to draw what I felt during one counseling session, I sketched a little girl, alone, gazing out of a barred window at a beautiful meadow. Peace, love and joy were seemingly outside. My dream became to go *outside* and play.

As though the angels were listening, very shortly after this revelation, a friend gave me a book detailing Lower Mainland parks and trails where dogs were welcome. The author described each place and rated the difficulty of the trails. Having shared with my husband that being in nature would be extremely beneficial for me, he promised that we would discover a new place to take Batza every weekend. Greatly anticipating our family adventures, during the week I researched various places. To my delight, I found a wonderful park a mere ten-minute drive from our home. Ten steps along the trail, I knew I'd found an oasis for my soul. Beautiful tall evergreens reached into the sky; native salal and blackberry bushes trailed along the pathway; birds spurted from branch to branch, singing when so inspired; squirrels leapt and chattered in celebration of play; and, as Batza rushed through them, the large sword ferns waved and bobbed as though saying, *yes, yes, you are welcome.* I felt welcomed. Nature reached out and I willingly took her hand.

Visiting the multi-trailed park became a near-daily ritual for Batza and me. Each afternoon, we'd pause at the mouth of the forest, ask permission to enter and await her response. Mysteriously and soothingly, the forest and I would intuitively link and she'd let me know if it was safe to enter. The trails varied in length and ease of navigation. Which one I chose depended on my level of hip pain. No matter though, there was a vital place within nature's arms that I had to reach.

I'd discovered a splendorous spiritual secret during my initial summertime visit. At the crossroads of the lower and upper trails, there stood a magnificent first-growth maple tree with multiple trunks sprouting out from its prodigious base. Its canopy of foliage spanned the breadth of the lower trail, providing a kaleidoscopic filter that scattered sunlit dancing shapes about the greenery. Awestruck, I laid my hand on the moss-threaded bark of this majestic wonder. Our connection was immediate and powerful. Bonding with this ancient earthly gift brought me closer to God and the angels. In my mind's eye, I saw the roots of the tree extending through earth's core to the other side of the globe, and the branches above reaching deep into Heaven. Feeling the life vibration of the tree, in my heart I knew for that pause in time, I was no longer alone.

"Let's go see our tree!" became the cue for Batza to jump off the armchair and head for the door. No matter how thick the darkness enshrouded my mind, or how intense the pain in my hip, I knew that all would be okay when I laid my hands on the trunk of the stately maple that pulsated nature's love. As soon as this *oh, so magical* tree was within sight, my pace would quicken. The tree became my trusted confidant, a measure of hope, a receiver of gratitude, and a spiritual shoulder where tearful pleas fell on God's ears and counsel came from the divine. Under its canopy, I could freely unburden my emotional and physical pain without fear of hurting another or repercussions for myself. I asked for guidance and listened for the answer. Without fail, the pain that poured out from within would dissipate, slowing my thoughts so that I could embrace insights from my higher-self, God and the angels. Each time we parted, I felt more confident, healed and at peace. *If only I could take this sacred tree home with me.*

Nearing the date of my hip replacement, the pain in my upper thigh worsened. But rather than weaken, it strengthened my resolve to daily reach nature's tall green manifestation of hope and love. Throughout recovery, my focus was on healing enough to visit my inspirational comrade. Within six weeks of receiving my new hip, cane in one hand, Batza's leash in the other, off we went to see our friend. As expected, our tree had patiently awaited our return.

The maple stretching skyward at the crossroads of the upper and lower trails remains a hallmark of my healing journey. Under the protection of its branches, my hands on its energy-emanating trunk, angst and fear gradually moved toward inner-peace and self-love.

Boy Scout wisdom asserts that when lost in the forest, hugging a tree while you await rescue is one's surest survival strategy. It's seems apropos, that when I was totally lost, by anchoring myself in the tree's magical enchantment, I connected with me.

Though I'd written multitudes of business letters, training manuals, reports, and such, I never identified with being a writer. Writing about my inner-longings, dreams and illusions never entered my mind. How was it possible that when my friend suggested we take an informal creative writing class, I agreed to attend? The pre-requisite was to bring a special pen—a bold pen. I did as instructed.

Equipped with paper and my special new bold pen, I timidly knocked on the door. There were only four of us at the writing table, which was a little daunting in that I couldn't disappear among a sea of others. Self-exposure was a much dreaded state.

Standing at the flip chart, marker in hand, the instructor urged, "Shout out the first word that comes into your mind."

"Love," yelled my friend.

"Woman," said another.

"Beach," I offered, my angst quickly waning. This exercise was fun.

"Life!"

"Fear!"

I quickly glanced at the middle-age blond woman who'd associated 'life' with 'fear.' My journey through the darkness was not one reserved solely for me.

"Poem!" yelled someone, followed by about a half-dozen more rapidly fired words that came easily to this creative group.

"Patricia, call out a phrase that includes the word *love*," our teacher enthusiastically commanded.

"Love is in the air!" I blurted.

"Perfect!" she responded, her expression pleased. "I want everyone to begin with 'Love is in the air.' Additionally, I want you to incorporate all of the remaining words on the flip chart into your story. You have five minutes."

"*Really?* You've got to be kidding," I thought, readying to put prose on paper that others might later read. *I'm not a writer!* Pen in hand, I inhaled a deep breath. It was an intimidating task, until our teacher said the most freeing words I'd ever heard.

"Remember, there is no right or wrong way of writing. Just write."

No wrong way of writing? Did she mean that anything I wrote would be okay? It didn't have to be perfect? I didn't have to be perfect? I'd just been handed the key to free-flowing, no holds barred, self-expression. And I liked it! No censorship. No judgment. No course grade to define or deflate me, just the absolute freedom to write what I thought and felt. I'd been liberated! Finally! *Well, at least for the six weeks the course lasted.*

Writing, similar to cross-stitching and communing with my maple tree, slowly connected me with my *true* self. Through these three simple, innocent and heartwarming activities I came to realize that, for much of my adult life, I'd functioned and performed without any true awareness or understanding of my inner self—an inner self that often contrasted and sometimes *conflicted* with my outer self.

In striving to be accepted, maybe admired—good career, nice home, fancy car, meticulous grooming, handsome husband—I'd not only compromised my spirit, I'd caged it! Striving for perfection came with a prison of my own fashioning.

In my teenage years, I'd celebrated being free-spirited and welcomed the realization that I didn't always think like other people. However, in my twenties, my biggest fear became not being accepted and finding myself alone. What I didn't realize was that my determination to conform, fit in and be loved—disconnected me from my heart-centered self.

When our six-week writing course ended, my friend and I delved into Julia Cameron's *The Artist's Way*. Ms. Cameron championed free-flowing, uncensored daily journaling, in what she called 'morning pages.' I liked the idea, so vowed to begin a ritual of starting my day by making a cup of tea, and then sitting down at the dining room table to write three pages, free hand. I'd write whatever came to my mind, whether it made sense or not. It excited me that these pages were for my eyes only—no regard for sentence construction, grammar or spelling. I'd compose multitudes of beautiful, flowery sentences similar to those I'd written during the creative writing course. The freedom would be bliss!

My shock was considerable, when it wasn't beauty, but dark strands of horrendous thoughts—suicide, hatred, despair, madness—that blemished my pretty journal paper. As if in a trance, I couldn't stop myself from writing—facing—the darkest parts of my psyche. Pages and pages of tortuous prose emerged while I looked on in absolute disbelief. *Were these thoughts really coming from my head? They couldn't be.* However, trusting that good would come from what was an excruciating exercise, I persevered, each day completing my three pages before laying my pen to rest.

With time, and what I must assume was the healing of the darker side of myself, my journaling exercise became one of repetitive questioning. *Who am I? What is my purpose in this life? Where am I to go from here?*

Perplexingly and discouragingly, though I rewrote the questions numerous times, no answers emerged.

It wasn't until a few weeks into this turbulent, crazy-making journaling journey, that I started to understand the benefits. The first gift realized was that I hadn't acted on the unspeakable deliberations that had initially popped out of my brain and onto paper. I was thankful for that! I was also hopeful that much of what must have been harbored anger, resentment and self-loathing, had been sufficiently soothed. The second gift was realizing that I was free to move forward in any direction I chose. For the umpteenth time, again I wrote: *Who am I?*

What is my purpose in this life? Where am I to go from here? But this time a new question emerged—*Am I strong enough to carve my own path?*

Then it happened. Out of the corner of my right eye, cascading iridescent plumes flanked the full length of my body. Quickly turning my head to the left, I saw a mirror image of the same beautiful enormous shimmering feathers. They were angel wings. In awe and reverence, I continued sitting at the table, pen in hand, eyes closed, allowing this glorious divine being to envelope me in love. Slowly inhaling, I breathed in the magnificent heavenly energy at my sides, my back and head. Exhaling, I released the love swelled within. For one omnipotent moment, I was acutely and comfortingly aware of my interconnection with the universe. The angel had come to let me know I was not alone—had never been alone. God held a space in His heart for me.

Life didn't vastly improve. Disenchantment, disappointment and fear of an earthly making still ebbed and tided. However, the realization of my heavenly connection allowed me to view the positive transpiring in my present. There forward, derisive self-talk and doubt took a backseat. Hope, gratitude and love were what would steer me forward in peace.

Over the next few months, my journal filled with gratitude for my teachers. I thanked Batza, my gorgeous, thick-furred white Polish sheepdog, for his unconditional, abundant and precious love. I expressed appreciation for my cross-stitched canvases for revealing my internal splendor, and for bringing me such joy through crafting and gifting. Many pages recounted my blessed visits to see my broad-leafed friend always waiting within the forest's arms. I wrote about the creative writing process, and how grateful I was for the words that allowed me to express and connect with my inner and outer worlds. Tears streaming, I acknowledged my thankfulness for the angel, who by embracing my back with a potent and powerful love, had connected me with my inner-strength, showing me that my spine was akin to a maple tree's trunk: strong, yet flexible. Like my tall green comrade, no matter how strong the wind, I could bend with whatever storm blew my way.

Strengthened by my experiential, emotional and soulful connections to the universe, nature, animals and myself, I once again reached out into the human world. *This time I was prepared. This time I was safe.*

Out, Out—Damn Thought!

Louise E. Morris

We colored in silence.

It was three in the afternoon on Monday, and most of my students had scattered. Brenda, a thin, pretty young lady with bright brown eyes and a hesitant smile, had chosen to stay behind. It was a rare treat. Most often this semester, she packed up her things fifteen minutes before class ended, skipping out the door along with the sounding bell. Brenda had a boyfriend.

A few minutes later, it was Brenda who broke the silence and my heart.

"I showed him, Mrs. M. He thought he could get away with hitting me, but I showed him. I went back to his house and cracked him one right in the face, just like he did to me."

Eyes down, her coloring strokes quickened. Mine stopped.

Attempting to flick her over-the-counter dyed blond hair out of her eyes with the jerk of her head, she huffed out a labored sigh before pushing her bangs off of her forehead. Like Brenda, her bangs had a mind of their own.

It had taken her almost two years to trust me enough to disclose such a personal story. *Don't overreact, Louise. Overreact, and she'll shut down and you won't be able to help her.*

"Now that he knows not to hit me, we're getting along just fine," she continued, a triumphant smirk puffing her cheeks. Still, she wouldn't make eye contact.

Brenda mistook her boyfriend's jealousy as him caring too much. His abusive reaction to her a new reality, she obviously believed that by physically standing up to him, she could protect herself from future harm.

"What do you think of my drawing?" I asked, futilely trying to squelch the anxious soup in my stomach, while staying engaged with Brenda.

"The way you shaded the leaves yellow makes the tree look more real," she remarked, smiling sweetly. "I like it!"

Treading into what I knew was tender territory, I softly asked, "What will happen the next time he hits you?"

"I'll crack him one again! Nobody hits me and gets away with it," she declared, her angry eyes dancing defiantly as she glanced down, her crayon now heavy on the paper.

There was little sense in discussing the obvious—anger was Brenda's only defense. This was her first love. I'd taught enough years, lived enough years, to know that beneath her indignant bragging, lay a downward snowball of anger and disappointment rolling over layers of confusion, hurt and fear.

"What will happen if the hitting doesn't stop?" I asked, knowing this was a couple who partied every weekend. Another physical altercation was inevitable.

Doodling with her pencil crayon, a solemn mask replaced her earlier smirk.

I waited for a bit before saying, "Brenda, you know I want you to be happy. Didn't you tell me you're angry with your mother because she won't leave your dad, even though he keeps hitting her?"

I paused, hoping what I'd said would sink in. Brenda continued doodling.

"But aren't you being hit too?" I gently probed. "Your boyfriend shouldn't be hitting you, and neither should *you* be hitting him. It's not good for you to hit anyone." Fearing I might have said too much, I jokingly added, "So the next time he hits you, call me and *I'll* hit him for you."

Brenda's coloring stopped as she studied my mischievous, twinkling eyes. Once certain I was joking, her hip jerked sideways and her eyes rolled skyward, as she quipped, "Well, that's just stupid, Mrs. M."

An eruption of side-splitting laughter provided the comedic relief needed to take the edge off. We resumed coloring in silence, but this time with grins on our faces.

Daring to broach my concerns again, I said to Brenda, "I know you're trying to be strong, and I'm proud of you for that. Let me tell you what *strong* people do. If someone hits them, they walk away. They do not stay with that person. If you can walk away with a broken heart from someone you love who is hurting you, then *that's* being strong."

In hopes of easing the thinking that might soon swirl about her young mind should she regret having confided in me, and wanting to empower her at the same time, before she left my office, I added, "If you choose to walk away from him, if you want…and only if you want, come and tell me about it. And Brenda, if you don't want to tell me about it, that's okay too."

Decades earlier, Brenda's story had been her teacher's story. Resonating utmost was her *boasting* that she'd punched him back. I'd swathed myself in the same misplaced pride.

Like Brenda, rather than feeling the emotional pain of a physically abusive relationship, and unwilling to perceive myself as an underdog, I constructed a *victim-hero* story. One unwittingly created to transform a nightmarish encounter into a Sunday afternoon movie special, with me starring as victor—vindicated and triumphant—not broken and bruised.

Brenda may have left my office that day, but I was not alone, for I've always been in the company of my thoughts. Unfortunately, during my younger years they were often negative.

Through guiding my young student to raise her victim-hero story to another level—from a tale of hitting back to one of letting go—she helped me.

Sitting at the colorful, cluttered table worrying about her, I realized how much of my life had been spent searching for happiness, striving to overcome the painful consequences of my childhood, and attempting a multitude of strategies to gain mastery over my shortcomings. All noble feats, too often undermined by compulsive, self-oppressive thinking that kept me locked in shame.

Brenda's victim-hero story reminded me that our words mirror our beliefs. As we journey in our healing and awareness, our stories align with our progress, making it crucial that we *hear* our own words. This was an awareness for which there was no going back.

He's getting closer and closer. *Where can I hide? If he catches me, he's going to kill me. He's usually careful around people—tonight he's too angry to care. Why didn't I just listen to him?*

Exhausted, lungs stinging, knees near buckling, heart thundering each time he hollered my name, I raced for cover in a stranger's backyard. *Please God, don't let them come outside—I couldn't take any more humiliation.*

Barely avoiding tripping over a flattened lawn chair that I spotted courtesy of a nearby streetlight, my panic soared. *Oh, my God! Can he see me too?* Hysterical, I ran toward the darkness near the back fence. Desperately trying to climb over it, my sandals kept slipping. I was trapped. Diving into a decaying heap of leaves, grass and twigs that had been windswept against the fence, I burrowed until only my nose and eyes peeked through. My nostrils recoiled at the putrid smell of decomposing debris that poked and itched. But I didn't dare scratch.

Shivering violently, fear of being embarrassed switched to silent pleas for my life. *Please, God, let them come outside.* Sounds magnified by heightened instincts, I listened. He wasn't more than twenty feet from me.

Chattering teeth silenced by widening my jaw, I rolled my eyes leftward to see him flop forward, panting as he planted his massive hands on his kneecaps.

"I'm going to kill her," he puffed between curses. "I'm going to kill her." Catching his breath, he straightened and glared in my direction. "Bitch!"

Had he spotted me? *Stop shaking, Louise. Stop it. Stop it. Stop it!*

"Bitch!" he spat again.

Oh, my God! Can he see me? Is he talking to me? Muscles primed for flight, I watched as he suddenly turned and trudged out of the yard. *Would he return?* Shrouded beneath rotting vegetation, I waited. Eventually, my spastic shivering subsided, the moist leaves becoming soothingly cool against my adrenaline-fevered skin. Slowly, I crept out of hiding...listening...watching...fearing.

Later that night, rag-doll empty, body and soul spent, I cried myself to sleep in an unfamiliar bed as a concerned friend looked on. I wondered, "Can you run out of tears?"

Like Shakespeare's Lady Macbeth who tried to *will* away the bloody "damn'd spot" staining her hands and conscience, I tried to will away my haunting marathon of *what ifs*, but lamentably could not. *Out, out—damn thought!*

I couldn't deny or dismiss the terror and humiliation of that backyard. Re-run after re-run of how that night could have ended, played through my mind. *What if I'd tripped over the lawn chair? What if he'd heard my clattering teeth, or I'd sneezed? What if he'd killed me?*

Gradually, needing to escape the paralyzing truth—if he had found me, he was crazed enough to murder—my story became one of heroism.

Ignoring the emotional scars littering my thoughts, for days afterward I reveled in the kudos and sympathy of friends, as my cleverly cloaked anger, fear and humiliation became a humorous account of how *I'd* outsmarted and outrun *the beast.* Distorted, my pain became bearable. Rationalizing that the laughter generated by my victim-hero story lessened the impact on others, allowed me to deny the truth—there were no heroes that night. My fantastical accounting was merely a vain attempt to shield myself from my true feelings.

As a young woman, I dreamed of becoming a missionary and helping others; saw my adult-self as spiritual, worldly and wise. *How was it that I ended up in such an unhealthy relationship?*

Living in a small town, feeling trapped financially and without real recourse, explained *why* I stayed—until that dreadful night—but it did not explain *how.* What were the building thoughts and beliefs that framed my skewed destiny? *Could unresolved shame be helming my life?*

Repeatedly told, "It's your own fault," childhood traumas became a lesson well-taught—there was something inherently wrong with me. Suffering in silence was safest; bruises heal quicker on the outside than on the inside.

Too young to see the unfairness in blaming a child, and too vulnerable to shield myself from such harmful accusations, those harsh words echoed into my adult life. Being unable to protect my siblings compounded layers of guilt onto an already fragile ego.

Naively believing my intrinsically defective character was to blame for every travesty and misstep, I felt undeserving of anyone's love, including Jesus's. Fearing further ridicule and rejection, speaking about my self-deprecating thoughts and feelings was out the question, even though there were many visible clues of their existence—mainly, the slow destruction of flawed Louise.

If happiness wasn't possible, then having fun was. Partying, drinking and recounting the hilarious exploits of the weekend became my primary focus. To protect myself from what I saw as a world filled with self-indulgent manipulators, I sometimes became opinionated, critical and judgmental—quickly rejecting anyone I thought was about to reject me.

Unfortunately, some of those who might have had a positive influence on my life were also warded off with deliberately wounding wit. Rationalizing that I was only *unkind* to unkind people, I still managed to view myself as a 'nice' person. Ignoring that even some of those close to me feared my barbed tongue, for years, I remained armored with my *who cares* brashness.

Eventual motherhood didn't slow or alter my course. To shield my children from my partying, I compartmentalized my life into three sections—family, work and nightlife. Rarely did I allow the three areas to overlap. Thankfully, wishing to be a better parent and resolving to fill the void in my soul rather than run from it, I moved away from the numbing craziness. With this brave move toward normalcy, however, came my painful past.

As the years rolled by, witnessing the pain my children endured—some because of my bad choices, others due to life's hard knocks—added a weighty layer of remorse to my already deep-seated shame. Wanting to heal, I turned to our modern self-help gurus, soaking up their wisdom in one book after another.

Studying these masters brought some peace to my run-amuck, troubled mind; especially, when I learned that my feelings and reactions—anger, hyper-vigilance and depression, to name a few—were reasonable under the circumstances. Like the palm trees in Dr. Wayne Dyer's book, *Living the Wisdom of the Tao: Change Your Thoughts, Change Your Life,* whose "so-called weakness somehow gives them the strength to survive devastating storms"—my *vulnerability* was also one of my greatest *strengths.* For instance, my *fear of criticism* fueled my early work ethic, becoming an integral characteristic that led me to achieve success in university and later as a teacher.

Reading that the road to happiness required *purpose* paved with a *positive outlook*—living positively became my purpose, setting me on an urgent pursuit to correct my character defects. Unfortunately, this 'righted' thinking made me the poster girl for what Wayne Dyer referred to as Maslow's "deficiency motivation," in that much of my life was spent 'trying to fix myself.' It took a long while to realize that when you concentrate on your defects, you actually nurture them.

Naturally, at first, it was much easier to notice other people's flaws. A pursuit thoroughly enjoyed until Gary Zukav in his book *The Mind of the Soul: Responsible Choices* pointed out that: "What you discover when you look inside are the very things you find most repulsive in others." Somewhat humbled, I took another hard look inward.

Somersaulting through incessant self-reflection became increasingly counterproductive. Old wounds bled among the new cutting deep into my spirit—triggering more twisted stories starring me victim-turned-hero. Like my young student, simmering pain, fear and shame became anger that I flipped into a ceaseless series of reframed tales to ease my suffering. Until it eventually dawned on me that these creative fables didn't erase my frustrated anguish—they kept me stuck in muddy despair.

Having taken a major healing step, without being critical but merely observant, I began to notice the victim-hero stories of others. Amazingly, it quickly became apparent that many of us suffer a similarly skewed self-protection pattern. Victimhood is rampant.

Trusting that I'd be unbiased, two coworkers asked me to mediate their dispute. Before our agreed upon mediation session, both of these ladies made certain to speak with me in private. Cornering me in the washroom, each recounted her slant of the truth. That day, I heard two victim-hero stories! Believe me, neither of these women was truly a victim; yet, in their minds, they were.

The mediation was mostly successful despite each one's fear of being wrong. Sitting face-to-face, each woman's story gradually crept closer to the truth. It struck me that their shared underlying motivation was not wanting to be *the villain*, and thereby, the one who should apologize.

Afterward, in private again, each lady added a piece or two to her story, portraying herself as having taken the higher-road during mediation, explaining that it was sometimes better to just let things go. It seemed that each one's real après mediation goal was to save face.

Neither lady wanted to be wrong, and if the truth was that they were both right, then each desperately sought to be just a little more right. *Could not wanting to be wrong be a reason for this type of victim-hero story?*

Pondering this question sparked a shift in consciousness for me. Had I also adopted victimhood without truly being victimized? *Was being a victim easier than taking responsibility for my own feelings, actions and reactions? Did I need to be right one hundred percent of the time?* My answers were humbling.

In a quest to *be seen* as wise, kind and likeable, I masked negative emotions and thoughts with humorous anecdotes and *positive* talk. Pretty laughter and language all dressed up for the sake of my fragile ego. Like my coworkers, I wasn't being deliberately deceptive, I simply wasn't confident that inclusive of my warts and wrongs, I was still loveable. Being *wrong* equated with being flawed. Unaware that fear of criticism was at the wheel of my frail ego, I was victim to a deceptive master—me.

Throughout my healing voyage, packing my bags and starting over somewhere else sometimes crossed my mind. Until it occurred to me that, no matter where I went, my thoughts were along for the ride. Louise couldn't escape Louise, because I was at the helm of every negative thought that led to inner screams of "Out, out—damn thought!"

In his book *A New Earth,* Eckhart Tolle describes self-talk as "the voice in your head that never stops speaking." Reading his depiction of compulsive thinking, I realized that every feeling, obsession, and interpretation is fueled by thought. It was then that I wondered, *"Could compulsive thinking be an addiction?* And if compulsive thinking is indeed an addiction, it must be the catalytic addiction, more powerful than the others, because it feeds and nourishes each of them. Wow!"

Once I finally understood that the journey to happiness and inner-peace rested in the palm of *self*-acceptance, not *acceptance by others,* my life flourished. I no longer agonized over my own or anyone else's flaws. Take it from someone who's viewed life both negatively and positively: peace and happiness are best achieved with your eyes and heart opened wide in grace and love, not closed in fear. In *The Kindness Ambassador,* there is a great quote by Joyce M. Ross: "Be grateful for your shadows, light and dark, as they are your compass to the life you are meant to love."

Healing is a continual journey. To this day, occasional painful childhood memories and current hurts sneak into my thoughts. But now they remind me of how far I've come, no longer taunting me for endless hours. Nor do I need to banish them with "Out, out—damn thought." Instead, I accept 'what is' and who 'each of us is'—choosing not to fire back at those who sometimes bruise my tender heart or shake my still healing ego.

Whenever retelling stories or sharing insights, I'm now vigilantly aware of the adjectives and adverbs employed to describe incidents and others. Occasionally still catching myself spinning words to protect or illuminate my ego, I stop midsentence and ask myself, "Where did that come from?" Unkind words don't hurt as much as they once did, and when they do upset me, I view it as an opportunity for self-reflection, sometimes chuckling at how easily some situations and people provoke me.

Feeling defensive has actually become a favored red flag, because it alerts me that my ego is again at the wheel as my thoughts become feelings. In response, I quickly check my physiological reactions for further clues while contemplating, "What am I *afraid* or *ashamed of?*" Answering honestly provides me the opportunity to once again accept that judgment and perfection are not my allies—they're sneaky saboteurs of happiness and inner-peace. Eckhart Tolle, my revered distant teacher, summarized this truism best when he wrote in *The New Earth* that "thinking without awareness is the main dilemma of human existence."

What helps me stay centered, and aware, is Wray Herbert's HALT principle: don't let yourself become too *hungry, angry, lonely,* or *tired.* When my body, mind and spirit get the rest and fuel needed to be healthy, I'm more likely to make better decisions and to manage my ego.

Over the years, in my journey toward self-awareness and acceptance, some healing strategies worked better than others. One was casting out victim-hero stories and replacing them with positive or neutral alternative interpretations. Naturally, this was easier said than done. Extended alone time, such as while driving home from work, I'd often become aware of my negative thinking. Sometimes unable to spin a particular thought positively, I'd simply change the channel of my thoughts to a mundane task; for instance, what I would make for dinner or what ingredients were in a favorite recipe. Failing that ploy, I'd sing along with the radio. One of these tactics usually worked in freeing me from nourishing negativity.

Visiting with my sister often led to our exchanging victim-hero stories. Although needing to share and process our feelings, rolling about in the muddy waters of our childhood or dwelling on current negative situations, was harming our current sibling relationship. Wanting to share more joy, we put a time limit on talking about bothersome issues. When our agreed upon reflection session was up, we switched topics or activities. Unfueled, the past became far less significant.

Consciously choosing to support and encourage myself as I would a close friend, led to kinder self-reflection and acceptance. Although I didn't always understand the adage that you must love yourself first, I do now. Loving yourself is crucial for attracting positivity. Out of self-love, you are predisposed to think, choose and live negatively. By feeling *less than* you unconsciously invite situations and relationships that reinforce your unworthiness. The opposite is equally true: by feeling deserving, you invite situations and relationships that reinforce your worthiness.

Mahatma Gandhi said, "A man is but the product of his thoughts. What he thinks, he becomes." I choose awareness, gratitude and love.

These days, although occasionally in the company of negative thoughts, their power to dominate and wound is vastly diminished, making it easier to switch tracks and get back to feeling worthwhile and loved. Thought—is a powerful friend or foe. A lifetime of searching, led to discovering that the only thing keeping me from achieving happiness was my thinking.

Most new discoveries are suddenly-seen things that were always there.
—Susanne K. Langer

Surviving or Thriving? It's Your Life!

Maria Ganguin

"Under the 'B'—52," the caller announced, sending my heart racing and my gratitude heavenward. Playing bingo with my older brother and down to our last dollar, we'd just minutes before agreed to pool our resources. If by some miracle we won, we'd share our winnings.

"BINGO!" I hollered, waving the winning card in the air. "I can't believe it. We just won!"

"How much did we win?" Georg asked, dollar signs alive in his young eyes as we headed toward the caller to have our bingo card checked.

Vibrating, we waited while our card was verified as a winner.

"Good for you two," the caller said, smiling at our obvious thrill. "You're a thousand dollars richer."

My brother held out his hand as fifty-dollar bill after fifty-dollar bill was placed in his shaking upturned palm. "Here you go," Georg said, tipping the last fifty-dollar bill to the caller.

"Are you crazy?" I thought, but didn't say. Fifty dollars is a lot of money to be giving away!

It was late at night and we were at Vancouver's notorious Pacific National Exhibition known for its scary carnival rides, amazing fast food, and various exhibitions we didn't care about. We were there for the thrill of the rides and the high of playing bingo, which we'd just experienced to the max.

Unable to contain our excitement, we called home to tell Mom and Dad of our great fortune. Dad answered, sounding genuinely pleased when I babbled on about our big win. Before hanging up, I arranged with our father to pick us up at 11:00 p.m. Georg, however, was quick to say he wasn't going home. He was going to stay and play more bingo!

While on the phone with my father I noticed my school chum John standing nearby. When he didn't approach me, hanging up the phone and too thrilled to be social, I simply walked off with my brother. Knowing Georg had an actual hole in his pocket, I took the majority of our cash home, leaving him only a small amount to gamble.

Arriving at home and feeling millionaire rich, I tossed the bundle of money into the air, letting it fall on the bed, where I rolled in it. Although I had a two-thousand-dollar paycheck in my wallet—wages earned from working the summer at my cousin's campground on Vancouver Island—the multiple fifty-dollar bills was a first. Never before had I possessed so much actual cash. It was a heady experience for a young lady of sixteen. Unbeknown to me at the time, our big win would become a lifelong lesson.

Georg arrived home at 2:00 a.m., broke, needing money to pay the cab driver, and asking for more of his share of our win so he could return to the PNE and continue gambling. (I later learned that he'd won an additional two hundred dollars after we parted, but had managed to gamble that away in a couple of hours.)

Unfortunately, Dad had confiscated our cache for safekeeping. After scouring our bedrooms and finding enough to pay the cab, too excited to sleep, Georg and I spent the rest of the night playing cards.

Monday morning, I was suddenly the most popular girl at school. Apparently John had overheard my conversation with Dad and had been busy telling all the students about Georg's and my win. So there I was, hitherto a misfit who was keenly aware that she didn't have a lot in common with her classmates, suddenly a sought after friend.

Gratitude that my win had rocketed me to near Prom Queen Status quickly dissolved as I recognized that being popular was fun, but having money also came with a much bigger responsibility. Instead of 'buying new friends' I decided to only spend money on my family, my closest classmate and another girlfriend who didn't attend our school, but loved me *broke* or *rich*.

The next few months were spent buying fun times and lunch for loved ones. Too young to fully comprehend the consequences of my generosity, my big win and much of my hard-earned paycheck soon disappeared. Georg was also busy spending his windfall on renting cars and having his version of a great time.

While checking my nearly depleted bank account, it hit me—without a goal for my money, being generous with family and friends would keep me perpetually broke. Quickly exchanging generosity for establishing credit, saving and material goals, I secured a credit card at a department store, charged a stereo system and then paid it off. Feeling incredibly grown up and responsible, I set a second and third goal of saving for a car (including one year's insurance) and then a house that would one day suitably house my own children and husband.

Before leaving home at age twenty-one, I had the car and insurance. At twenty-eight I'd saved the down payment for a house. Unable to fully qualify for the monthly payments, my common-law boyfriend co-signed the first mortgage. For a few years, the two of us were quite the financial duo: I worked at the credit union and was wise with money; he was a mechanic and earned a great wage.

Wanting to stretch my financial wings, I started a Party Lite business retailing candles and crystals via home party demonstrations. A year later, I left the credit union to pursue Party Lite fulltime. My goals fueled by warrior determination and effort, it was a successful adventure—until, I broke my ankle. The stress of my being in a wheelchair for months proved too much for our relationship, and my romantic partner and I separated. He moved out, taking our hot tub, car and fair compensation for his half of the house.

Word to the wise: two incomes stretch much further than one; especially, when you're self-employed in a small business. Maintaining the house on my own was tough, but I couldn't sell it, for within its walls lay my dreams. It was the perfect family home: nice residential area, schools nearby, four bedrooms, two bathrooms, and a big treed yard. Just because I was now single and struggling, I wasn't about to forfeit the house that would one day be a home for my family. I'd simply be a better financial warrior!

Unable to drive a stick shift with a broken ankle, I sold my vehicle via a series of promised payments. Unfortunately, the buyer didn't make even one payment. Needing cash, I repossessed the car. Still short each month, I took in international exchange students and rented rooms to the occasional traveler.

For the next several years, paying the mortgage was my sole priority. Though it was tough, I was proud to be accomplishing so much on my own, or at least mostly on my own. Noticing my year-after-year struggle, after explaining that she'd already given my siblings money but hadn't given me any because I'd always been self-sufficient, Mom helped me out financially. I was grateful, but beginning to wonder if I'd be able to maintain my goal to keep my house.

While still actively working my Party Light business in the evenings, I took a day job driving a coffee truck. When the opportunity arose to co-own a truck with a girlfriend, I jumped. Now having equity in my home, I was able to afford the start-up cost, and was fairly convinced that being partners in an owner-operator coffee truck business would make ends meet much more easily. But as is the case with many small businesses, my financial troubles continued. Together, my partner and I decided to buy a second truck. Forever fighting to make two trucks profitable, the pursuit of money began to takes its toll.

The fun in achieving my goal had long been spent. What was supposed to give me the means-to-an-end was sucking away the time needed to fulfill the dream at the end of my goal. So busy surviving, there was little room in my schedule for family, friends or meeting Mr. Right. If anything, my warrior-self was emitting the signals that I neither had the time nor desire for a man. My heart didn't sing, it howled!

For years I'd been too busy to hear my own tearful laments. *But tied directly to my dreams, how could I let go of my house and/or business?* It was during this period that I started to wonder about how best to balance my personal needs with my well-ingrained sense of financial responsibility. I wondered, *"Did one have to be exchanged for the other?"*

I'd learned early that choices—big and small, financial and personal—have long-term consequences. Though winning five hundred dollars had boosted me to schoolyard fame, followed by a quick realization that without a worthy goal money evaporates, it also instilled a runaway determination in me so doggedly ingrained that my end-goal dream of a family took backseat.

The house and business (and all the headaches that went with them) that were supposed to carry me toward my personal goals were pushing them further and further away. I wanted a family and a warrior husband/father to go with it. But instead, I'd become the warrior, too busy and independent to give any guy a chance to steal my heart. At forty-one, I made a decision to let go of my business and house in favor of rediscovering the lost me.

How had I become so incredibly insignificant in my own dream? While working at the credit union, I counseled numerous clients on the merits of saving and investing. At the time, it disheartened me that so many people were living beyond their means. Safe in my banking uniform, I generally assumed they were financially irresponsible, never considering that perhaps their over-spending was a reflection of some deeper unfulfilled need. Looking back, I now wonder how many of our deeply-in-debt clients were actually 'self-medicating.' It's so easy to point a finger at what society calls 'spendaholics.' But what lies beneath the need to buy for a high? Is it simply that we've all been seduced by materialism, or is something more complicated and furtive at the tiller of a sea of debt?

Averaged over the entire country, Canadians have a personal debt-to-asset ratio of 1-1.5, meaning we owe one-and-half times what we own. Yet, survey after survey, the majority of our citizens claim not to be concerned. When asked if it's troubling that a slight rise in interest rates could force many young families into selling their homes or defaulting on their mortgages, many of us simply shrug. *Why is that?*

Being a typical Canadian, I know that it's not because we don't care about our fellow countrymen, because we do. Is it that we believe our government will bail us out? Not likely, because we've witnessed the recent financial horrors of our friends in the United States and Europe. Is it that we don't feel we have a choice but to continue on with a wait-and-see attitude? Maybe it is. Is it that many simply haven't learned how to handle money? Yes, but not entirely. Is it that most Canadians equate the attainment of material goods with success? Yes, partially. Is it that many of us in free-market economies believe that our self-worth somewhat equates with what we accomplish and own? Sadly, this is truer than most of us wish to acknowledge.

Money is a tricky emotional issue as much as it is a means of exchange. From the time you first hear that 'money is dirty' or that someone is 'filthy rich,' wealth becomes equated with guilt and greed. Add in images of retired seniors eating dog food and street people begging for change, and you have fear fueling the train. One only has to pick up a newspaper or novel, listen to the radio, or watch television or a movie to be bombarded with the message that money can buy both love and happiness. Discombobulating the matter further is that many citizens of the industrialized world believe it is their free-market *right* and *semi-obligation* to own a car, home and vacation cottage. Never mind the pressure to save enough to send your offspring to university and build a nest egg for retirement. In Canada we don't have to worry about health care costs, but many around our globe do. Notorious for wearing our hearts on our sleeves, most Canadians donate to charity and worry about those less fortunate. Then, of course, there are government taxes. Wow!

Managing money is infinitely more overwhelming than many of us realize. Though I learned early that having *goals* for my cash was important, by doggedly pursuing my goals, for a very long time, I unwittingly sacrificed my dreams. *So what's the answer?* How does one achieve a healthy balance of living life fully while saving and accumulating desired material wealth?

Foremost, it's important to realize that money is an emotional part of our lives. The conundrum comes when we view money as being separate from how we see ourselves, needs and desires. I'm not a psychologist, but I can easily see that by assuming I needed a house before marriage and children, and then becoming a slave to that assumption, was falsely based on the additional assumption that 'I had to have it all' before 'I could have it all.' *How crazy is that?* My worth on the romantic market was never about what I owned or didn't own. How could it be? No one that I'd fall in love with would marry me for the sake of a house. I wanted a lifelong partner who loved me for who I was on the inside, not one who loved me because I was good at accumulating and managing money.

Spending wisely is important, but in order to truly nurture and fulfill your dreams, there must be a balance between living fully and investing wisely. Though I continue to save for the future, I've taken a job as a caregiver for an elderly lady who daily brings me pure joy. I've also started dating and spending time with family and friends. My life now has balance, hope and financial security. When the time is right I will marry and hopefully have children; albeit, maybe because the man I marry has offspring he joyfully shares.

Brendon Burchard in *Life's Golden Ticket* asks his readers to consider the following three powerful questions that we will all ask ourselves toward the end of our time on earth: *Did I live? Did I love? Did I matter?* Unfortunately, many of us never frame these questions until very late in life. Fortunately, simply thinking about how you'd like to be able to answer them provides the blueprint to finding happiness and balance while attaining your financial and material goals.

I invite you to answer Brendon's questions, beginning with his third question: *Did I matter?* Considering that one-third, or more, of your life will likely be directed toward accumulating wealth, what does your answer to this question look like? Oprah Winfrey has a great quote: "I've come to believe that each of us has a personal calling that is unique as a fingerprint and that the best way to succeed is to discover what you love and find a way to offer it to others in the form of service, working hard, and also allowing the energy of the universe to lead you." What is your personal calling? What could you do for a living, or what business could you start that would make your heart sing while helping others? Your answer holds the key to a lifetime of personal fulfillment, so take ample time to fully consider your desires.

Did I love? Humans are meant to be connected with other humans. Too often, we sacrifice our relationships for the sake of our goals or because of fear. Yes, fear. Knocked down once or twice, it's easy to convince yourself that having a romantic relationship isn't important, which is fine, provided that you find another way to connect with your fellow beings, or at the very least with animals and nature. The adage that 'no man is an island' applies romantically and goal-wise. Working toward the attainment of goals is great, but is it worth sacrificing time with loved ones? From personal experience, I know that it is not. Life must be balanced to be fulfilling.

I've left Brendon's first question for last because the answer to this question sometimes overshadows the significance of the other two and leads one down an unfulfilling path. As Brendon Burchard suggests, *Did I live?* is best answered in context with the previous two: *Did I love? and Did I matter?* What does really living look like to you? Does it include love and purpose? Does having love and purpose make your dreams of travel or adventure seem a little sweeter? I'm betting that it does and recommend that you read all three of Brendon Burchard's amazing bestselling books: *Life's Golden Ticket, The Millionaire Messenger,* and *The Charge.*

I also invite you to take a long and hard look at your attitude toward money. Do you *know* that there is sufficient wealth in the world? Do you feel worthy of having money? Do you feel capable of accumulating wealth? If you answer negatively to any of these three questions, I'm happy to tell you that you're mistaken. There *is* plenty of abundance in the world, and you are both capable and worthy of accumulating wealth. Perhaps that wealth won't be billions or even millions, but wealth isn't simply about accumulated cash or material goods. It's more about lifestyle and having a healthy balance of love, happiness, adventure, and purpose, as well as the financial freedom to enjoy it all. Working as a caregiver affords me the opportunity to have it all. On the other hand, slaving at a business I didn't love for the sake of material goals *robbed* rather than *fulfilled* my dreams.

I once heard a joke about a penny-pinching movie star. In answer to a friend's quip, "Hey, you can't spend it when you're dead!" the frugal star replied, "Who cares? I don't spend it now!" Cute parable, with a hidden message: Life is meant to be loved in the present, not put off until a tomorrow that never seems to arrive. However, to one day be able to handle gobs of money, you need a starting place. *If you can't manage two thousand dollars, how will you ever wisely manage two hundred thousand dollars?* Investment-wise, think as big as you like, but start by budgeting the small amounts, as they are the stepping stones to your personal fortune.

I continue to set goals and recommend that you do too. Big and small, short and long-term, having goals that are clear, attached to timeliness, written down, and believed by you to be doable, is essential to ensuring you live life to the fullest. But don't be a blind slave to those goals. Twice a year, take a 'personal fulfillment test' and ask yourself the following questions: 1) What are the emotional *whys* behind your goals? Are your goals motivated by 'positive' emotions such as love and joy, or by 'negative' emotions such as lack, fear and greed? Are you on a perpetual wheel of gathering, rather than enjoying your life? Always consider the possibility that your solution might lie in managing what funds you already have, rather than thinking that you need more, then more again, until all you are doing is chasing the ever-elusive pot of gold. 2) Are the goals previously set by you still goals you truly desire? 3) Are all areas of your life—health, family, work/business, spiritual, and recreational/downtime—in balance? If not, what changes do you need to make? 4) Is your current goal-attainment plan moving you forward or has it become stagnant? If your answer is the latter, it may be time to let go of your current plan. It's your life—set goals to thrive, not merely to survive.

"My mission in life is not merely to survive, but to thrive;
and to do so with some passion, some compassion,
some humor, and some style."
—Maya Angelou

MEET THE HEARTMIND WISDOM COAUTHORS

ARNOLD VINGSNES

"Escape from the Green Room"

Midway in life, Arnold Vingsnes's world shipwrecked. Suddenly unemployed and seemingly unemployable, he moved into a windowless room on skid row in East Vancouver, British Columbia. Initially, he took comfort in blaming outward. It wasn't until he retook the helm of his destiny that he managed to "Escape from the Green Room."

Arnold is a Labor Relations and Negotiations Specialist. His career includes time as a sailor, captain and trade union leader. He lives in Abbotsford, British Columbia and has a daughter, step daughter and one grandchild. He enjoys writing, cooking, traveling, and helping others.

Arnold is available to speak to audiences
on a variety of topics, including:
Rough or Calm Waters: Captain Your Destiny.
He can be contacted via www.heartmindwisdom.com/arnoldvingsnes

BILL STRENG

"Eternally High"

Bill Streng is a gentle, kind and spiritual man. His early years were speckled with misguided pursuits and the use of illicit drugs. His life totally transformed after a spiritual encounter-series with a beautiful angel, Jesus and then God. In his chapter "Eternally High" Bill shares his incredible journey to Heaven and back; and why, there forward, his life became a spiritual high.

Bill lives in Surrey, British Columbia. Currently, he is a semi-retired real estate agent. Most days he can be found at his computer researching the connection between divinity and science. He enjoys dancing, hiking and visiting with friends. Above all, he treasures his daughter, son and stepson.

Bill is available to talk to audiences on *Eternally High; Here's Why.* He can be contacted via www.heartmindwisdom.com/billstreng

BROCK TULLY

"Bouncing Back from Brock-Bottom"

At age twenty-three, Brock Tully hit what he refers to as 'Brock-bottom.' In his mission to help himself and encourage others to be kind, he cycled ten thousand miles throughout Canada, the United States and Mexico—an enlightening, yet grueling feat, he has since repeated twice. His chapter, "Bouncing Back from Brock-Bottom," is a heartfelt collection of his experiences, reflections and poetry.

Brock is the founder of the annual World Kindness Concert. (www.worldkindnessconcert.com) He lives in Vancouver, British Columbia with the love of his life, Wilma. His career includes time as a college football and basketball coach, a drug rehabilitation counselor, a recreation therapist, and as an inspirational speaker.

Brock is available to speak to groups on the inherent magic and miracles of self and other kindness. His most popular talks include: *Goodbye Bullying; Hello Self!—Preventing school and cyberspace bullying. Workmates Are People Too!—Boosting workplace morale through self-love and community. Head-Heart Alignment—Love YOU, regardless!* And, *Reflections—A journey toward Wholeness and Oneness.* He can be contacted via www.brocktully.com

DAISY LANDRIGAN

"Till Death Do Us Part"

Though separated, Daisy Landrigan stayed by her husband Robbie's side throughout his battle with colon cancer. Her chapter, "Till Death Do Us Part," is a heartfelt glimpse into how she put aside all past hurts, and dedicated her life to ensuring their children had a treasure chest full of happy memories with their father.

Daisy lives in Delta, British Columbia with her two daughters. Now alone to "hang the moon in the sky to chase away the darkness," she is continuing Robbie's legacy by coaching their girls' sports teams and by making sure her children feel loved and safe. Daisy enjoys dancing, cooking and traveling.

Daisy is available to talk to audiences on a variety
of topics, including *Intentional Living*.
She can be contacted via www.heartmindwisdom.
com/daisylandringan

E. PATRICIA CONNOR

"Heart Connections—A Matrix"

E. Patricia Connor is an ordained minister and a cofounder of Kindness is Key Training and the Heartmind Wisdom Collection. From the delight-filled day when she taught the family maid to tell time by a clock, Patricia recognized her inner-calling to inspire, educate and empower others. In her chapter, "Heart Connections—A Matrix," she shares her insights and the tools that helped free her from an extended period of dark depression.

Patricia is happily married and lives in Delta, British Columbia. Her desire to propagate spiritual, as well as emotional and physical health for all, led her to become a practitioner of aromatherapy, herbology, Bach flower remedies, Reiki, and reconnective-healing. She has worked as a *Stop the Violence* Counselor for Battered Women Support Services, was a Director of Development Resources for the Surrey Women's Center, and was a director of Human Resources at Radarsat International Inc.

Patricia is available to speak to audiences on the *13 Kindness Keys to Living the Life You are Meant to Love.* She can be contacted via www.heartmindwisdom.com/joyandpatricia

ELIN NASH

"Lessons from an Uninvited Houseguest"

When Elin Nash moved into an apartment with her 'dream view,' strange incidents started happening. Having recently lost her sister, Anita, at first, Elin wondered if the odd occurrences were simply a manifestation of her grief. They weren't. "Lessons from an Uninvited Houseguest" is a heartwarming account of how Elin transformed her fear of the unnerving 'shenanigans' into an exciting spiritual awakening.

Elin has traveled and worked throughout Norway and Canada. She has fished in oceans and lakes at 40 degrees below, climbed mountains and landed jobs in places where she couldn't speak the language. She attributes her intuitive and empathetic nature to her practice of Transcendental Meditation. She lives in North Vancouver, British Columbia. She has two daughters and two grandchildren.

Elin is available to speak to audiences, and invites you to share your insights and spiritual experiences on her blog—www.heartmindwisdom.com/elinnash.

ERIKA TAYLOR

"From Neediness to Wholeness"

Erika Taylor's chapter, "From Neediness to Wholeness," is a candid account of her need to be in a romantic relationship to view herself as being 'whole.' Metaphysical wisdom infused with love has served as the guiding principle in her awakening. It is her desire to encourage others to explore limiting patterns that cause suffering, and to empower people with tools of transformation.

Erika has a Bachelor of Arts in the social sciences. She has worked as an ESL tutor, yoga instructor and a psychometrist in the field of neuropsychology. Always eager to learn and grow, she has five counseling certificates from various organizations.

Erika lives in Vancouver, British Columbia. Dancing, singing and chanting are the activities that lift her into pure joy—a state of consciousness she has been able to access more frequently as the wounds of her past have healed.

Erika is available to speak to audiences on a
variety of healing modalities and topics.
She can be contacted via www.heartmindwisdom.com/erikataylor

GEORGINA GRACE

"From Emptiness to
Living, Loving and Laughing"

As a child, "angry at being transported to the planet Zircon, and overwhelmed by the thousand-plus students in her new high school," Georgina Grace's "chatterbox self, coiled inward, clamped closed, and became mute." It was the beginning of an 'emptiness' that haunted and hurt until she gradually unearthed the keys to her motto: 'live…love…laugh. Her chapter, "From Emptiness to Living, Loving and Laughing," is a humorous and delightful account of her journey.

Georgina adores animals, helping others and being in community. When she discovered her cat was allergic to smoke, there was only one solution—toss the tar and nicotine sticks. Her quest inward and outward led her to become an intuitive counselor, inspirational speaker and author. Georgina is studying to become an ordained minister.

Georgina is available to speak to audiences on *Living,*
Loving and Laughing: The Miracle of Connection.
She can be contacted via http://facebook.com/Georgina.Grace2012.

J. DENNIS ROBERT

"Fearless, No Matter What!"

Born with Horner's syndrome, J. Dennis Robert quickly learned that the keys to fitting in and making friends were ingenuity and fearlessness. Though admirable qualities, when younger, his ingenious and fearless endeavors often invited 'trouble.' Dennis's free-spirited nature led him into a lifelong love of entrepreneurial ventures, the first of which was shoveling snow off neighborhood driveways. His chapter, "Fearless, No Matter What!" is a delightful glimpse into his youthful shenanigans, including one that landed him front of a judge.

Dennis lives in Surrey, British Columbia. He enjoys organic gardening, creating and working with his hands. He doesn't believe in giving up or shying away from any circumstance, predicament or challenge.

Dennis is available to talk to audiences about
being *Fearless, No Matter What!*
He can be contacted via www.heartmindwisdom.com/jdrobert

JOYCE M. ROSS

"Rainbows, Butterflies and Other Miracles"

Joyce M. Ross is a cofounder of Kindness is Key Training and the Heartmind Wisdom Collection. Her chapter, "Rainbows, Butterflies and Other Miracles," is a lighthearted glimpse into the magic of family and spiritual connectedness.

Joyce lives in Delta, British Columbia. For over seventeen years, she ran singles dances for the forty-plus crowd. She has been writing since the age of fourteen. Her books *Direct Sales: Be Better Than Good-Be Great!* and *The Kindness Ambassador and The Sugarholic Prosecutor* are available in *KiK's* Online Library and on Amazon.com.

Joyce is available to speak to audiences on the *13 Kindness
Keys to Living the Life You are Meant to Love.*
She can be contacted via www.heartmindwisdom.com/joyandpatricia

KARIE-ANNE HAWTHORNE

"Born to be Weird"

From an early age, Karie-Anne Hawthorne questioned the meaning of life. In 2009, when she discovered Inner Garden Balance Point Chapel, a non-denominational/inter-denominational church, she found answers and, surprisingly, that she wasn't 'weird' at all. Her chapter, "Born to be Weird," is a delightful account of how she came to celebrate her own and others' uniqueness. *Did her family ever find her great granddad's fortune?*

Karie-Anne is married with children and lives in Langley, British Columbia. She regularly teaches classes and lectures on a number of healing and spiritual modalities. She is studying to become an ordained minister.

Karie-Anne is available to talk to audiences
about finding *Your Unique Voice.*
She can be contacted via www.heartmindwisdom.com/karieanne

KATHARINE FAHLMAN

"Bankrupt! What I learned about Life."

Katharine Fahlman's lifelong dual roles of teacher and student have provided her with invaluable lessons and abundant wisdom. Her candid and insightful account of bankruptcy—*trials* and *gifts*—reflects her resilience, loving ways and faith. Katharine also once won a large cash lottery, so she is familiar with both ends of the financial spectrum.

Katharine is happily married and lives in Surrey, British Columbia. As a wife, mother, grandmother, working administrator, and a business woman, she has always utilized her intuitive abilities to help her make decisions, anticipate situations and connect with people. Posted above her bed is a sign that reads: 'Good morning. Know that today you are in good hands. You can relax. Thank you for your trust and understanding.'

Katharine is available to speak to audiences on
Thriving through Anything and Everything!
She can be contacted via www.heartmindwisdom.com/katharine

LARRY CHASE

"Decision Day—To Live or Die"

Prior to taking Kindness is Key's Inspirational Authorship Course, Larry's writing experience was limited to emails and a few letters. After completing his chapter, "Decision Day—To Live or Die," he now plans to write an entire book! When you read his journey from death-by-weight to fitness and happiness, you'll understand his burning desire to help others stop self-medicating with food.

Larry lives in Surrey, British Columbia and is available to inspire audiences—big and small.

Larry's talk *The Skinny Guy Inside* is a poignant
and humorous account of his remarkable
two hundred and ten pound weight loss. (He
has since lost another twenty pounds!)
He can be contacted via www.heartmindwisdom.com/larrychase

LOUISE E. MORRIS

"Out, Out—Damn Thought!"

As a mother and teacher, Louise Morris learned early about the power of words. Her chapter, "Out, Out—Damn Thought!" describes how she became aware of her inner voices and overcame her negative thinking. Like many people, rather than admit to shaming details, Louise gaily recounted colorful victim-hero stories to entertain and shock her friends. Her life began to flourish when she realized that the journey to happiness and inner-peace rests in *self*-acceptance.

Louise lives in Surrey, British Columbia. She holds B.A. and M.A. in education with a focus on special education, leadership and mentoring. Believing in natural consequences and restitution over discipline, and always aware of how difficult it is to change because of her own challenges overcoming negative thinking, she guides her students with caring wisdom.

Louise is available to speak to audiences about *Changing Your Story.* She can be contacted via www.heartmindwisdom.com/louisemorris

MARCUS DWAYNE HARRIS

"Social Laryngitis"

In his chapter, "Social Laryngitis," Marcus Dwayne Harris shares how misguided youthful perceptions almost cost him everything he held dear. Once he realized that *"pleasing others* had morphed into *disappointing everyone,* like water doused on fire," his flame expired. Finding his voice was a long and emotional journey back to himself and his family.

Marcus Dwayne Harris lives in Surrey, British Columbia. He is happily married and a 'work at home' father of three. He has a Bachelor of Arts in computer programming and a minor in business. Marcus is a self-taught web and graphic designer. His wife, Shabena, is a coauthor in *Heartmind Wisdom* Collection #2.

Marcus is available to talk to audiences about
discovering *Your Authentic Voice.*
You can follow him on Facebook and at www.
heartmindwisdom.com/marcusdharris

MARIA GANGUIN

"Surviving or Thriving? It's Your Life"

As a teenager, Maria Ganguin learned the value of a 'buck' when she and her brother won a thousand dollars playing bingo. In her chapter, she shares the wisdom nugget: *If you can't manage two thousand dollars, how will you ever wisely manage two hundred thousand dollars?* She also recommends, twice a year taking a 'personal fulfillment test' to determine if you are on track financially and personally.

Maria lives in Delta, British Columbia. Once a banker, she now enjoys caring for the elderly. Her favorite pastimes are cooking, walking her dog in the park and finding creative ways to save money. A 'giver' by nature, she is always the first to offer a helping hand.

Maria is available to talk to audiences about
Thriving Through Everything.
She can be contacted via www.heartmindwisdom.com/mariasserenity

MONICA FORSTER

"Tears in My Ears"

The unbelievable news that Monica Forster was pregnant came three weeks after being diagnosed with Non-Hodgkin's Lymphoma. *Was this a cruel joke or the best thing that could happen?* Monica and Brad had been trying to get pregnant for three out of their four year marriage. When Monica delivered the news, Brad thought she was kidding. She wasn't.

In her chapter, "Tears in My Ears," Monica vividly recounts the gift of her pregnancy. At a difficult time in her journey, she's never forgotten the words of her hospital roommate: "Pray as though your prayers are already answered. There is no room for doubt in miracles."

Monica, Brad and their handsome son Alexander Matthew, live in Vancouver, British Columbia. Watch for more of her writing by following her on Facebook at www.facebook.com/monicaf

Monica is available to speak to audiences on *Love and Other Miracles.* She can be contacted via www.heartmindwisdom.com/monicaforster

ROSWYN NELSON

"Lonely Choices"

Roswyn Nelson's chapter, "Lonely Choices," is a down-to-earth and somewhat humorous account of the joys and trials of raising four kids—mostly by herself. Working as a waitress allowed her "to provide a decent life for my kids—if it was a good day we ate well; if not, there was always a can of pork and beans." Her recollection of being attacked by a lobster is sure to make you laugh.

Roswyn is semiretired and lives in White Rock, British Columbia. A people lover and believer in natural products, she is actively involved in network marketing. She is extremely proud of her children, twelve grandchildren and ten great-grandchildren.

Roswyn is available to talk to audiences on a variety
of topics, including *The Freedom of Choice!*
She can be contacted via www.heartmindwisdom.com/roswyn

SHIRLEY J. BUECKERT

"Alchemy of Grief"

In just over three years, Shirley Bueckert lost six beloved souls, including her husband Lou. One year later, her beloved dog Rufus died. Beginning with the diagnosis that her husband had Non-Hodgkin's Lymphoma, her "world lurched, teeter-tottered and reversed one hundred and eighty degrees." Eventually, she found solace in the anonymity of travel, and through learning that she didn't have to die with Lou as he would be part of her forever. Among other healing endeavors, she found comfort in the 'safe container' offered by a women's circle.

Shirley has two children and lives in Langley, British Columbia. She loves gardening, traveling, hand drumming, and dragon boating. Through nature she has found peace and gratitude. Each day, her intention is to live a full and enriching life.

Shirley is available to talk to audiences about *Living an Enriching Life.*
She can be contacted via www.heartmindwisdom.
com/shirleyjbueckert

SUDIPTA BANERJEE

"There is Always a Solution"

While living in India, Sudipta Banerjee's husband Bishu died. As they said goodbye, she promised to fulfill his last wish: "I have only one request, take good care of Gina...she is my soul." To provide every opportunity for their young daughter Sudipta immigrated to Canada. Sudipta's chapter, "There is Always a Solution," is an insightful and heartfelt account of her struggles as a single parent in a foreign country.

Sudipta lives in Surrey, British Columbia and is a retired high school teacher. She loves to educate younger people, and encourages everyone to be a socially conscientious humanitarian. She has a Master's Degree in Physics and also in Education. She has traveled extensively. Her dream is to explore East Africa.

Sudipta is available to talk to audiences about *Finding Your Solutions.* She can be contacted via www.heartmindwisdom. com/sudiptabanerjee

SUSAN BERGER THOMPSON

"Dying to Live"

Released from the hospital on her thirty-ninth birthday, three weeks after suffering a burst cerebral aneurysm, Susan Berger Thompson relished in the *normalcy* of being with her two children. Grateful for a second chance, she examined what in her life needed to be changed, nurtured or scrapped. "Dying to Live," is a poignant glimpse into the bittersweet journey *within* that led Susan to her authentic self.

Susan Berger Thompson lives in Surrey, British Columbia. Spending time with her children and grandchildren is her greatest joy. Her love of writing and art began in her teens.

Susan is available to speak to audiences on how to
Live your Perfectly Balanced Passionate Life.
She can be contacted via www.heartmindwisdom.
com/susanbthompson

COAUTHORS' COMFORT FOOD RECIPES

"Food is so primal, so essential a part of our lives,
often the mere sharing of recipes with strangers
turns them into good friends."
—Jasmine Heiler

ARNOLD'S FAMOUS POTATO SALAD

Arnold Vingsnes

Tasting and adjusting the amount of mayonnaise and spices is the key to success with this recipe. I'm asked for this salad everywhere I go.

INGREDIENTS:

2	large russet or Yukon Gold potatoes
2	large eggs
½ to ¾ cup	mayonnaise (not salad dressing)
2	fresh garlic cloves, minced
1½ tablespoons	fresh green onion, finely chopped
1 teaspoon	fresh parsley, finely chopped
1½ teaspoons	dry mustard
⅛ teaspoon	paprika
⅛ teaspoon	fresh ground pepper

DIRECTIONS:

1. Peel and boil potatoes. Drain water. Let potatoes cool completely.
2. Hard boil eggs, cool completely and peel.
3. Cut 1 potato and 1 egg into small chunks and place in a large mixing bowl.
4. Add ½ of the remaining ingredients.
5. Repeat steps 3 and 4.
6. Mix thoroughly.
7. Cover bowl and refrigerate overnight.
8. Taste next morning and adjust by adding more mayonnaise and/or spices. Mix well and return to refrigerator.

9. Taste again before serving and adjust spices if needed.

Makes 4 large servings.

GARLIC MASHED POTATOES

Bill Streng

INGREDIENTS:

6	unpeeled red potatoes, washed and quartered
¼ teaspoon	salt
2	garlic heads
½ teaspoon	olive oil
¼ cup	butter
¼ cup	milk, cream or sour cream
pinch	salt and/or white pepper

DIRECTIONS:

1. Cut top off of garlic heads. Rub olive oil on exposed top of garlic. Wrap in tinfoil. Place on baking dish and bake at 350°F for 30 minutes or until garlic is soft. Remove garlic from outside peel and set aside.
2. Boil potatoes in lightly salted water. When cooked, drain.
3. Add baked garlic, butter, milk, salt and/or white pepper to potatoes. Mash.

Makes 6 servings.

RAIN-CITY CRACKERS

Brock Tully

I put my name on this recipe, but it's really Wilma's delicious and healthful creation. These crackers are a staple in our home. Enjoy!

INGREDIENTS:

2 cups	spelt flour
2 tablespoons	flax seeds (ground or whole)
2 tablespoons	sesame seeds
2 tablespoons	millet
1 cup	pumpkin seeds
½ cup	sunflower seeds
1 cup	dried cranberries
2 teaspoons	crumbled rosemary
1 teaspoon	salt
¼ cup	brown sugar
2 ½ teaspoons	baking soda
2 cups	soured milk
¼ cup	molasses

DIRECTIONS:

1. Mix dry ingredients together.
2. Stir milk and molasses together.
3. Fold wet mixture into dry ingredients and stir.
4. Pour into 2 small greased loaf pans.
5. Bake at 350°F for 50 – 60 minutes. Cool slightly. Remove from pans and finish cooling on a rack.

6. Wrap cooled loaves in waxed paper or foil and refrigerate overnight.
7. Unwrap and preheat oven to 250°F.
8. Slice the loaves as thinly as possible with a bread knife. Lay slices on a cookie sheet, sprinkle with additional salt to taste, and dry at 250°F until crispy – 45 minutes or longer.

Makes 12 servings.

Lentil Soup with Rice

Daisy Landrigan

This hearty soup is a comfort food that my mother made when I would get sick or had an upset stomach. Now, I make it for my kids, and they love it!

INGREDIENTS:

2 tablespoons	olive oil
5	garlic cloves, minced
1 tablespoon	ginger, minced
2 teaspoons	cumin seeds
1	large onion
1	large tomato, chopped finely
1 tablespoon	sea salt
1 teaspoon	turmeric
1 cup	red lentils, washed
8 cups	water
½ cup	rice, washed
2 teaspoons	masala
2 tablespoons	cilantro chopped finely for garnish

DIRECTIONS:

1. In a large pot, heat olive oil on medium heat. Add minced garlic and ginger and give it a quick stir. Add cumin seeds and sauté for 1-2 minutes until flavor of the cumin seeds is released.
2. Add onions and continue to sauté for another 5 minutes until onions are cooked.

3. Add finely chopped tomato and cook the mixture for another 2-3 minutes.
4. Add salt and turmeric and cook for another few minutes. (Turmeric needs to be cooked in oil first for best results.)
5. Add washed red lentils and stir the mixture well.
6. Add 8 cups of warm water and bring to a boil. Continue to cook the lentils for 20 minutes on medium heat.
7. Add washed rice to mixture and cook it for another 10 minutes.
8. Add masala and chopped cilantro; then, stir.
9. Allow the soup sit for at least 5 minutes before serving.

Makes 6 servings.

CLASSIC Caesar Salad

E. Patricia Connor

Garlic lovers will be hooked on this recipe. Add cooked chicken cubes or sautéed prawns to make this salad a complete meal.

INGREDIENTS:

6	anchovy fillets
5	large garlic cloves, peeled
2 teaspoons	brown sugar
2 teaspoons	Dijon mustard
6 tablespoons	red wine vinegar
2	eggs, coddled
1 cup	olive oil
½ cup	Parmesan cheese
¼ cup	croutons
2	heads of romaine lettuce

DIRECTIONS:

1. Place eggs in boiling water for 3 minutes. (Cool slightly, before scooping egg from shell.)
2. Mix first six ingredients in electric blender until smooth.
3. Slowly add olive oil to mixture.
4. Wash, tear and place lettuce in large salad bowl.
5. Add salad mixture to coat lettuce. (You may have some dressing left over.)
6. Add Parmesan cheese and croutons.
7. Toss well.
8. Serve.

Makes 12 servings

TART & SWEET SALAD

Elin Nash

This is a refreshing, easy and quick recipe that is a perfect accompaniment to any meal.

INGREDIENTS:

1	large carrot
1	large Granny Smith apple
½ lemon	freshly squeezed juice
¼ teaspoon	organic brown sugar
2 tablespoons	chopped dried fruit (optional)
garnish	parsley or coconut slivers

DIRECTIONS:

1. Peel carrot and apple. Grate both into a bowl.
2. Pour in lemon juice and add sugar.
3. Toss well and place in serving dish.
4. Garnish.

Makes 4 to 6 servings.

HERB AND GARLIC PRAWNS

Erika Taylor

This flavorful prawn dish works well as an appetizer or as a main course. Accompany it with cubes of crusty bread and a citrusy green salad for an elegant, easy-to-prepare meal.

INGREDIENTS:

½ cup	olive oil
2 heads	garlic, minced
½	lemon, juiced
4	bay leaves, whole
2 containers	(28 grams each) fresh basil, chopped
½ container	(14 grams) fresh oregano, chopped
4 – 6 pieces	sundried tomato packed in oil, chopped
¼ teaspoon	cayenne pepper
½ teaspoon	salt (to taste)
¼ teaspoon	black pepper
1½ pounds	fresh prawns, shelled and deveined

DIRECTIONS:

1. Place garlic, lemon juice and bay leaves in olive oil and cook on medium to low heat for about 10 minutes. (Be careful that the garlic doesn't turn brown.)
2. Chop the basil, oregano, and sundried tomato; then add to the mixture and cook for another 5 minutes. Stir often.
3. Add cayenne pepper, salt, and black pepper.

4. Increase the heat and add the prawns. Turn often to coat well with the seasoned oil. Cook just until the prawns have turned pink.
5. Remove the bay leaves before serving. (Bay leaves are a choking hazard.)

Makes 4 – 6 servings.

Grandma's Baking Powder Biscuits

Georgina Grace

As a kid, I made these biscuits with my grandma. Great with stew or cabbage rolls.

INGREDIENTS:

1 cup	flour
2 teaspoons	baking powder
¼ teaspoon	salt
¼ cup	shortening
1/3 cup	milk
½ cup	grated cheese (optional)

DIRECTIONS:

1. Pre-heat oven to 425°F.
2. Sift flour.
3. Add baking powder, flour, salt and sift.
4. Add shortening to dry ingredients.
5. Cut shortening into flour until it looks like small peas.
6. Mix well and pour in milk. (Optional: Add grated cheese.)
7. Mix with fork, then roll into a ball.
8. Knead 8 – 12 times on floured board.
9. Roll flat with rolling pin so that the mixture is ¾ inch thick.
10. Use the mouth end of a drinking glass to cut out biscuits.
11. Put on ungreased pan one inch apart.
12. Bake 15 minutes.

Makes 8 – 10 biscuits.

EASY SWEET POTATO SOUP

J. Dennis Robert

This recipe is easy to make and warms you up in the winter.

INGREDIENTS:

4 cups	water (from boiled potatoes, if possible)
3	celery stalks
2	green onions, chopped
1	large chicken bouillon cube
1 handful	chopped cilantro
1 – 2	small sweet potatoes (orange)
3 tablespoons	salted butter (optional)
½ cup	2% milk or cream (optional)
1 – 2	crushed garlic cloves(optional)

DIRECTIONS:

1. Place first six ingredients in a large pot and bring to a boil. Cook until vegetables are tender.
2. Remove from stove and let cool for 10 minutes; then, puree in a blender.
3. Place back in pot and reheat.
4. Optional: add butter, milk or cream and crushed garlic. Mix well.

Makes 4 servings.

MOM'S TURKEY SOUP FOR THE SOUL

Joyce M. Ross

Tasty and easy to adjust to your own ingredient/spice preferences.

INGREDIENTS:

4 cups	unsalted chicken broth
2 cups	cold water
3	celery stalks
1	large yellow onion, chopped
2 - 3 lbs.	turkey thighs (or chicken)
3	garlic gloves
1 teaspoon	Italian herbs
1 teaspoon	sweet curry
1 ½ cups	uncooked macaroni (or rice)
16 oz.	canned stewed tomatoes
1 cup	frozen or canned corn

DIRECTIONS:

1. Place first 8 ingredients in a large pot and bring to a boil. Cook until turkey is done.
2. Add macaroni and cook to desired tenderness. (See note below.)
3. Add stewed tomatoes and corn. Continue cooking for 5 minutes.
4. Serve with crackers or your favorite biscuits.

Note: I prefer to cook the macaroni separately so that the pasta doesn't soak up all the broth after the soup is refrigerated.

Makes 4 servings.

SWEET POTATO CASSEROLE

Karie-Anne Hawthorne

INGREDIENTS:

Casserole

2¼ pounds	sweet potatoes, peeled and chopped
1 cup	half-and-half cream
¾ cup	brown sugar, packed
1 teaspoon	salt
2 teaspoons	vanilla extract
2	large eggs
	cooking spray

Topping

1 ½ cups	miniature marshmallows
½ cup	all-purpose flour
¼ cup	sugar
¼ teaspoon	salt
2 tablespoons	chilled butter, cut into small pieces
½ cup	chopped pecans, toasted

DIRECTIONS:

Preheat oven to 375°F.

Casserole

1. Place potatoes in a Dutch oven, and cover with water.
2. Bring to a boil. Reduce heat, and simmer 20 minutes or until very tender. Drain; cool slightly.
3. Place potatoes in a large bowl. Add half-and-half, first amount

of sugar, salt and vanilla. Beat with a mixer at medium speed until smooth.
4. Add eggs; beat well. (Mixture will be thin.)
5. Scrape mixture into a 13 inch x 9 inch baking dish, pre-coated with cooking spray.

Topping
1. Lightly spoon flour into a dry measuring cup; level with a knife.
2. Combine flour, second amount of sugar and salt in a bowl.
3. Cut in butter with a pastry blender until mixture resembles coarse meal or small peas.
4. Stir in pecans.
5. Sprinkle mixture over casserole.
6. Distribute miniature marshmallows over top of casserole.
7. Bake at 375°F for 30 minutes or until golden brown.

Makes 8 – 10 servings.

BAKED CUSTARD

Katharine Fahlman

This old fashioned baked custard was one of my mom's best. It's simple to make and easy to clean up.

INGREDIENTS:

2 cups	whole milk
2	eggs
2 tablespoons	vanilla
½ cup	white sugar
Sprinkle	nutmeg
Sprinkle	cinnamon

DIRECTIONS:

1. Combine all ingredients except nutmeg and cinnamon in a blender.
2. Blend on high speed for 1 minute.
3. Pour into round glass baking dish – 6 inch diameter and 5 inch deep.
4. Sprinkle nutmeg and cinnamon on top.
5. Bake at 350°F – 375°F degrees for approximately 45 minutes.

Makes 4 servings.

CHICKEN A LA KING

Larry Chase

This recipe is simple and delicious.

INGREDIENTS:

½ pound	mushrooms, sliced
½ cup	butter or margarine
½ cup	flour
2 cups	chicken broth
2 cups	light cream
2	egg yolks, beaten
3 cups	cooked chicken or turkey, diced
½ cup	pimento, cut into strips
1 teaspoon	salt
¼ teaspoon	pepper

DIRECTIONS:

1. Sauté mushrooms in butter in medium to heavy skillet.
2. Mix flour with chicken broth and add to skillet. Stir.
3. Add cream and simmer for 5 minutes.
4. Add egg yolks, chicken and pimento. Stir until thoroughly hot; however, don't let mixture boil.
5. Add salt and pepper.
6. Spoon over rice or pasta.

Makes 6 – 8 servings.

PASTA SURPRISE

Louise E. Morris

Made with leftovers, this meal is both nutritious and cost-effective.

INGREDIENTS:

1 pound	macaroni or preferred type of pasta
1 pound	ground beef
1	large onion, chopped
5	large mushrooms, chopped
1	large celery stalk, chopped
1 24 oz. jar	marinara sauce
1 10 oz. jar	tomato sauce
1 12 oz. jar	kidney beans
1 teaspoon	dried basil
1 teaspoon	dried parsley
	salt and pepper

DIRECTIONS:

1. Cook pasta according to package directions. Drain and return pasta to pot.
2. In large skillet, cook ground beef, onions, mushrooms and celery. (Stir often. Cook until beef is well done.)
3. Drain off fat and stir remaining mixture into pasta.
4. Add marinara sauce, tomato sauce, kidney beans, spices, and chopped leftovers.
5. Cook over medium-low heat, stirring occasionally for 8 – 10 minutes.
6. Add salt and pepper to taste.

Makes 12 servings.

CURRIED CAULIFLOWER

Marcus Dwayne Harris

Cauliflower never tasted so good.

INGREDIENTS:

4 cups	cauliflower (1 head)
1 tablespoon	milk
½	10 oz. can cream of chicken soup
¼ cup	mayonnaise
½ cup	cheddar cheese, grated
1 teaspoon	curry powder
2 tablespoon	butter, melted
1 cup	Saltine cracker crumbs

DIRECTIONS:

1. Cook cauliflower until tender-crisp and set in a large casserole dish.
2. Combine milk, chicken soup, mayonnaise, cheese, and curry powder. Pour over cauliflower.
3. Mix melted butter and cracker crumbs. Sprinkle on top of cauliflower.
4. Bake at 350°F for 30 minutes.

Makes 6 servings.

SPINACH SALAD MARIA STYLE

Maria Ganguin

With a whole lot of love and raspberry vinaigrette, it's ready to serve.

INGREDIENTS:

Big bag or container	fresh spinach, washed and tossed
2 handfuls	sugar snap peas
1 handful	strawberries, washed and sliced
4 tablespoons	feta cheese
½ cup	mix of soya nuts, sunflower seeds and cranberries
	raspberry vinaigrette

DIRECTIONS:

1. Toss all together and serve.

Makes 4 - 6 servings.

Mini-Quiche Recipe

Monica Forster

This easy mini-quiche recipe is perfect for a party appetizer or an after school snack.

INGREDIENTS:

1 cup	Black Forest ham, finely diced
3 tablespoons	green onion, finely minced
1	egg
½ cup	whipping cream
¼ teaspoon	dill weed
dash	pepper
12	unsweetened tart shells
1 cup	Swiss cheese, shredded

DIRECTIONS:

1. Preheat oven to 375°F.
2. Preheat tart shells for 5 minutes.
3. Remove from oven. Add ham and green onion to each shell.
4. Beat together egg, whipping cream and dill.
5. Put 2 tablespoons into each tart shell.
6. Top with Swiss cheese and bake in the oven for 15-20 minutes or until the edges are brown and the centers appear firm.
7. Cool 5 minutes and serve warm

Makes 12 mini-quiches.

Spicy Lentil Soup

Roswyn Nelson

Red, brown or green lentils cook quickly and never require soaking. This rich, spicy soup cooks in minutes and can be frozen for later use.

INGREDIENTS:

¼ teaspoon	olive oil or coconut oil
1	large onion, chopped
3	medium celery stalks, chopped
1 teaspoon	garlic, minced
2 cups	lentils washed (about 1 pound)
1 28 oz. can	stewed tomatoes, diced
8 cups	vegetable stock or organic chicken broth
1	bay leaf
1 teaspoon	cayenne pepper
1 teaspoon	chili powder
1 teaspoon	paprika
1 teaspoon	dried basil (optional)
1 teaspoon	sea salt
½ teaspoon	ground cumin (optional)
½ teaspoon	freshly ground black pepper

DIRECTIONS:

1. Pre-heat a fairly large stock-pot over medium heat.
2. Add the olive or coconut oil to lightly coat the bottom of the pot.
3. Add the onion, celery, and garlic.
4. Cook until the onion has softened (about 2-3 minutes).

5. Stir in the lentils, tomatoes, stock, bay leaf, cayenne, chili powder, cumin, paprika, basil, salt, and pepper.
6. Bring to a boil, reduce heat, and simmer until the lentils have softened (about 20 minutes).
7. Remove the bay leaf before serving. (Bay leaves are a choking hazard.)
8. Add a spoonful of either Greek Yogurt or sour cream before serving.

Makes 12 one cup servings.

COMFORTING, COLORFUL CORN BREAD

Shirley J Bueckert

Comforting flavors of corn, cheese and peppers bring sunshine to your plate and palate.

INGREDIENTS:

1 cup	all-purpose white flour
1 cup	cornmeal
4 teaspoons	baking powder
½ cup	butter
½ cup	granulated sugar
3	eggs
½ cup	green and red peppers, chopped
14 oz.	can of cream style corn
1 cup	Monterey Jack or cheddar cheese, shredded
dash or 2	hot sauce

DIRECTIONS:

1. Combine flour, cornmeal and baking powder. Set aside.
2. Combine and mix butter and sugar. Then, one at a time, beat eggs into mixture until light and fluffy.
3. Stir in green/red peppers, corn, cheese, and hot sauce.
4. Add flour mixture, blend well.
5. Pour into 13" x 9" greased baking pan.
6. Bake in 325° F oven for 45 minutes.

Makes 16 - 20 slices.

INDIAN RICE PUDDING

Sudipta Banerjee

Savor the taste of Chaler Payesh—an Indian treat!

INGREDIENTS:

¾ cup small grained special rice or basmati rice

8 cups Half-and-half cream

¾ cup Indian jaggery, or brown sugar

DIRECTIONS:

1. Bring half-and-half cream to a boil. Then, lower heat and continue cooking until half-and-half is reduced to approximately one liter. (About half.)
2. Soak rice in cold water for 15 minutes. Drain excess moisture.
3. Add rice to reduced half-and-half.
4. Stir continuously until the rice softens. (Keep stirring or rice will stick to bottom of pan.)
5. Add brown sugar (or jaggery). Stir until the sugar dissolves.
6. Remove from the stove.
7. Garnish with slivered almonds.
8. Once cooled, refrigerate.
9. Serve chilled.

Makes 12 servings.

SHEPHERD'S PIE
with a TWIST

Susan Berger Thompson

Easy to make and comforting on a cold winter day.

INGREDIENTS:

4	large potatoes, peeled and cubed
1 tablespoon	butter
1 tablespoon	onion, finely chopped
¼ cup	cheddar cheese, shredded
5	carrots, chopped
1	pie shell (homemade or bought)
1 tablespoon	vegetable oil
1	onion, chopped
1 pound	lean ground beef
2 tablespoons	flour
1 tablespoon	ketchup
¾ cup	beef broth
¼ cup	cheddar cheese, shredded

DIRECTIONS:

1. Boil potatoes and carrots separately. Drain and mash separately.
2. Add butter, finely chopped onion and first ¼ cup of shredded cheese to potatoes.
3. Preheat oven to 375°F.

4. Cook chopped onions in pre-heated large frying pan. Cook until clear.
5. Add ground beef to frying pan and cook until well browned. Drain off any fat. Stir in flour and cook 1 minute. Add ketchup and beef broth. Bring to a boil. Reduce heat and simmer for 5 minutes.
6. Spread the ground beef in an even layer on the pie shell. Spread the mashed carrots on top, then the potato mixture and top with remaining shredded cheese.
7. Bake for 20 minutes or until golden.
8. If desired, just before serving, pour a small amount of hot gravy over each piece.

Makes 6 – 8 servings.

Love Now and Then

Simer Dhillon

Am I but a stranger, with struggles far from yours?
Am I but a beggar, someone you abhor?
Do you even see me?
Is it your habit to ignore?

Am I but my title, with mysteries far from yours?
Am I but a saint, a myth of your folklore?
Do you even know me?
Is it your habit to adore?

Whether
I
sit upon your pedestal
or have fallen from your grace
I
breathe
laugh
cry

and one day we will fly.

Will you know me then—
in the glorious rays of love
from whence we came?

See my soul now—
and when we greet above
call out my name.

About the

THE KINDNESS AMBASSADOR
AND THE SUGARHOLIC PROSECUTOR

A Semi-Autobiographical Inspirational Novel

Written by Joyce M. Ross
Inspired and Edited by E. Patricia Connor

The Kindness Ambassador and the Sugarholic Prosecutor is loosely based on the lives and experiences of the co-founders of Kindness Is Key (*KiK*) Training Inc., Joyce M. Ross and E. Patricia Connor. The *13 Kindness Keys* woven throughout are the cornerstones to everything Patricia and Joyce believe and encourage in their seminars and inspirational authorship training. The spiritual awakenings of the characters are fact-based and meant to inspire you to explore your purpose-path—on earth and eternally—and bring greater meaning, abundance and love into your personal journey.

Fiction or Fact?
The truth about the real lives of our characters.

Joyce's journey through gaming addiction is accurately portrayed in the novel, including the divine *aha* message she received from her spiritual guides that led her to become an activist for gaming reform. Over three million Canadians and ten million Americans are severely, moderately, or in danger of becoming addicted gamblers. For this vulnerable segment of society, what begins as a fun activity slowly becomes a nightmarish addiction that destroys their finances, self-worth and families. Incorporating the 13 Kindness Keys into her life allowed Joyce to release shame and transform her shadows into a purpose-path of helping others.

Since her early twenties, Patricia has moved forward and lived fully through what for someone else might have been debilitating depression. Through her character in *The Kindness Ambassador,* Patricia shares some of her healing techniques. Our next inspirational novel, *The Wooden Nickel Wellness Spa,* chronicles Patricia's life in more detail, and is a must read for anyone who suffers from this under-recognized and under-diagnosed condition.

Patricia and Joyce have been close friends since they met in 1984 while retailing Mary Kay Cosmetics. Their friendship is based in: mutual respect; similar views, values and goals; and, a shared purpose-path. Discounting no one's religious or spiritual beliefs, throughout the book, our originating divinity is referred to as *Source.* Both women believe in what His Holiness the 14th Dalai Lama of Tibet espoused when he said: "My religion is very simple. My religion is kindness."

To order *The Kindness Ambassador and the Sugarholic Prosecutor,*
please visit: www.kiklibrary.com or
http://bookstore.balboapress.com/

HEARTMIND WISDOM
Inspirational Anthology Collection

WRITING CONTEST

Our global brothers and sisters are invited to enter Kindness is Key's *Heartmind Wisdom* Writing Contest. For contest details please visit www.heartmindwisdom.com.

Kindness is Key's

Annual 'Largest Human Peace Sign' Concert and Guinness World Records Attempt

Gregg Braden in his book *The Divine Matrix* states that "the minimum number of people required to 'jump-start' a change in consciousness is the square root of one percent of a population." Known as the *Maharishi Effect*, this principle translates into ten people affecting one hundred thousand. To this end, Kindness is Key annually attempts the world record for the 'Largest Human Peace Sign.' We invite you to help us seed global peace, hope, love, and kindness by challenging your neighborhood, business, organization, or school to surpass our current Human Peace Sign participant numbers.

www.humanpeacesign.com

Kindness is Key's

Annual 'Peace Sign Event' Contest

Everyone is encouraged to enter *KiK's* annual 'Peace Sign Event' contest. To enter, simply host and video a peace sign event or project. Make certain that you include our sponsors' names and/or logos. Then enter to win in one of the following categories:

- Outstanding Creative Peace Sign Event
- Outstanding Creative Inclusion of Sponsors
- Outstanding Creative Use of Nature
- Outstanding Creative Inclusion of Recycled Materials
- Outstanding Creative Entry from a Grade/Elementary School
- Outstanding Creative Entry from a High School
- Outstanding Creative Entry from a University or College
- Outstanding Original Peace Song

Help seed worldwide peace—visit www.humanpeacesign.com

81% surveyed want to write a book.
Sadly, only 1% of wannabe writers are published.

Kindness is Key Training Inc. has greatly
increased the odds of being published!

HEARTMIND WISDOM
Inspirational Authorship Course

Kindness is Key Training Inc. guides *new* and *published* writers through the joys of inspirational authorship. Graduates are published in *Heartmind Wisdom—An Anthology of Inspiring Wisdom From Those Who Have Been There.* All twenty-one coauthors with a submission in a *Heartmind Wisdom* anthology share equally in royalties. Each published *Heartmind Wisdom* coauthor benefits from a Personal Replicated Website that has blogging capabilities and is connected to *KiK*'s Online Library. Coauthors may 'co-link' other blogs/websites (of a healing or inspirational nature) and promote other published works (books, e-books, DVDs and CDs) on their Personal Replicated Website.

If you are interested in sharing your educational,
healing or inspirational story with a global audience,
please visit www.heartmindwisdom.com.

Recommended Reading

Braden, Gregg. *Deep Truth: Igniting the Memory of Our Origin, History, Destiny and Fate.* USA: Hay House, Inc., 2011.

Braden, Gregg. *The Divine Matrix: Awakening the Power of Spiritual Technology.* USA: Hay House Inc., 2007.

Burchard, Brendon. *Life's Golden Ticket: An Inspirational Novel.* New York: HarperCollins, 2007. *The Millionaire Messenger.* New York: Free Press, 2011. *The Charge.* New York: Free Press, 2012.

Cameron, Julia. *The Artist's Way.* New York: Penguin Putman, 2002.

Dyer, Wayne W. *Change Your Thoughts, Change Your Life – Living The Wisdom of the Tao.* USA: Hay House Inc., 2007.

Dyer, Wayne W. *Wishes Fulfilled: Mastering the Art of Manifestation.* USA: Hay House Inc., 2012.

Evers, Anne Marie. *Affirmations: Your Passport to Happiness.* USA: Affirmations International Publishing Company, 1989.

Fromm, Erich. *The Art of Loving.* New York: Bantam Books Inc., 1956.

Gibran, Kahlil. *The Prophet.* (Originally published in 1923) England: Oneworld Publications, 1998.

Gray, John. *Men are from Mars, Women are from Venus.* USA: Barnes & Noble Inc., 2004.

Hay, Louise L. *You Can Heal Your Life.* USA: Hay House Inc., 2004.

Herbert, Wray. *On Second Thought: Outsmarting Your Mind's Hard-wired Habits.* USA: Random House Inc., 2010.

Kohn, Rachael. *The New Believers: Re-Imagining God.* Australia: Harper Collins, 2005.

Kuntz, Ted. *Peace Begins With Me.* Coquitlam: Ted Kuntz, 2005.

Leonard, Barbara. *Don't Just Stand There Sucking Your Thumb ....* New Westminster: Balance Point – Inner Garden Awareness Institute, 2003.

Maltz, Maxwell. *Psycho-Cybernetics: A New Way to Get More Living Out of Life.* New York: Pocket Books, 1960.

Ross, Joyce M. *The Kindness Ambassador and the Sugarholic Prosecutor--13 Keys to Living the Life You Are Meant to Love.* USA: Balboa Press, 2012.

Bolen, Jean Shinoda. *The Millionth Circle: How to Change Ourselves and the World--The Essential Guide to Women's Circles.* USA: Conari Press, 1999.

Tolle, Eckhart. *A New Earth: Awakening to Your Life's Purpose* USA: Dutton/Penguin Group, 2005.

Tully, Brock. *Reflections* Series. Vancouver: B. Tully, 1983.

Wieder, Marcia. *Making Your Dreams Come True.* New York: Harmony, 1999.

Zukav, Gary. *The Mind of the Soul: Responsible Choices.* USA: Free Press, Simon & Schuster Inc.

Recommended Music

Hagan, Denise. *For Those Who Hear.* Rosa Records, Sneezer Publishing, 2006. www.denisehagan.com

Recommended Websites

www.brocktully.com
www.denisehagan.com
www.letmeoutcreative.com/
www.heartmindwisdom.com
www.humanpeacesign.com
www.innergarden.com
www.kindnessiskey.com
www.mercyships.ca/
www.mercyships.org/
www.mooncoinproductions.com (Kindness Rocks)
www.peacebeginswithme.ca/
www.worldkindnessconcert.com

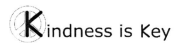

CPSIA information can be obtained at www.ICGtesting.com
Printed in the USA
LVOW121128070713

341725LV00002B/202/P